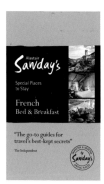

French Bed & Breakfast

Italy

British Bed & Breakfast

British Hotels & Inns

Ninth edition
Copyright © 2016
Alastair Sawday Publishing Co. Ltd
Published in 2016
ISBN-13: 978-1-906136-76-5

Alastair Sawday Publishing Co. Ltd,
Merchant's House, Wapping Road,
Bristol BS1 4RW, UK
Tel: +44 (0)117 204 7810
Email: info@sawdays.co.uk
Web: www.sawdays.co.uk

The Globe Pequot Press,
P. O. Box 480, Guilford,
Connecticut 06437, USA
Tel: +1 203 458 4500
Email: info@globepequot.com
Web: www.globepequot.com

Series Editor Alastair Sawday
Editors Patrick Henry, Jennie Coulson,
Nicky de Bouille
Editorial Assistance Stephanie Hare,
Laura Siegler, Florence Sivell
Senior Picture Editor Alec Studerus
Production Coordinators
Lianka Varga, Sarah Barratt
Writing Jo Boissevain,
Ann Cooke-Yarborough, Lucy Cowie,
Nicola Crosse, Donald Greg, Monica
Guy, Wendy Ogden, Honor Peters,
Helen Pickles, Annie Shillito
Inspections Ann Cooke-Yarborough,
Jennie Coulson, Jill Coyle, Nicky de
Bouille, Gilles Denis, Georgina Gabriel,
Diana Harris-Sawday, Patrick Henry,
Nicky Hilyer, Rosie Jackson, Patricia
Shears, Alison Skinner, Nikki Varney,
Jo Wilds, Elizabeth Yates.

And thanks to those people who did an
inspection or two.

Thanks to Ann Cooke-Yarborough and
Annie Shillito for their invaluable support.

Marketing & PR 0117 204 7810

*We have made every effort to ensure the accuracy
of the information in this book at the time
of going to press. However, we cannot accept
any responsibility for any loss, injury or
inconvenience resulting from the use of
information contained therein.*

Production: Pagebypage Co. Ltd
Maps: Maidenhead Cartographic Services
Printing: Pureprint, Uckfield
UK distribution: The Travel Alliance, Bath
Diane@popoutmaps.com

Cover photo credits.
Front  1. Hostellerie Bérard & Spa, entry 332  2. Hotel de France, entry 148
3. Hôtel Maison de Lucie, entry 89
Back:  1. Hostellerie Bérard & Spa, entry 332  2. Château de la Commanderie, entry 290
3. Château de Bonnemare, entry 94
Spine: La Baronnie Hôtel & Spa, entry 201

# Alastair Sawday's

## Special Places to Stay

# French Châteaux & Hotels

# 4    Contents

Nobody can take the Frenchness out of France. Other countries may have been overwhelmed by outside interference, but France sticks to her guns.

Our publishing began with *Alastair Sawday's Guide to French Bed & Breakfast*, displaying the sheer vitality of French culture, ways and style. We focused on farmhouses and rural areas, and I still think that rural France is a European treasure. Every visitor helps to keep people in their villages. The same is true of its hotels, many of them oases of economic dynamism.

It is fun to see France adapting to, and part-defining, this century. The bicycle is known in France, affectionately and perceptively, as La Petite Reine, and she is benignly running amok. You can now cycle the length of the Loire, all the way to the Atlantic. This is wonderful, and adds new perspectives for visitors. Paris was bike-friendly before most other cities, and you can pootle about everywhere on hired bikes. These things make a difference.

The food scene is as alive as ever, despite criticisms – often valid – that fast food is intruding dangerously. Look for the symbol 'Maître Restaurateur' at the door of a restaurant, awarded to restaurants that make everything from scratch. If we all avoid fast food it will surely wither.

An interesting new seduction is the glut of antiques for sale in flea-markets and auction houses. The weak euro is also good for most other things, such as these hotels themselves. Have a look at L'Hôtel, once the Paris home of Oscar Wilde, and the Hôtel de la Paix in Montparnasse. We have châteaux galore, in many of which I would happily spend my last days. There is a heated pool carved into the rock at Demeure de Vignole – utterly bizarre, and irresistible.

These hotels need us, for they are being throttled by the big booking companies; and we need them, for we, too, are being throttled by the internet, the media and the frenzy of life. Leaf through these pages and then dive in; there is everything to gain.

*Alastair Sawday*

Photo above: Tom Germain

## How do we choose our Special Places?

It's simple. There are no rules, no boxes to tick. We choose places that we like and are fiercely subjective in our choices. We also recognise that one person's idea of special is not necessarily someone else's so there is a huge variety of places, and prices, in the book. Those who are familiar with our Special Places series know that we look for comfort, originality, authenticity, and reject the insincere, the anonymous and the banal. The way guests are treated comes as high on our list as the setting, the architecture, the atmosphere and the food.

## Inspections

We visit every place in the guide to get a feel for how both house and owner tick. We don't take a clipboard and we don't have a list of what is acceptable and what is not. Instead, we chat for an hour or so with the owner or manager and look round. It's all very informal, but it gives us an excellent idea of who would enjoy staying there. If the visit happens to be the last of the day, we sometimes stay the night. Once in the book, properties are re-inspected every few years, so that we can keep things fresh and accurate.

## Feedback

In between inspections we rely on feedback from our army of readers, as well as from staff members who are encouraged to visit properties across the series. This feedback is invaluable to us and we always follow up on comments. So do tell us whether your stay has been a joy or not, if the atmosphere was great or stuffy, the owners and staff cheery or bored. The accuracy of the book depends on what you, and our inspectors, tell us. A lot of the new entries in each edition are recommended by our readers, so keep telling us about new places you've discovered too. Please email us on info@sawdays.co.uk.

However, please do not tell us if your starter was cold, or the bedside light broken. Tell the owner, immediately, and get them to do something about it. Most owners, or staff, are more than happy to correct problems and will bend over backwards to help. Far better than bottling it up and then writing to us a week later!

## Subscriptions

Owners pay to appear in this guide. Their fee goes towards the high costs of inspecting, of maintaining our website and producing an all-colour book. We

Photo: Bastide de Marie, entry 308

only include places that we find special for one reason or another, so it is not possible for anyone to buy their way onto these pages. Nor is it possible for the owner to write their own description. We will say if the bedrooms are small, or if a main road is near. We do our best to avoid misleading people.

### Disclaimer

We make no claims to pure objectivity in choosing these places. They are here simply because we like them. Our opinions and tastes are ours alone and this book is a statement of them; we hope you will share them. We have done our utmost to get our facts right but apologise unreservedly for any mistakes that may have crept in. The latest information we have about each place can be found on our website, www.sawdays.co.uk.

You should know that we don't check such things as fire alarms, swimming pool security or any other regulation with which owners of properties receiving paying guests should comply. This is the responsibility of the owners.

## Using this book
### Finding the right place for you

All these places are special in one way or another. All have been visited and then written about honestly so that you can take what you want and leave the rest. Those of you who swear by Sawday's books trust our write-ups precisely because we don't have a blanket standard; we include places simply because we like them. But we all have different priorities, so do read the descriptions carefully and pick out the places where you will be comfortable. If something is particularly important to you then check when you book: a simple question or two can avoid misunderstandings.

### Maps

Each property is flagged with its entry number on the maps at the front. These maps are a great starting point for planning your trip, but please don't use them as anything other than a general guide – use a decent road map for real navigation. Most places will send you detailed instructions once you have booked your stay.

### Symbols

Below each entry you will see some symbols, which are explained at the very back of the book. They are based on the information given to us by the owners. However, things do change: bikes may be

Photo above: Le Domaine des Prés Verts Spa, entry 44
Photo right: Auberge de Concasty, entry 251

under repair or a new pool may have been put in. Please use the symbols as a guide rather than an absolute statement of fact and double-check anything that is important to you – owners occasionally bend their own rules, so it's worth asking if you may take your dog even if they don't have the symbol.

Wheelchair access – Some châteaux and hotels are keen to accept wheelchair users into their hotels and have made provision for them. However, this does not mean that wheelchair users will always be met with a perfect landscape, nor does it indicate that they have been officially assessed for such a status. You may encounter ramps, a shallow step, graveled paths, alternative routes into some rooms, a bathroom (not a wet room), perhaps even a lift. In short, there may be the odd hindrance and we urge you to call and make sure you will get what you need.

Limited mobility – The limited mobility symbol 🚶 shows those places where at least one bedroom and bathroom is accessible without using stairs. The symbol is designed to satisfy those who walk slowly, with difficulty, or with the aid of a stick. A wheelchair may be able to navigate some areas, but these places are not fully wheelchair friendly. If you use a chair for longer distances, but are not too bad over shorter distances, you'll probably be OK; again, please ring and ask. There may be a step or two, a bath or a shower with a tray in a cubicle, a good distance between the car park and your room, slippery flagstones or a tight turn.

Pets – Our 🐕 symbol shows places which are happy to accept pets. Do let owners know when booking that you'd like to bring your pet – particularly if it is not the usual dog! Be realistic about your pet – if it is nervous or excitable or doesn't like the company of

Photo: Hôtel Sainte Beuve, entry 55

other dogs, people, chickens, children, then say so.

Owners' pets – The  symbol is given when the owners have their own pet on the premises. It may not be a cat! But it is there to warn you that you may be greeted by a dog, serenaded by a parrot, or indeed sat upon by a cat.

## Practical Matters
### Types of places

Hotels can vary from huge, humming and slick to those with only a few rooms that are run by owners at their own pace. In some you may not get room service or have your bags carried in and out; in older buildings there may be no lifts. In smaller hotels there may be a fixed menu for dinner with very little choice, so if you have dishes that leave you cold, it's important to say so when you book your meal. If these things are important to you, then do check when you book.

### Rooms

Bedrooms – these are described as double, twin, single, family or suite. A double may contain a bed which is anything from 135cm wide to 180cm wide. A twin will contain two single beds (usually 90cm wide). A suite will have a separate sitting area, but it may not be in a different room. Family rooms can vary in size, as can the number of beds they hold, so do ask. And do not assume that every bedroom has a TV.

Bathrooms – all bedrooms have their own bathrooms unless we say that they

don't. If you have your own bathroom but you have to leave the room to get to it we describe it as 'separate'. There are very few places in the book that have shared bathrooms and they are usually reserved for members of the same party. Again, we state this clearly.

### Meals

Breakfast is included in the room price unless otherwise stated.

Some places serve lunch, most do Sunday lunch (often very well-priced), the vast majority offer dinner. In some places you can content yourself with table d'hôte, in others you can feast on five courses. Most offer three courses for €25-€50, either table d'hôtes or à la carte. Some have tasting menus, occasionally you eat communally. Some large hotels (and some posh private houses) will bring dinner to your room if you prefer, or let you eat in the garden by candlelight. Always ask for what you want and sometimes, magically, it happens.

Photo: Hôtel de Londres, entry 74

## Prices and minimum stays

We quote the lowest price per night for two people in low season to the highest price in high season. Only a few places have designated single rooms; if no single rooms are listed, the price we quote refers to single occupancy of a double room. In many places prices rise higher when local events bring people flooding to the area.

The half-board price quoted is per person per night unless stated otherwise, and includes dinner, usually three courses. Mostly you're offered a table d'hôte menu. Occasionally you eat à la carte and may find some dishes carry a small supplement. There are often great deals to be had, mostly mid-week in low season.

Most small hotels do not accept one-night bookings at weekends. Small country hotels are rarely full during the week and the weekend trade keeps them going. If you ring in March for a Saturday night in July, you won't get it. If you ring at the last moment and they have a room, you will. Some places insist on three-night stays on bank holiday weekends.

## Booking and cancellation

Most places ask for a deposit at the time of booking, either by cheque or credit/debit card. If you cancel – depending on how much notice you give – you can lose all or part of this deposit unless your room is re-let.

It is reasonable for hotels to take a deposit to secure a booking; they have learnt that if they don't, the commitment of the guest wanes and they may fail to turn up.

Some cancellation policies are more stringent than others. It is also worth noting that some owners will take the money directly from your credit/debit card without contacting you to discuss it. So ask them to explain their cancellation policy clearly before booking so you understand exactly where you stand; it may well avoid a nasty surprise. And consider taking out travel insurance (with a cancellation clause) if you're concerned.

## Arrivals and departures

Housekeeping is usually done by 2pm, and your room will usually be available by mid-afternoon. Normally you will have to wave goodbye to it between 10am and 11am. Sometimes one can pay to linger. Some smaller places may be closed between 3pm and 6pm, so do try and agree an arrival time in advance or you may find nobody there.

## Closed

When given in months this means for the whole of the month stated. So, 'Closed: November–March' means closed from 1 November to 31 March.

# Sawday's
## Vineyard collection

It's always a glorious
time to expand your
knowledge of the
French grape!
Stay in one of our hand
picked Special Places
on wine estates
scattered across some
of the best wine
regions in France.

www.sawdays.co.uk/vineyards

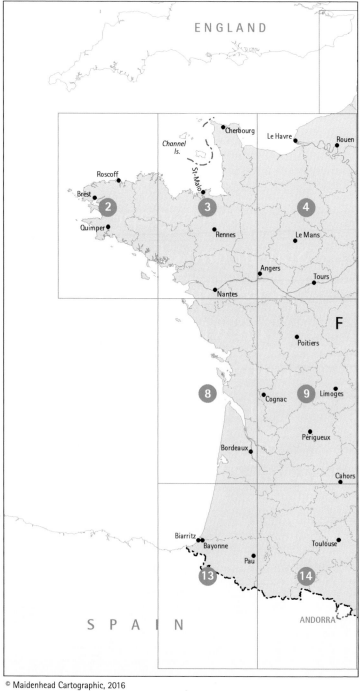

© Maidenhead Cartographic, 2016

© Maidenhead Cartographic, 2016

# Map 1

17

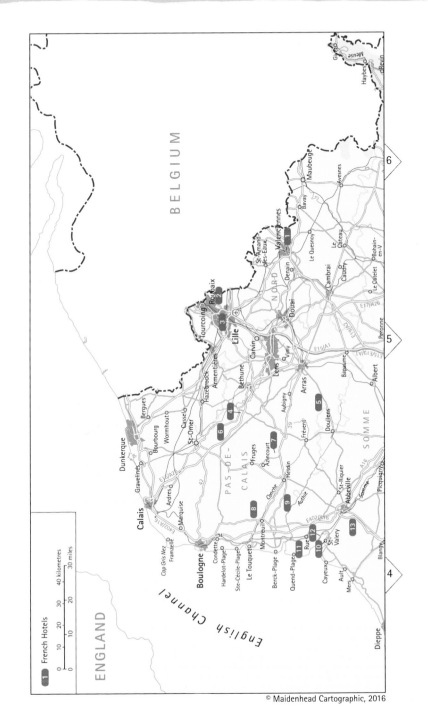

© Maidenhead Cartographic, 2016

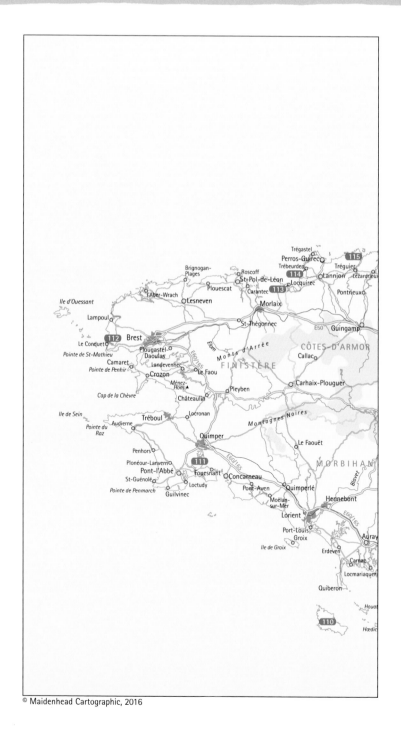

# Map 3

19

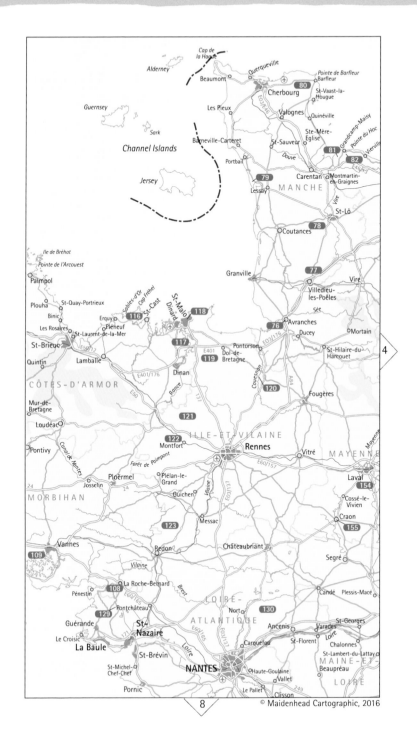

© Maidenhead Cartographic, 2016

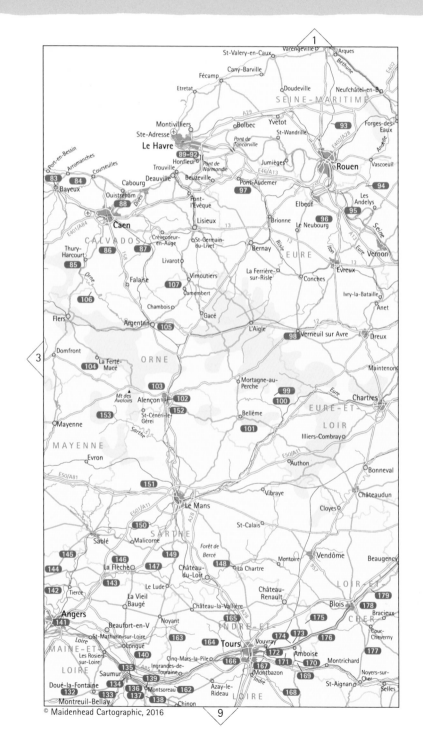

© Maidenhead Cartographic, 2016

# Map 5

21

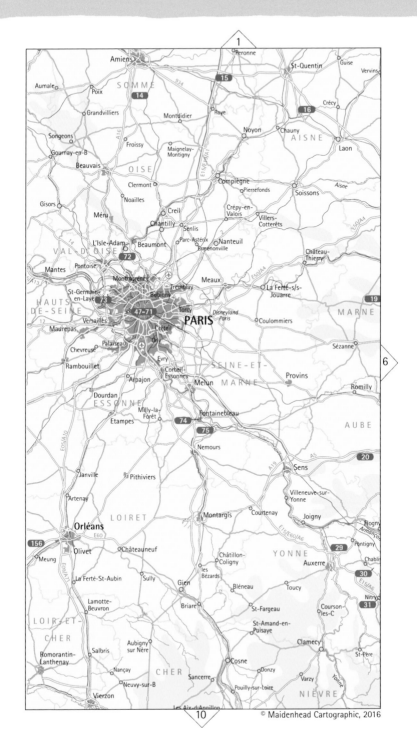

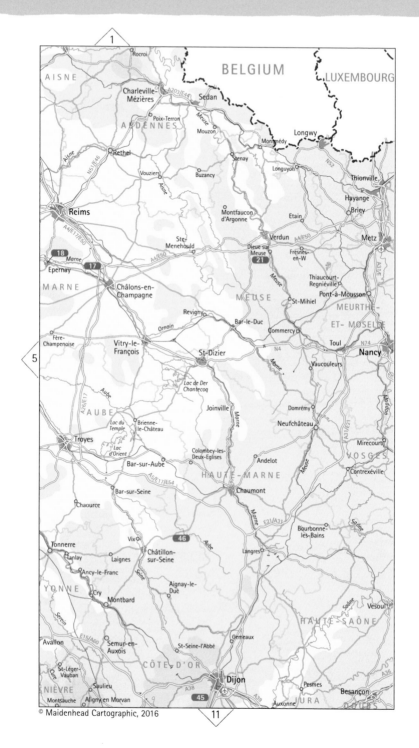

© Maidenhead Cartographic, 2016

# Map 7

23

© Maidenhead Cartographic, 2016

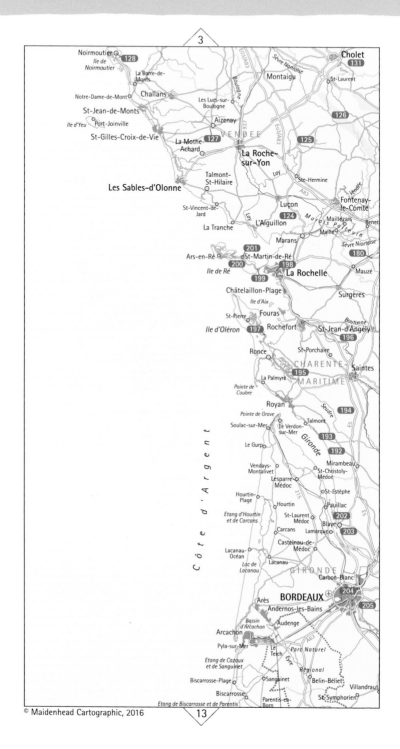

3

Noirmoutier
Île de
Noirmoutier
128
La Barre-de-
Monts
Cholet
131
Montaigu
St-Laurent
Sèvre Nantaise
Notre-Dame-de-Mont
Challans
Les Lucs-sur-
Boulogne
St-Jean-de-Monts
Île d'Yeu  Port-Joinville
St-Gilles-Croix-de-Vie
Aizenay
126
VENDÉE
125
La Mothe-
Achard
127
La Roche-
sur-Yon
Les Sables-d'Olonne
Talmont-
St-Hilaire
Loy
Ste-Hermine
St-Vincent-de-
Jard
Luçon
Fontenay-
le-Comte
La Tranche
L'Aiguillon
Loy
Maillezais
Maillé
Benet
Marais Poitevin
Marans
Sèvre Niortaise
180
Ars-en-Ré
201
St-Martin-de-Ré
200
198
Île de Ré
199
La Rochelle
Mauzé
Châtelaillon-Plage
Surgères
Île d'Aix
St-Pierre
Fouras
St-Jean-d'Angély
Ile d'Oléron
197
Rochefort
196
Boutonne
Ronce
St-Porchaire
CHARENTE
Saintes
La Palmyre
195
MARITIME
Pointe de
Coubre
Royan
194
Seudre
Pointe de Grave
Soulac-sur-Mer
Le Verdon-
sur-Mer
Talmont
Gironde
193
Le Gurp
192
Vendays-
Montalivet
Mirambeau
St-Christoly-
Médoc
Lesparre-
Médoc
St-Estèphe
Hourtin-
Plage
Hourtin
Pauillac
Côte d'Argent
Etang d'Hourtin
et de Carcans
St-Laurent-
Médoc
Blaye
202
Carcans
Lamarque
203
Lacanau-
Océan
Castelnau-de-
Médoc
Lac de
Lacanau
Lacanau
GIRONDE
Carbon-Blanc
204
BORDEAUX
Arès
205
Andernos-les-Bains
Bassin
d'Arcachon
Audenge
Arcachon
Pyla-sur-Mer
Le
Teich
Parc Naturel
Eyre
Etang de Cazaux
et de Sanguinet
Régional
Biscarrosse-Plage
Sanguinet
Belin-Béliet
Villandraut
Biscarrosse
Parentis-en-
Born
St-Symphorien
Etang de Biscarrosse et de Parentis
13

Map 9 25

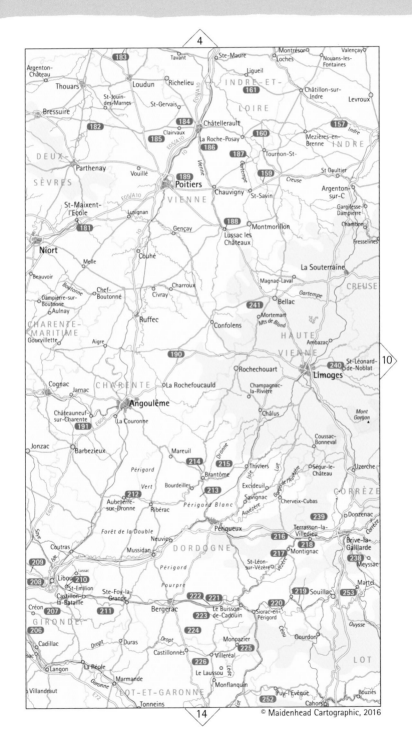

© Maidenhead Cartographic, 2016

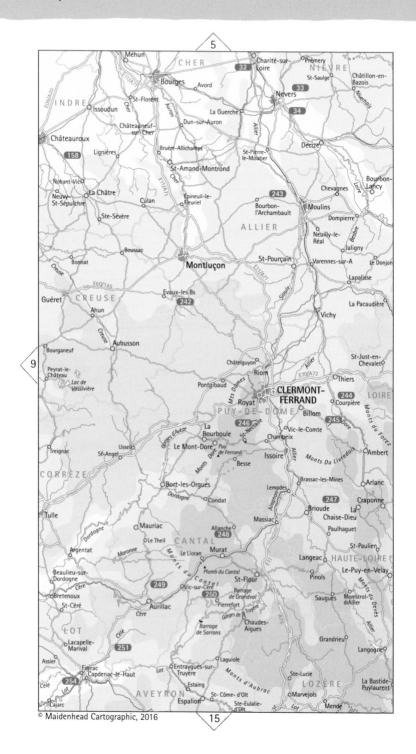

# Map 11

27

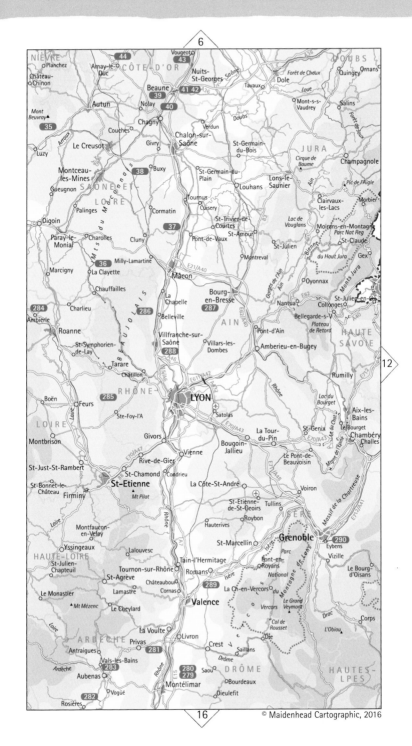

© Maidenhead Cartographic, 2016

Map 13                                                                29

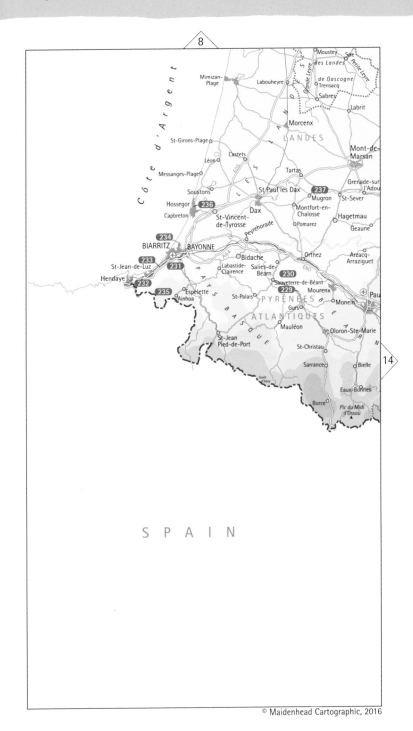

© Maidenhead Cartographic, 2016

# Map 15

31

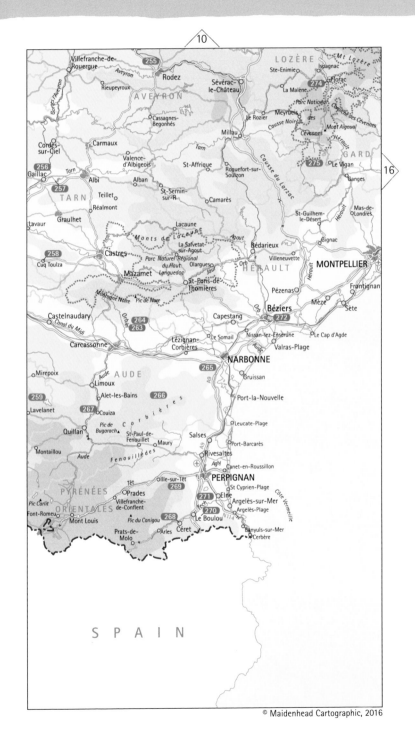

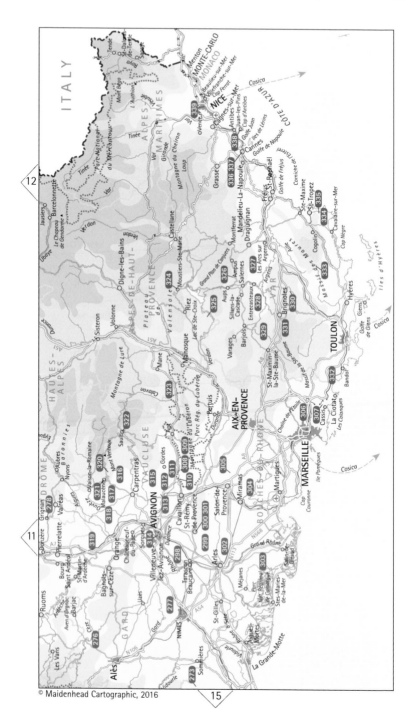

# The North • Picardy • Champagne–Ardenne

## Auberge du Bon Fermier

Forget your stilettos, the cobbles in the flowered courtyard continue into the deeply attractive bar and restaurant of this 16th-century haven in a rebuilt town. It is a maze of passageways, burnished beams and tiny staircases. A copper washbasin greets you at the top of the stairs leading to the rooms. Looking down from a glassed-in corridor, you can almost hear the clatter of hooves arriving in the courtyard, now a quiet terrace for afternoon tea and snacks; the passengers jostling between Paris and Brussels were probably delighted to be delayed at this bustling staging inn. Bedrooms are all differently quirky, one with tapestried curtains and walls, another with red bricks and wooden struts, some not too well lit, all with baths and bathrobes. There are two larger, lighter ground-floor rooms with post-modern lamps and tables. Downstairs, where a suit of armour guards a wooden reception dais, the evenings sparkle when the main restaurant is lit by candles. Monsieur Beine takes great trouble devising new menus with his chef and most diners would raise a glass in his direction.

| Rooms | 14 doubles: €94–€115. |
|-------|------------------------|
|       | 2 singles: €78–€115. |
| Meals | Breakfast €10. |
|       | Lunch & dinner €26–€52. |
| Closed | Rarely. |

Monsieur Beine
Auberge du Bon Fermier,
64 rue de Famars,
59300 Valenciennes, Nord

| | |
|---|---|
| Tel | +33 (0)3 27 46 68 25 |
| Email | beinethierry@hotmail.com |
| Web | www.bonfermier.com |

### Château de Courcelette

A quiet cul de sac beside Lannoy church leads to unexpected 18th-century elegance surrounded by tree-filled grounds. It's the oldest château left standing in the area, and you're just 20 minutes from the centre of Lille (easy to reach by bus or tube), yet all is leafy and peaceful. The big walled garden is superb, and there's a beautiful brick and cobble terrace where you can relax and plan your forays into the lively town: galleries and museums, boutiques, bustling Sunday markets, outdoor cafés, Flemish roots. Energetic new hosts plan to introduce contemporary touches while preserving classical features – pilasters, panelling, marble, medallions... A downstairs room for guests is being created soon too. Upstairs, pale, peaceful bedrooms with original doors and handsome antiques are quietly luxurious. Breakfast is served on the first floor too: bread and croissants from the local baker, cheese, charcuterie and from time to time a homemade cake – as early or as leisurely as you like. *Parking on-site.*

| Rooms | 3 doubles: €90-€100. |
|---|---|
| | 1 suite for 4 (2 adults & 2 children): €100-€160. |
| | Extra bed/sofabed available €20 per person per night. |
| Meals | Dinner, 3 courses with wine, aperitif & coffee, €40. |
| | Restaurant 5-minute walk. |
| Closed | Rarely. |

**Virginie Tuffery**
Château de Courcelette, 17 rue César Parent, 59390 Lannoy, Nord

| Tel | +33 (0)3 20 75 45 67 |
|---|---|
| Mobile | +33 (0)6 23 64 02 84 |
| Email | chateau.lannoy@gmail.com |
| Web | www.chateau-de-courcelette.com |

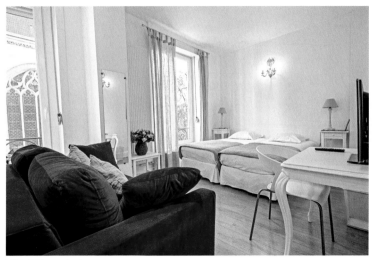

## Hôtel Brueghel

Perfectly positioned on a pedestrianised street in the heart of the city is a tall, quaint, traditional hotel painted a groovy grey. Reception is friendly and cosy (mahogany panels, corduroy armchairs, Art Nouveau radiators) while the tiny cast-iron lift – the original! – takes you up to six soft-carpeted floors. Bedrooms range from small to extremely small (and they tell you this on booking). Warm, comfortable, well-furnished, they have elegant new bathrooms, painted bedside tables, antique desks, and prints of Bruegel and others on the walls. Go for a room with a view of the church tower (many do, while the rear rooms have no view at all). You pay extra for breakfast but it sounds very nice and it'll set you up for the day: charcuterie, cheeses, croissants, fruits, crepes with maple syrup, two sorts of bread. Thanks to Eurostar, Lille is a great place for a city break: old churches, charming houses, narrow streets, Sunday markets (Place du Concert is one for foodies) and astonishing pâtisseries… try Aux Merveilleux de Fred, regal Méert, or both. We loved it all. *Cot available.*

| Rooms | 16 doubles: €70–€104. |
|-------|------------------------|
|       | 4 singles: €65–€76. |
|       | Extra bed €15. |
| Meals | Breakfast €11.50. |
|       | Restaurants 1-minute walk. |
| Closed | Never. |

Florence .
Hôtel Brueghel,
5 parvis St Maurice,
59000 Lille, Nord

| Tel | +33 (0)3 20 06 06 69 |
|------|------------------------|
| Email | contact@hotel-brueghel.com |
| Web | www.hotel-brueghel-lille.com |

## Le Château de Philiomel

Unwind on a 15-acre estate – the owners live next door – in immaculate solitude. Never mind the slightly incongruous, beet-factory surroundings, the Château de Philiomel is a haven of peace. At the end of a long avenue of trees, overlooking lake and leafy park, this commanding Italianate mansion has the right ingredients to give you grand ideas, yet is run with a light touch. Pillars, portico, marble fireplaces, all are here, in excellent order, but there's no standing on ceremony and your hosts give you a great welcome. Large lofty bedrooms, uncarpeted, uncluttered, are immaculate in muted colours with new furniture and family antiques; the suite has its own balcony; bathrooms are large and new. You wake to buffet breakfast at private tables in a light-flooded dining room with white walls and polished parquet – a super spread of homemade jams, pastries, fresh orange juice, and coffee poured from a crested silver pot. With the A26 close by, this is a good stopover on the way to or from Calais. Walk into the town for dinner, or drive to a Michelin-starred restaurant (there are two!).

| Rooms | 3 doubles: €90–€100. |
| | 1 suite: €130. |
| | Extra bed/sofabed available €25 per person per night. |
| Meals | Restaurants 2km. |
| Closed | Rarely. |

Frédéric Devys
Le Château de Philiomel, Rue Philiomel,
62190 Lillers, Pas-de-Calais

| Tel | +33 (0)3 21 61 76 76 |
| Mobile | +33 (0)6 09 10 81 95 |
| Email | contact@philiomel.com |
| Web | www.lechateaudephiliomel.com |

## Château de Saulty

The re-lifted stately face looks finer than ever in its great park with apple orchards (15 varieties!) and horses grazing: a special house in a special setting. Inside? A warm, embracing country home with a panelled breakfast room (with secret doors), an amazing, museum-worthy, multi-tiled gents' cloakroom and, up the wide old stairs, four pleasing, peaceful bedrooms, all large and bright, some huge, uncluttered with floral fabrics, traditional furniture and immaculate white linen. All have wooden floors and plain walls in sunny tones, perhaps an old fireplace or a mirrored armoire, but stay in 'Pink Lady' if you can (all are named after apples) with its pretty antique bed, its great big bathroom and its gentle garden views. Breakfast is the best of continental: fresh fat croissants, homemade jams, and (of course) apple juice like you've never tasted. This is a great place for visiting the Canadian National Vimy WWI Memorial and the quaint town of Arras, a half hour drive. Quiet and intelligent, Sylvie is a natural at making guests feel at home – and enjoys practising her English.

| Rooms | 1 double: €70. |
| | 1 family room for 4: €100. |
| | 2 triples: €80. |
| Meals | Restaurants 16km. |
| Closed | January. |

**Emmanuel & Sylvie Dalle**
Château de Saulty,
82 rue de la Gare, 62158 Saulty,
Pas-de-Calais

| Tel | +33 (0)3 21 48 24 76 |
| Email | chateaudesaulty@nordnet.fr |
| Web | www.chateaudesaulty.com |

## Château de Moulin le Comte

Huge tall windows, great big doors and a checker-tiled hall are original touches still on show in this small château, renovated recently and completely by the Van der Elsts. Your Belgian hosts – father, mother, son, recently moved from Brussels – are serious about succeeding in their new venture and you will excuse the wonderfully kitsch china chihuahuas when you are relaxing in one of their immaculate rooms. Expect textured wallpapers, swish showers, hotel standards and heaps of space; we particularly liked the Green Room for its original wooden polished floor and garden view. Dinner in the elegant green and gold dining room might feature local watercress, colourful St Omer cauliflowers or veal with mustard, cooked by Francis who speaks seven languages, including Japanese! Nothing is too much trouble for your very welcoming hosts. The heritage site of Aire sur la Lys is a walk away, St Omer and war cemeteries are close, and the exciting new Louvre-Lens is a 45-minute drive. Great value for such an excellently run house.

| Rooms | 4 twin/doubles: €99–€139. |
| --- | --- |
| | 1 family room for 4: €119–€159. |
| | Singles €79–€99. |
| | Dinner, B&B €108–€177 per person. |
| | Extra bed/sofabed available €20 per person per night. |
| Meals | Dinner €15–€20; 5 courses, €27; 5 courses with wine, €49. |
| | Restaurant 1.5km. |
| Closed | Rarely. |

Francis Van der Elst
Château de Moulin le Comte,
44 rue Principale, Moulin le Comte,
62120 Aire sur la Lys, Pas-de-Calais

| Tel | +33 (0)3 21 88 48 38 |
| --- | --- |
| Mobile | +33 (0)6 24 21 08 91 |
| Email | info@chateaudemoulinlecomte.com |
| Web | www.chateaudemoulinlecomte.com |

Entry 6   Map 1

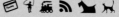

## La Cour de Rémi

A raved-about bistro, seven delicious rooms round the quadrangle, a romantic treehouse, two new rooms in the cottage, all in a fine, tranquil and rectilinear domaine: the ingredients for a very spoiling weekend. In the expert hands of Sébastien these farm buildings have become informally, fabulously chic. A manger skirts the old stables, a glassed-over brick well glows softly in the three-tier former tack room, floor-to-ceiling glass replaces high barn doors, grain storage attics have become vast beamed spaces with views to both sides, one suite has a jacuzzi, another has two baths side by side… but the cherry on top is surely the four-metre-high treehouse, wrapped spectacularly round a venerable sycamore, with a big decked balcony under the leaves. Breakfast can be delivered to your door as you consider your options: abbeys, châteaux, gardens, WWI sites, a bike ride, seal-spotting by the Somme. Whether you do all of these things or nothing at all, make sure you're back for Sébastien's 'râbles de lapin' (rabbit) or 'colvert rôti' (duck), served in the designer-chic, bistro-friendly dining room. La Cour de Rémi is sublime.

| | |
|---|---|
| Rooms | 6 doubles: €85-€100.<br>3 suites for 2: €140-€160.<br>1 treehouse for 2: €160. |
| Meals | Breakfast €12.50. Dinner €30.<br>Wine €15-€100. |
| Closed | Christmas. |

Sébastien de la Borde
La Cour de Rémi,
1 rue Baillet, 62130 Bermicourt,
Pas-de-Calais

| | |
|---|---|
| Tel | +33 (0)3 21 03 33 33 |
| Email | sebastien@lacourderemi.com |
| Web | www.lacourderemi.com |

## Auberge d'Inxent

Sommelier in a restaurant in Lille, Jean-Marc won a Perrier contest on the luck of a draw. Off he tripped with his young wife and two children to a most emerald green valley and claimed a whitewashed, geranium-spilled, 18th-century country inn. Order a trout on the vine-covered terrace and back comes a live one in a bucket from their trout farm across the road by the river. Needless to say Jean-Marc's exceptional wine list and creative use of local produce should lead to a prolonged stay (the nearby ramparts of Montreuil sur Mer are well worth a visit). Inside: wonky beams and low ceilings, a battery of copper pans behind the old zinc counter, deep green walls in the smaller dining room (our favourite), and all the cosiness of a modest country kitchen with open fires on chilly days. Bedrooms are snug, smallish and beamy, furnished with repro cherrywood antiques and refreshed with modern leather and wicker; bathrooms are spacious and airy. This may not be grand-chic but it's an endearing address: an uncommon treat to find such good food combined with such perfect service.

| Rooms | 3 doubles, 2 twins: €75–€81. |
|---|---|
| Meals | Breakfast €10. |
| | Lunch & dinner €19–€42. |
| Closed | Christmas & New Year. |

**Laurence & Jean-Marc Six**
Auberge d'Inxent,
318 rue de la Vallée de la Course,
62170 Inxent, Pas-de-Calais
Tel        +33 (0)3 21 90 71 19
Email      auberge.inxent@wanadoo.fr
Web        www.auberge-inxent.fr

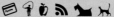

## Le Clos de la Prairie

If it's worth doing, it's worth doing well – a maxim that could certainly be applied to this elegant small hotel. Sandrine and Sébastien, young and attentive, have transformed what was once a typical bunch of whitewashed farm buildings in deepest meadowy France into a perfectly put-together place to stay. No need to tear round the countryside trying to find that elusive, 'just what we wanted' spot for dinner – it's here. Sebastian worked in every aspect of hospitality, from wine waiter to maître d'hôtel, before training as a chef in Nice; now he has his own place to show off his skills, and the food is divine. Contemporary rooms, all on the ground floor, are handsomely dressed in neutral hues with fine bed linen while state-of-the-art bathrooms are definitely worth lingering in; little terraces accessed through sliding glass doors are great spots from which to admire long green views punctuated by mature trees, and make up for the lack of a large guests' sitting room. Oodles to see and do nearby – beaching it at Le Touquet, cycling, birdwatching, meandering, or, of course, in this region, just dreaming.

| | |
|---|---|
| Rooms | 5 doubles, 1 twin: €95–€127.<br>1 family room for 4,<br>1 family room for 3: €135–€167. |
| Meals | Breakfast €15. Dinner €15–€37.<br>Wine €19–€138. |
| Closed | Rarely. |

Sandrine Adam
Le Clos de la Prairie,
17 rue de St Rémy,
62870 Gouy St André, Pas-de-Calais

| | |
|---|---|
| Tel | +33 (0)3 21 90 39 58 |
| Email | leclosdelaprairie@orange.fr |
| Web | www.leclosdelaprairie.com |

## Château du Romerel

In wooded grounds in the heart of the town, with private parking and views over the bay, this early-19th-century villa exudes quiet privilege. Gracious interiors include two chandeliered salons – lavish with curtains and deep sofas – and a polished dining room with small tables for breakfast, a feast of eggs, pastries, yogurts, local cheeses and jams, homemade apple juice and home-grown fruits. Dinners sound just as good. Romerel combines the luxuries of a hotel with the warmth of a B&B: hostess Amélie keeps the honesty bar stocked and takes delicious care of you. Light-flooded bedrooms are country-house luxurious with soft colours, thick carpets and fine antiques, bathrooms are being renovated, and most rooms have a bay view. Wander the gardens with their secret bowers and a 200-year-old Cedar of Lebanon… lodges too, sheepfold, historic ice house and unheated pool. The popular town overlooks the Baie d'Authie; hop on a boat and spot the seals; drive to the Parc du Marquenterre, famous for birdlife. Or visit the gardens at Valloires Abbey, the Château de Rambures, Amiens Cathedral: all are within an hour's drive.

| Rooms | 3 doubles: £183–£223. |
| | 1 triple: £243–£263. |
| Meals | Dinner €35, on request. |
| | Restaurant 5-minute walk. |
| Closed | Rarely. |

**Amélie Bordier**
Château du Romerel,
15 quai du Romerel,
80230 St Valery sur Somme, Somme
Tel     +33 (0)3 22 23 68 70
Email   info@chateaudenoyelles.com

## Le Fiacre

The 300-year-old farmhouse, all gnarled beams and cosy nooks, holds a popular restaurant with a seasonal menu from Picardy's land and sea. You can start with a colourful cordial from the tiny bar, and move on to homemade foie gras, filleted pigeon and strawberry soup. You'll find the rest of the hotel – and staff – just as delightful. Modern bedrooms, built sensitively in the same country-farmhouse style, are set around a flower-filled courtyard garden with a patio and pond. Spacious, beamed ground floor rooms open out to here while suites, with two bedrooms and a shared living room, suit families or two couples. In summer you can take a dip in the heated pool, laze on sun loungers and enjoy a generous continental breakfast on a dining terrace surrounded by pines. The flat, lush countryside around the Baie de Somme is replete with golf courses, bike routes, horse-riding trails and bird-watching spots like the famed Parc du Marquenterre. And the closest beach is just two kilometres away near Fort Mahon. Convenient for Calais and Dieppe, this is a relaxing place for a break or stopover.

| Rooms | 2 doubles, 6 twins: €90-€134. 1 suite for 2, 2 family suites for 4: €100-€315. 3 triples: €125-€190. |
| Meals | Breakfast €15. Dinner €24-€49. Wine list €30-€100. Restaurant closed 13 November to 12 March. Restaurants 2km-3km. |
| Closed | 11 December to 6 February. |

André Szymczak
Le Fiacre, 6 rue des Pommiers,
Hameau de Routhiauville,
80120 Quend, Somme

| Tel | +33 (0)3 22 23 47 30 |
| Email | lefiacre@wanadoo.fr |
| Web | www.hotel-le-fiacre.fr |

## Château de Noyelles en Baie de Somme

The village of Noyelles stands at the head of the magical Baie de Somme, the 19th-century château stands on the edge of the village, a pretty peach and white gâteau in a seven-acre landscaped park with orchards, neat lawns, rose beds and a terrace scattered with smart parasols. It's more guest house than hotel, with rooms spread generously over three floors. A balcony runs past the first-floor rooms; snug tower rooms on the second and third floors flaunt jaunty angles. Whites, pearly greys, oyster greens, hazy blues and sand-toned paintwork and panelling make for sober, sophisticated, TV-free spaces; Chinese antiques and objets d'art – an opium pipe here, a courtesan's fan there – provide delightful detail. And now two *roulottes* in the grounds offer a more exotic stay. Three airy reception rooms and two drawing rooms please the eye with their considered variety: a Starck chair slipped into the classic, plush décor; deep crimson sofas set before a handsome marble fireplace. Fabulous local seafood and organic veg, fruit from the garden: you will eat well here. Masses of things to do and it's easy to ignore the rush-hour traffic. *Some rooms interconnect.*

| | |
|---|---|
| Rooms | 3 doubles, 3 twin/doubles: €95–€189. 2 suites for 2: €200–€240. |
| Meals | Breakfast €14. Picnic available. Dinner €35; book ahead. Wine €16–€40. |
| Closed | Christmas & 2 January to 5 February. |

Pascal De Zotti
Château de Noyelles en Baie de Somme,
30 rue Maréchal Foch,
80860 Noyelles sur Mer, Somme
Tel     +33 (0)3 22 23 68 70
Email   info@chateaudenoyelles.com
Web     www.chateaudenoyelles.com

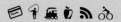

## Château de Béhen

Donkeys to stroke, bicycles to hire and ponies to ride: horsey folk and families will be in clover. Surrounded by wooded parkland, the red-brick building with a limestone trim started life as a holiday house; later its ground floor was extended. In the 1950s the Cuveliers moved in, adding paddocks and a pond for swans, deeply traditional decoration with strong colours and some ornate oh-so-French flourishes. Today there are six large bedrooms for guests, with solid oak floors and rugs, bedspreads plain or toile de Jouy, and furniture in Louis XV style. Two-tone panelling graces the first-floor rooms while those above have sloping ceilings and a beam or two. Bathrooms are hotel-perfect with double basins of mottled marble. Norbert-André, who managed stud pacers in Australia, has come home to cook and does a grand job, at one convivial table, or single tables if preferred. Cheeses are local, vegetables are just-picked, banquets can be arranged. Saddle up and enjoy a guided trek – for a day or even two. Lovely friendly people, perfect peace and 15 horses to ride.

| Rooms | 2 doubles, 1 twin: €125-€213. |
| | 1 suite for 2: €180-€202. |
| | 2 family rooms for 4: €185-€244. |
| Meals | Dinner with wine, from €43; |
| | book ahead. |
| Closed | Rarely. |

Cuvelier Family
Château de Béhen,
8 rue du Château,
80870 Béhen, Somme
Tel    +33 (0)3 22 31 58 30
Email  norbert-andre@cuvelier.com
Web    www.chateau-de-behen.com

### Château de Chaussoy Epagny

Welcome to a marvellous old family château, a registered *monument historique* built in 1777. This is no 'Relais et Châteaux' experience: La Chambre d'Hélène, up the sweeping stair, is as authentic as can be. It comes with 10-foot high shuttered windows, French polished parquet, meadow views and much period charm; the bathroom is entirely modern. Breakfast with homemade jams is served beside the marble chimney (its fire lit on cool days) in the dining room — a sunny space with painted wood panelling typical of the Louis XVI style, photos of the children and grandchildren and a life size bust of Général de Caffarelli, soldier of Napoleon; you can eat outside in the summer. Madame is delightful and loves to tell you about the history of the building and her family. You can stroll through the wooded grounds, guides for local walks can be provided and Amiens, with one of the greatest gothic churches in the world and lots of restaurants, is worth the 20-kilometre drive. Compiègne, Chantilly, Senlis and Paris are all within an hour's drive.

| | |
|---|---|
| Rooms | 1 double: €75. |
| Meals | Restaurant 6km. |
| Closed | 1 November to 1 April. |

**Christine de Caffarelli**
Château de Chaussoy Epagny,
38 rue du château,
80250 Chaussoy Epagny, Somme

| | |
|---|---|
| Tel | +33 (0)3 22 41 05 07 |
| Email | chdecaffarelli@cegetel.net |
| Web | www.chateaudechaussoy.com |

## Château d'Omiécourt

On a working estate, Omiécourt is a proudly grand 19th-century château and elegant family home (the Thézys have four children, mostly grown now), with tall slender windows and some really old trees. Friendly if formal, communicative and smiling, your hosts have worked hugely to restore their inheritance and create gracious French château guest rooms, each flooded with light with an ornate fireplace. The 1900 room has a sweep of polished floor and a turn-of-the-century bed, the more modern Chambre des Ormieux sits brightly under the eaves in a separate 'maison'; near the two pools (one outdoor, one in), it comes with a super new blue and white tiled bathroom and a guest kitchen on the ground floor. Enjoy a buffet supper in your room one night – aperitifs, candlelight, champagne – and a Michelin-starred dinner in Roye the next. Breakfast is continental and something of a feast. There's table football and table tennis for the children, a boutique of pretty things and rambling green parkland to explore. A house of goodwill, deeply traditional, naturally hospitable.

| Rooms | 3 doubles: €153–€156.<br>1 suite for 3: €165–€195.<br>Separate maison – 1 family room for 4<br>with kitchen: €195.<br>Extra bed €30. |
|---|---|
| Meals | Gourmet dinner, room service, €35.<br>Restaurants 12km. |
| Closed | Rarely. |

Dominique & Véronique de Thézy
Château d'Omiécourt,
80320 Omiécourt, Somme

| Tel | +33 (0)3 22 83 01 75 |
| Email | contact@chateau-omiecourt.com |
| Web | www.chateau-omiecourt.com |

## Domaine Le Parc

Down a tree-lined drive between tailored lawns you approach this 18th-century mansion built on castle foundations, now a family-run guest château. The river Oise slides gently by. There are ten lawned, tree'd and statued acres here and, at the back, a brick-walled belvedere terrace with soaring views over woodland, untamed countryside and river. Inside, wander at will between a gracefully decorated dining room, breakfast room and library, and a sitting room with gorgeous soft sofas. Up the spiral oak staircase are the bedrooms, classically and elegantly decorated, some with more of those views. Strong colours with floral fabrics stand out against striped or patterned fabric walls; luxurious bathrooms have jacuzzi baths; clusters of antique bottles on the window ledges and an antique hobby horse add whimsical touches to a formal décor. Dutch Jos has previously won Michelin stars for his cooking, Anne is a former maître d'hôtel, both are efficient, consummate, multi-lingual hosts. Don't miss the fortified churches and great Gothic cathedrals. *Babies (non-crawling) and children over 10 welcome. Dinner compulsory on first night only. No credit cards.*

| | |
|---|---|
| Rooms | 3 doubles, 2 twins: €75–€95. |
| Meals | Dinner, set menu, with wine, €38, booking required for first night. |
| Closed | 23 December to 5 January. |

Jos & Anne Bergman
Domaine Le Parc,
Rue de Quesny,
02800 Danizy, Aisne
Tel       +33 (0)3 23 56 55 23
Email   contact@domaineleparc.fr
Web     www.domaineleparc.com

Entry 16   Map 5

## Château de Juvigny

Oozing old-world charm, this handsome 1705 château wraps you in its warmth. The family have occupied one wing for 200 years and, thanks to Brigitte, it has a wonderfully easy-going elegance. There are chandeliers, polished floorboards, antiques, old-fashioned bathrooms, cracked floor tiles, rustic outbuildings. Bedrooms, in the old servants' quarters, are informally stylish with marble fireplaces, original wooden wrap-around wainscoting, pretty floral or toile de Jouy wallpapers with colour-matched bed covers and green views. The surrounding parkland has a fine selection of mature trees, formal areas and a beautiful natural lake with boating and swimming; a moat encircles the whole château. You breakfast in an attractive dining room beneath a vast (and deteriorated!) portrait of an ancestor – the long table is set with pretty china and flowers, warm pastries and homemade jams. Head out for walks, fishing and champagne vineyards; explore Epernay and Reims; return to courteous, unfussy country comfort.

| | |
|---|---|
| Rooms | 3 doubles, 1 twin: €95–€150. |
| | 1 suite for 4: €150–€200. |
| | Extra bed €25. |
| Meals | Restaurant 10km. |
| Closed | Mid-October to 1 April (except by arrangement). |

**Brigitte Caubère d'Alinval**
Château de Juvigny,
8 av du Château, 51150 Juvigny,
Marne

| | |
|---|---|
| Mobile | +33 (0)6 78 99 69 40 |
| Email | information@chateaudejuvigny.com |
| Web | www.chateaudejuvigny.com |

## La Villa Eugène

On the prestigious Avenue de Champagne, this 19th-century mansion was the home of champagne magnate Eugène Mercier; old family photos still line the staircase and the staff can tell you which room belonged to whom. Then there's the décor, an enticing balance of traditional French with contemporary touches: walls the colour of whipped cream, furniture Louis XVI or 'colonial' (dark wood, leather and wicker), soft yielding curtains, gracious parquet floors. There's modernity in flat-screens and WiFi, pampering in the bathrooms – all a good size – with fluffy towels and luxurious products by Keiji; it earns the five stars of which the owner is so proud. The buffet breakfast is an array of homemade cakes, tarts, yogurts and breads, served in the light-filled conservatory – whose mosaic floor has been lovingly restored – or in the garden with its heated summer pool, colourful beds and young palm trees. Just 30 minutes from Reims and its mesmerising cathedral, a smart launch pad for the three major Routes de Champagne. Then return to the luxurious cocoon that is the bar.

| Rooms | 15 twin/doubles: €160-€398. Extra bed/sofabed available €35 per person per night. |
|---|---|
| Meals | Breakfast €21. Restaurants 2km. |
| Closed | Never. |

Agnès Rafik
La Villa Eugène,
82-84 av de Champagne,
51200 Epernay, Marne
Tel      +33 (0)3 26 32 44 76
Email   info@villa-eugene.com
Web     www.villa-eugene.com

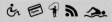

## Château d'Étoges

Etoges, used as a stopover by French kings on journeys east, is a moated 17th-century château: through the wrought-iron gates then over the footbridge to a little island fortress, transformed into a hotel by the family who have lived here for generations. The grounds are lovely, too, with their fountains, lawns and ponds. It is, indeed, fit for a king, from the fully French rooms with their delicious fabrics and linen to the elegant meals with home-grown veg. Opulent bedrooms glow with antiques and fresh flowers, some have four-posters and two have mezzanine beds over bathrooms; rooms in the orangery have less character. The handsome restaurant, also in the orangery, has a majestic fireplace and, fittingly, deep orange curtains. If you fancy breakfast in bed, smart staff will bring it to your lace-covered table: breads, croissants, jams, fruit. If you prefer to breakfast downstairs, take your pick from the buffet and drift onto the terrace. This intimate hotel is right in the middle of champagne-growing country; easy for cycling and fishing, too, with a well-stocked lake a ten-minute drive.

| | |
|---|---|
| Rooms | 26 twin/doubles: €99–€298. 2 suites for 2: €300. |
| Meals | Breakfast €18. Lunch & dinner €45–€89; children's menu €20. Wine €20–€200. |
| Closed | Christmas & 24 January to 11 February. |

**Marie Champenois**
Château d'Étoges,
4 rue Richebourg,
51270 Etoges, Marne

| | |
|---|---|
| Tel | +33 (0)3 26 59 30 08 |
| Email | contact@etoges.com |
| Web | www.etoges.com |

## Domaine du Moulin d'Eguebaude

The secluded old buildings house two owner families, a restaurant, several guest rooms and 15 tons of ever-present live fish. Fishing folk gather on Sundays to catch trout in the spring water that feeds the ponds; groups come for speciality lunches. Meals may include trout terrine, home-reared salmon, a neighbour's potatoes, wild asparagus in buttery sauce, cinnamon custard. For breakfast round the big table there's brioche, baguettes, croissants, yogurt, fruit salad, cereals, apple juice and their own jams and honey. Created in an old mill 40 years ago, the bedrooms under the eaves are mostly small-windowed, simply furnished and prettily decorated in rustic or 'grandmother' style. Other rooms are in the newly built half-timbered cottage across the drive. At one end of the shop – packed with cottage-industry goodies (charcuterie, honey, jams, wine and champagne) – is a wide floor of thick glass under which immense fish can be seen swimming to and fro between the water tanks. A pony wanders freely in the grounds. Wonderful food and service – and good English spoken.

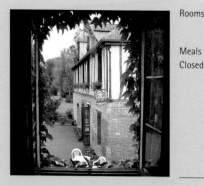

| Rooms | 2 doubles, 1 twin: €76-€81. |
| | 2 family rooms for 4: €111-€127. |
| | 1 triple: €86. |
| Meals | Dinner with wine, €28. Guest kitchen. |
| Closed | Rarely. |

**Alexandre & Sandrine Mesley**
Domaine du Moulin d'Eguebaude,
36 rue Pierre Brossolette,
10190 Estissac, Aube
Tel      +33 (0)3 25 40 42 18
Email    moulineguebaude10@gmail.com
Web      www.moulineguebaude.jimdo.com

Lorraine • Alsace

## Hostellerie du Château des Monthairons

If you seek peace and quiet in lovely large grounds, or a spot of fishing maybe – the river Meuse meanders through – this would be a good, utterly French, choice. Monthairons served as an American military hospital in the First World War and become a base for the Germans in the Second. It is now run by three offshoots of the Thouvenin family, who did a major refurbishment in the Eighties. One couple looks after the restaurant and food, the other two are in charge of the hotel and grounds. Because of this personal touch, there's a homely feel in spite of the proportions. Bedrooms are smart, classic French and come in all sizes, some with duplex suites ideal for families; we'd love a room facing the park. The restaurant is elegant and full of flowers, a place for a fancy dinner not a quick bite. You can swim and canoe here, too; a former owner diverted the river especially and the neighbouring meadow is now known as the 'old river'. Organised activities? They do several packages including introductions to fly-fishing, rides in a horse-drawn carriage, visits to Verdun. Return to be spoiled in the spa.

| Rooms | 12 doubles, 6 twins: €110–€240. 5 suites for 2-4: €185–€390. 2 apartments for 2-4: €290–€390 per night. |
|---|---|
| Meals | Breakfast €17–€18. Lunch €28, weekdays only. Dinner €48–€105. Wine €44–€96. |
| Closed | January to mid-February. |

**Madame Pierrat**
Hostellerie du Château des Monthairons,
26 route de Verdun, Le Petit Monthairon,
55320 Les Monthairons, Meuse

| | |
|---|---|
| Tel | +33 (0)3 29 87 78 55 |
| Email | accueil@chateaudesmonthairons.fr |
| Web | www.chateaudesmonthairons.fr |

## Château d'Alteville

Within exploring distance of Strasbourg, Nancy and Metz, the château has more than a whiff of history. It was built for one of Napoleon's generals and the two paintings that hang in the Louis XVI salon were gifts from the Emperor. David's family has farmed here for five generations; now he welcomes guests with huge kindness and eco-awareness. Bedrooms are authentically French and solidly traditional, with carved armoires, Voltaire armchairs, perhaps a draped bedhead or a small chandelier. Parkland views float in through the windows and bathrooms have been updated. Downstairs is more stylish: a library/billiard room, a many-windowed salon hung with portraits, a majestic dining room where splendid candlelit dinners are served several nights a week in the company of your lively, charming host (book ahead). The grounds are beautifully landscaped; enjoy the peace and quiet lazing on the terrace – or pull on your hiking boots and follow your nose through the woods and round the ponds. Tranquil, romantic and definitely special.

| Rooms | 4 doubles, 1 twin: €91. |
|---|---|
| Meals | Dinner €31–€38.50; book ahead. Wine €5–€15. |
| Closed | Rarely. |

**David Barthélémy**
Château d'Alteville,
Tarquimpol,
57260 Dieuze, Moselle

| Tel | +33 (0)3 87 05 46 63 |
| Mobile | +33 (0)6 72 07 56 05 |
| Email | chateau.alteville@free.fr |

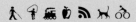

Entry 22   Map 7

## Auberge de La Cholotte

In a wooded valley filled with chattering birds, deer, foxes and wild boar sits a spacious pink sandstone farmhouse framed with bright blue shutters and rambling wisteria. A happy spot and spectacular in the autumn sunshine. Both the dining room with open-fire and the wood-panelled restaurant are open to the public and they host regular concerts here. Angelika serves up hearty local produce: ham baked in hay, local rabbit and trout, organic veg and German pastries; she'll even cook the mushrooms you forage from the forest. Stay for supper and some music or head to restaurants in Gérardmer or Saint Dié. Like the communal spaces, all five bedrooms have a rustic chic feel, artistic colour combinations and paintings on the walls; all are on the first floor with harmonious views of pond, garden or forest. There's much to do here: the Vosges mountains are nearby, the pilgrim's path Camino de Santiago passes the house, there are heaps of gardens, good walking and fishing. Such peace and quiet and such a friendly couple running the show, no wonder guests return again and again.

| Rooms | 3 doubles, 1 twin, 1 family room for 3: €90-€100. |
| Meals | Dinner €25. Wine €18-€32. |
| Closed | Rarely. |

Angelika & Patrick Colin
Auberge de La Cholotte,
44 La Cense de St Dié,
88600 Les Rouges Eaux, Vosges

Tel     +33 (0)3 29 50 56 93
Email   auberge@lacholotte.com
Web     www.lacholotte.com

## Le Saint Barnabé – Hôtel & Spa

At the top of its quiet valley, under the guidance of attentive and efficient owners, the whole hotel now has a modern, elegant feel: gone are the traditional Alsatian frills. Food is important here, and good. Éric is the chef. Trained with France's best and chef at Château d'Isenbourg for some years, he uses local, biodynamically-grown ingredients whenever he can. Clémence tends the colourful garden and can also advise on what to do between the Vosges hills and the Alsace plain: there are typical villages and wine-growers to visit, excellent hiking, bike rides and good fishing places (they also have mini-golf on the spot, and a spa). The ferny woods are full of paths and burbling brooks and there's skiing in season. Rooms, quietly elegant and comfortable, are of two kinds: in the main house they are big with smashing bathrooms and the odd balcony; in the separate building behind, they are smaller, with a shower each – and cheaper! A great place for nature lovers and gourmets, the Saint Barnabé is fabulously quiet – bar the birdsong – and carefully eco-friendly.

| | |
|---|---|
| Rooms | 26 twin/doubles: €108-€199. Discounts available mid-week – please enquire with owner. |
| Meals | Lunch €18.90, Mon-Sat. Picnic available. Dinner €29.49-€72 plus à la carte. |
| Closed | Christmas & 11 January to 8 February. |

**Clémence & Éric Orban**
Le Saint Barnabé – Hôtel & Spa,
53 rue de Murbach,
68530 Buhl, Haut-Rhin

Tel       +33 (0)3 89 62 14 14
Email   hostellerie.st.barnabe@wanadoo.fr
Web     www.le-stbarnabe.com

## Hôtel à la Ferme – L'Aigle d'Or

In a simple, colourful Alsatian village, this typical old farm is framed by shrubs, roses, manicured hedges and a pretty brick terrace. The welcome from the family, who have been here for generations, is as gracious as the setting. Bedrooms, in the main house or converted outbuilding, are splendid: a good size and comfortable, they have polished floorboards, oriental rugs and fine beds, one carved in Alsatian style. In the new, exquisitely decorated stable suites you'll find timber balconies, wonderful fabrics and an even greater sense of luxury. Here, too, are the spanking new Aigle d'Or restaurant and the breakfast room, where Jean-Philippe's delicious brioches and pastries are served. His father mans the bar, his mother and grandmother help in the kitchen, Brigitte meets and greets, Jean-Philippe is master chef and the food is outstanding. Chalked up on the board are escargots, foie gras, asparagus in season, choucroute, tarte flambée, apfelstrudel. Then retire to the wainscotted guest salon, warmed by a fine ceramic stove. A superb place run by a family that is professional, enthusiastic, endearing.

| | |
|---|---|
| Rooms | 12 doubles: €89–€154. |
| | 3 suites for 2: €134–€200. |
| Meals | Breakfast €15. |
| | Lunch & dinner €32–€78 (except |
| | Monday eve & Tuesdays). Wine €25. |
| Closed | Rarely. |

Jean-Philippe & Brigitte Hellmann
Hôtel à la Ferme – L'Aigle d'Or,
10 rue du Château,
67150 Osthouse, Bas-Rhin

| | |
|---|---|
| Tel | +33 (0)3 90 29 92 50 |
| Email | hotelalaferme@wanadoo.fr |
| Web | www.hotelalaferme.com |

## Ermitage du Rebberg

Beams, baby grands and a botanical guide, library, sauna, gym... tradition and luxury meet in a satisfying embrace. Thirty peaceful acres of deer, mature gardens, conifers and woodlands surround you, as do echoes of aristocracy. A summer villa for a family whose main home was in the shade, there is an innate cosiness here, in spite of the size and the flora-draped grandeur. Pine- and pear-panelled rooms are worthy of a small château; woodwork is fine and ubiquitous. This elegant décor is the life's work of Madame, whose welcome is genuine, whose advice is priceless. Aromatic pastries and charcuterie appear for breakfast, taken socially or in privacy according to guests' whims. Dinner is framed by the tropical conservatory or sunny patio, with menus fit for a gourmand and wines to match. Marvel at the genuine Alsatian stübe with its 1870s 'poêle en faïence'. Spacious rooms (four in a former barn) compete for the top spot – Citrine is a favourite – and jacuzzi baths abound. The pool is a refreshing island in a sea of cool green. Relax, spy on squirrels, visit Strasbourg, follow the Route des Vin.

| Rooms | 4 doubles, 5 doubles with sofabed: €135-€205. 1 family room for 5 with sofabed: €155-€190. Singles €125-€195. |
|---|---|
| Meals | Dinner with apéritif, €48. Children's menu, 5-12 years, €22, from 12 years €33. Restaurants 1km. |
| Closed | Rarely. |

**Elisabeth Goetzmann**
Ermitage du Rebberg,
49 rue de la Hoube,
67280 Urmatt, Bas-Rhin

| Tel | +33 (0)3 88 47 33 31 |
| Email | info@ermitagedurebberg.com |
| Web | www.ermitagedurebberg.com |

Entry 26   Map 7

## Hôtel du Dragon

At the hub of old Strasbourg, looking over river and cathedral, the Dragon is solidly 17th century on the outside, temperately 20th century within. Built as a private mansion – Louis XIV stayed on his way to visit Marie-Antoinette in Austria – it became a hotel in the 1990s. The peaceful little courtyard received a classically pedimented porch and potted shrubs: a pretty place for an evening drink. They took a deeply contemporary approach inside – it is sober, minimalist-stylish and extraordinarily restful. Variegated grey and white are the basics: mushroom curtains on white walls, superb grey pinstripe carpeting, an arresting pattern of grey and white tiles in the bathrooms, muted mauve bedcovers for a dash of colour, and some good abstract paintings and sculptures here and there, displayed to great advantage. Some have river views and others see the cathedral's lovely spire. After 20 years as a mountain guide, Monsieur Zimmer returned to his native Strasbourg and has made the Dragon as welcoming as it is elegant. He is quiet and gentle and has a predilection for English-speaking guests.

| | |
|---|---|
| Rooms | 30 twin/doubles: €98–€176. 2 apartments for 4 without kitchen: €179–€229. |
| Meals | Breakfast €12. Restaurants 5-minute walk. |
| Closed | Rarely. |

Jean Zimmer
Hôtel du Dragon,
12 rue du Dragon,
67000 Strasbourg, Bas-Rhin

Tel      +33 (0)3 88 35 79 80
Email    hotel@dragon.fr
Web      www.dragon.fr

## Le Moulin

The thermal waters of Niederbronn have drawn visitors since Roman times, and the town, in the Northern Vosges, retains an authentic Alsatian atmosphere. Madame and Monsieur welcome you in the same spirit to their peaceful estate, where a stream-driven mill, now gîtes, sits amid ancient trees, a pool and rose walk. The elegant manor has two history-filled guest rooms, pretty in pastel and catching the morning sun with views over courtyard and park. The lounge and dining room (where breakfast is served) are spacious with original open fireplaces, warm colours and Madame's paintings on the walls. Quietly green, your hosts run an electric car, serve organic home-pressed apple juice and homemade jams at breakfast, and are now installing a pond with a reed bed system for purification. Wander the pretty garden, follow the path of the mill stream, roam UNESCO forests. There's hiking, climbing, biking and hunting on the doorstep and a plethora of medieval villages and ruined châteaux to discover. All those in search of the 'real French experience', history-lovers and the environmentally aware will be happy here.

| Rooms | 1 twin/double: €90. |
|---|---|
| | 1 suite for 5 (bunkbeds & extra single bed in second room): €90. |
| Meals | Restaurant 1km. |
| Closed | 1 January to 31 March. |

**Henri & Marianne Mellon**
Le Moulin,
44 route de Reichshoffen,
67110 Niederbronn-les-Bains, Bas-Rhin

Tel     +33 (0)6 25 43 40 40
Email   marianne.mellon@gmail.com
Web     gite.moulin.free.fr

# Burgundy

Photo: Les Deux Chèvres,
entry 45

## Château de la Resle

Built for a dignitary who lost his head in the French Revolution, this handsome house sits on an impeccable estate of landscaped gardens, neat, gravelled, lavender-lined paths, plus *orangerie*, pond and hornbeam maze. Johan and Pieter, your smiley, engaging, humorous hosts, came from Holland several years ago and have made everything elegant, modern and stylish. A fine stone staircase with a wrought-iron banister leads to spacious, minimally furnished rooms painted in muted hues of moss and deep-blue; views ponder over the gardens to hilly horizons, and fabulous modern art hangs on the walls. A further huge suite with a fine dressing area lies under dramatic roof carpentry in a cottage outside. Bathrooms are spotless white with state-of-the-art showers, pale pebble floors, beautiful accessories and chunky towels. Tuck into breakfast in the vast dining room with its dark walls and limestone flags, then work it off in the first-floor fitness room. Or set off for the vineyards and the wine tastings, the pretty villages with their ancient half-timbered houses, the walks and the cycle rides. Fabulous in every way. *Min. stay: 2 nights at weekends, 2 in high season. Over 10s welcome.*

| | |
|---|---|
| Rooms | 1 double, 1 twin/double: €195–€295. 3 suites for 2, 1 suite for 4: €250–€475. Extra bed/sofabed available €25 per person per night. |
| Meals | Dinner available on request, depending on occupancy. Restaurant 2km. |
| Closed | January to mid-February. |

**Johan Bouman & Pieter Franssens**
Château de la Resle,
89230 Montigny la Resle, Yonne

| | |
|---|---|
| Tel | +33 (0)3 86 41 86 57 |
| Mobile | +33 (0)6 86 11 29 22 |
| Email | info@chateaudelaresle.com |
| Web | www.chateaudelaresle.com |

## Château de Béru

Château life as you'd dream it: noble arches, exposed stonework and shuttered windows that survey glorious miles of vineyards. It's a place that transports you to another era, yet the well-worn choice antiques and tasselled tie-backs harmonise with modern backdrops of plum purple, flowery chintz and bold monochrome. Home to the Comtes de Béru since 1627, the estate goes back to the 12th century and includes a working vineyard – a delectable extra as you can tour the cellars. You can also wander the château, where the legacy of things past is tangible: Joan of Arc once passed through the foothills and Louis XIV's great-grandson stayed here. There's an exquisite contemporary simplicity to the guest bedrooms, with their raw brickwork and pretty fabrics, fresh linens, generous beds and chic bathrooms; we loved 'Havane'. Have breakfast in the sitting-dining room, by the pool, or in bed; you'll like Madame de Béru's homemade jams. You are in one of Chablis' prettiest valleys where there are heaps of abbeys to visit and shops to plunder... but you'll most probably stay put, it's such an enchanting spot.

| Rooms | 3 doubles: €130–€150. 1 suite for 5: €220. |
| Meals | Dinner €30. Wine €12–€22. Restaurant 7km. |
| Closed | Rarely. |

**Laurence & Athénaïs de Béru**
Château de Béru,
32 Grande Rue,
89700 Béru, Yonne

Tel      +33 (0)3 86 75 90 43
Email   laurencedeberu@gmail.com
Web     www.chateaudeberu.com

## Hôtel de la Beursaudière

Monsieur Lenoble's attention to detail is staggering. Not content with creating a buzzing, cheerful restaurant he has lovingly transformed a priory and farm buildings — stables, dovecotes, stone structures on varied levels, wooden verandas topped with red-patterned Burgundian roof tiles — into a very seductive hotel. Each bedroom has a trade for a theme: a typewriter and old books for the 'writer'; antique irons for the 'laundress'; horse and ox collars for the 'ploughman'; vine-decorated wooden panels for the 'wine-grower'. The walls have been lightly skimmed in plaster in natural shades of ochre, pigeon-egg grey or light yellow. Floors are terracotta or flagstone, stone walls are painted, rafters exposed and windows round or cottage square with curtains of vintage linens and lace. Beds are king-size, mattresses are excellent and TVs are hidden in antique cabinets. Most bathrooms are open plan so as not to detract from the beams and volumes. There is even a sheltered sun lounge on the terrace only overlooked by sparrows. A nice place to sit and sample your chilled choice picked up in Chablis.

| | |
|---|---|
| Rooms | 6 doubles, 5 twins: €85–€125. |
| Meals | Breakfast €10. |
| | Lunch & dinner €20.50–€43.50. |
| | Wine €15–€100. |
| Closed | Last 3 weeks in January. |

Monsieur & Madame Lenoble
Hôtel de la Beursaudière,
5-7 rue Hyacinthe Gautherin,
89310 Nitry, Yonne

| | |
|---|---|
| Tel | +33 (0)3 86 33 69 70 |
| Email | message@beursaudiere.com |
| Web | www.beursaudiere.com |

## Château de La Marche

Marie-Paule and Yves – elegant, enthusiastic, engaging – live in a house of Palladian grandeur built on the banks of the river Loire and surrounded by lush lawns, great trees and expertly planted borders (their business is garden design). It's peaceful and quiet, the only sound is birdsong and the lovely church bell. Inside find an endearing slice of... Italy, all bathed in light. Find a hall with frescoes, a comfy salon, mirrors, chandeliers and generous, double aspect arched windows for long views over the ever-changing river. Bedrooms are themed and eclectic: 'Margeurite' is vast, with a cow theme; 'Florence' has light and creamy panelling; 'Marine' is slightly smaller but bathed in light with a crisp blue and white seaside feel. Bathrooms are newly-renovated, shiny and bright. This is a great place for folk looking for more than an overnight stay – you have free run of the salon with its cosy sofas and games, and the dining room, with microwave and Nespresso machine – so settle in! On your doorstep is La Charité sur Loire, a World Heritage treasure. Return to billiards, table tennis and a leisurely pool-side bask.

| Rooms | 3 doubles: €95-€132. |
| | Extra bed/sofabed available €30 per |
| | person per night. |
| Meals | Restaurants 5km. |
| Closed | 3 November to 3 April. |

Yves Wallaert
Château de La Marche,
Grande Rue,
58400 La Marche, Nièvre
Tel      +33 (0)6 63 13 46 38
Email    wallaert@wanadoo.fr
Web      www.chateaudelamarche.fr

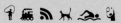

## Château de Nyon

A very pretty little château in a secluded valley in the heart of utterly unspoilt countryside. The remarkable Catherine inherited the house and has been doing B&B for 20 years. The bedrooms, all on the first floor, echo the 18th-century character of the house. Toile de Jouy is charmingly splashed across pink paper and fabrics, bathrooms have big tubs or walk-in showers, glorious views to the garden reveal an avenue of lime trees and a hornbeam maze. Friendly Madame serves breakfast on proper china in the dining room with windows north and south and blue and yellow painted panelled walls. Expect fresh pastries, good coffee, a choice of breads, homemade jam and home-produced honey. There's a comfortable sitting room ornately decorated with lots of floral fabrics and paper, and a very big garden at back and front which you may wander. Find lawns, borders, some fine ancient trees, a newly planted double 'square' of chestnut trees, and a walled garden turned over to vegetables. It's hard to leave this blessed setting but you must if you are to eat; the nearest good restaurant is ten kilometres away.

| | |
|---|---|
| Rooms | 2 doubles: €65–€85. |
| | 1 family room for 4: €150. |
| Meals | Restaurant 10km. |
| Closed | Rarely. |

Catherine Henry
Château de Nyon,
58130 Ourouër,
Nièvre

| | |
|---|---|
| Tel | +33 (0)3 86 58 61 12 |
| Email | chateaudenyon@gmail.com |
| Web | www.chateaudenyon.com |

## Château de Prye

The Queen of Poland, Marie-Casimire, lived here at the tail end of the 17th century – in this *château extraordinaire*, this architectural curiosity. The rooms are vast, the marble stables are palatial and the corridors heave with antlers and stag heads from previous ancestors; the history is intriguing. The young Marquis and Marquise have joyfully taken up the challenge of running both château and estate (they breed Charolais cattle) and host their national and international guests with grace and ease. Each cavernous bedroom is furnished with antiques – a triple-mirrored wardrobe from the Thirties, a Breton carved bedstead, a vintage oil-fuelled heater; bathrooms are en suite. Take a peek at the château kitchen with its wonderful old range and copper saucepans… from here breakfast is dispatched to an oak-panelled dining room with sumptuous views of the park. This rambling, asymmetrical, turreted château, its woodlands, gentle river and age-old trees of exotic and distant origins are contained within seven kilometres of walls… relish the fairy tale.

| Rooms | 3 doubles: €115-€190. |
| | 2 suites for 2-4: €115-€190. |
| Meals | Dinner €35; book ahead. |
| | Wine €8-€105. |
| Closed | Mid-October to mid-April. |

Magdalena & Antoine-Emmanuel
du Bourg de Bozas
Château de Prye,
58160 La Fermeté, Nièvre

| Tel | +33 (0)3 86 58 42 64 |
| Email | info@chateaudeprye.com |
| Web | www.chateaudeprye.com |

## Château de Villette

Coen and Catherine – he's Dutch, she's Belgian – fell in love with this little château in 2002, did it up together, then had their wedding here and now have two children: they love their adopted country. They've opened just five rooms to guests (the family rooms are twin-roomed) and one private cottage so they can spoil you properly and get to know you over dinner; though, should you prefer a romantic dinner for two, they'll understand. Deep in the Parc du Morvan, the château was built in 1782 as a summer retreat. Bedrooms, charmingly decorated by Catherine, are large, light and airy, with warm colours and polished floors. They are dressed in château-style finery with canopied four-poster or draped bedheads and sleigh beds. Bathrooms are as they should be – new claw-foot baths carry exquisite antique taps – and views sail out of great windows to meadows and woodland beyond. Your five-course dinner is served in a candlelit dining room or outside. The grounds are perfect for duck and pheasant shoots. Families would love it here; Beaune and the vineyards lie temptingly close.

| | | |
|---|---|---|
| Rooms | 1 double: €165–€235. 3 family rooms for 4, 1 family room for 2: €165–€350. 1 cottage for 2 with sitting room & kitchen: €245 per night. |  |
| Meals | Dinner €55; book ahead. Wine €18–€100. | |
| Closed | Christmas & New Year. | |

**Catherine & Coen Stork**
Château de Villette,
58170 Poil, Nièvre

| | |
|---|---|
| Tel | +33 (0)3 86 30 09 13 |
| Email | chateaudevillette@icloud.com |
| Web | www.chateaudevillette.eu |

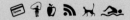

## Château de Vaulx

Described in 1886 as well-proportioned and elegant in its simplicity; Vaulx is as lovely now as then, and in the most beautiful position, in deep country, high on a hill with views that stretch to distant purple mountains. Marty, your charming, amusing host, and the animals (Nema the Jack Russell, Urga the filly, Otto the donkey… plus hens, sheep and beehives) welcome you to this generous estate. There's a panelled drawing room with chandeliers, a huge dining room with fresh flowers, curiosities and fashionable strong, exciting colours in big bedrooms. Sleep peacefully: not a hint of road rumble. The gardens are beautifully maintained: lawns manicured, box balls tightly topiaried, romantic avenues in dappled sunlight. The wonderful vegetable garden grows food for delicious table d'hôtes and Marty's peerless sense of hospitality will always go the extra mile. There's beautiful countryside all around and plenty of places to visit, including a 13th-century bell tower in the village. And moreover… Bernard Dufoux, one of the best chocolate makers in France, is in La Clayette and Saint Christophe has a weekly cattle market.

| Rooms | 2 doubles: €100–€120. |
| --- | --- |
| | 2 family rooms for 4: €145. |
| | 1 apartment for 5: €190. |
| Meals | Dinner €30. Wine €18. |
| | Restaurant 3km. |
| Closed | Rarely. |

Marty Freriksen
Château de Vaulx,
71800 St Julien de Civry,
Saône-et-Loire

| Tel | +33 (0)3 85 70 64 03 |
| --- | --- |
| Email | marty@chateaudevaulx.com |
| Web | www.chateaudevaulx.com |

## Carrion Cuisine Hôtel and Spa

The 17th-century façade of this limestone country inn — once a staging post in the heart of the village — conceals not a few surprises. Behind the muted peacock shutters lies a flashy, fun, excitingly unexpected lair of Designers Guild chic, and each of the ten bedrooms — from good-sized to palatial — is different. There's one in bright turquoise, another deep pink, a third with walls papered baroque-style in gold on white. Mattresses are divine, duvets plump, and one black-lacquer bed is lit from underneath. Bathrooms are suitably style-conscious, too — luxuriously functional, with sparkling tiles, some claw foot tubs, good-quality smellies and cosseting towels. There's scant outside space but how far do you wish to venture, when the Relais' restaurant is so enticing? Perfectionist owner-chef Frédéric Carrion only opened in 2009 and has already netted a Michelin star. Specialities include frogs' legs, Loctudy lobster and Grand Marnier soufflé… and gourmet picnics, accompanied by fine Viré-Clessé wine, can be arranged to take on walks amid the nearby vines. Bon appétit!

| | |
|---|---|
| Rooms | 7 doubles, 3 twins: €150–€290. |
| Meals | Breakfast €20. |
| | Lunch €30. Dinner €38–€94. |
| | Wine €20–€400. |
| Closed | Rarely. |

**Frédéric Carrion**
Carrion Cuisine Hôtel and Spa,
Place André Lagrange, 71260 Viré,
Saône-et-Loire

| | |
|---|---|
| Tel | +33 (0)3 85 33 10 72 |
| Email | contact@relais-de-montmartre.fr |
| Web | www.hotel-restaurant-carrion.fr |

## L'Orangerie

Ring the bell on the gate, to enter gardens that are secluded, charming, full of colour with a babbling brook. Here in the heart of Burgundy country you are immersed in the silence of a valley of vines. Light spills into the sitting room through arched vine-clad windows while cream walls and Indian rugs add to the simple elegance of this *maison de maître*. Antiques and travel are the owners' passion, and David's gentle Irish brogue is enchanting (no surprise to hear he has interviewed European royalty for a prestigious magazine). The grand staircase in the centre of this gracious house would not be out of place on a 1930s luxury cruise liner, while interesting paintings and handsome oriental fabrics add up to a mix of styles that work beautifully. Bedrooms vary in size and have lovely seersucker linen and antique prints; bathrooms are classically tasteful. Terraced lawns lead down to the heated pool, the meadows and trees, lavish breakfasts include unusual homemade jams, and the wonderful Voie Verte cycle route, along the former railway, runs nearby. *Over 12s welcome.*

| | |
|---|---|
| Rooms | 5 twin/doubles: €80–€110. |
| Meals | Hosted dinner with wine, €25–€40, on request. Restaurants 4km. |
| Closed | 3 November to 17 March. |

**David Eades & Niels Lierow**
L'Orangerie,
20 rue des Lavoirs, Vingelles,
71390 Moroges, Saône-et-Loire
Tel      +33 (0)3 85 47 91 94
Email    info@orangerie-moroges.com
Web      www.orangerie-moroges.com

## Le Clos du Colombier

Reach out of your bedroom window and pluck the grapes. Well, almost. This handsome town house – all pale-pink plaster and sky-blue shutters – sits in a sea of vineyards in the heart of Burgundy, surrounded by legendary names: Beaune, Pommery, Meursault … You've come to the right place for wine-tasting or stocking up your cellar. Or, you can check out a few châteaux, take a slow bike ride or just doze around the pretty pool. Although a hotel, the place has the feel of a relaxed, though rather smart, gîte. Rooms – some in a separate annexe – are airy and understated with tiled or polished-wood floors, cool whites and pale greys accented with, say, a splash of purple or charcoal. Sleek contemporary furnishings mix with vintage finds – perhaps a Baroque-style mirror or elegant writing desk – and all have garden or vineyard views. Some rooms have high ceilings and marble fireplaces. Stylish bathrooms have home-made organic soaps and soft bathrobes. Breakfast is continental and includes local honey, evening meals are available in the summer only. If the wine-tasting gets too much, chill out in the little spa overlooking the vines.

| | |
|---|---|
| Rooms | 10 doubles: €124–€163. |
| | 3 suites for 2: €185–€225. |
| | Extra bed €30–€45. |
| Meals | Breakfast €7–€15. |
| | Dinner €15–€45; children's menu €14. |
| | Restaurants 3-minute walk. |
| Closed | December – February. |

**Philippe & Véronique Barthelmebs**
Le Clos du Colombier,
1 rue du Colombier,
21630 Pommard, Côte-d'Or

| | |
|---|---|
| Tel | +33 (0)3 80 22 00 27 |
| Email | contact@closducolombier.com |
| Web | www.closducolombier.com |

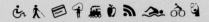

## Le Clos

A rustic-style hotel where you can have breakfast on the terrace overlooking the manicured *jardin de curé*. Then choose your suntrap in the garden – it's full of hidden corners; or wander, shaded by generous trees, among the quaint agricultural machinery that sculpturally dots the lawns. This white-shuttered farmhouse, in a peaceful semi-rural area, has been renovated to reveal exposed limestone walls and massive rafters; note the charming country breakfast room and the light and lofty sitting room whose ancient tiles have been garnished with oriental rugs and sofas. Big, neat, carpeted bedrooms have matching floral bed linen and curtains, some fine antique bedsteads and the odd exotic touch. Bathrooms are spotless and there are no half measures: big tubs, walk-in showers, an abundance of towels. There's no restaurant here, though there is a bar; the pretty village is just down the road. Montagny lès Beaune is deep in wine country – and when you've had your fill of burgundies and beaunes, there are mustards to try in a nearby village. Beaune is conveniently close.

| | |
|---|---|
| Rooms | 20 twin/doubles: €105–€140. |
| | 5 suites for 2: €160–€180. |
| | Singles €105–€180. |
| Meals | Breakfast €14. Restaurant 100m. |
| Closed | 24 November to 17 January. |

**Monsieur & Madame Oudot**
Le Clos,
22 rue Gravières,
21200 Montagny lès Beaune, Côte-d'Or

| | |
|---|---|
| Tel | +33 (0)3 80 25 97 98 |
| Email | hotelleclos@wanadoo.fr |
| Web | www.hotelleclos.com |

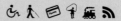

## La Terre d'Or

The night view of twinkling Beaune, five minutes down the hill, is glorious. Jean-Louis loves sharing 'his' Burgundy: the making of the elegant vintages, the best Burgundian chefs, great Romanesque art. All this by bike, horseback, jeep or hot-air balloon. The Martin family – Jean-Louis and Christine now joined by son Vincent – run three wonderful houses, each surrounded by mature trees and a terraced garden enlivened by Vincent's wife Jurga's sculpted figures. The modern, multi-levelled main house has five large and lovely bedrooms while the stone cottage, for B&B or self-catering, is traditional, the third house being more independent. The noble old beams and rosy tomette floors frame a fine new, pale, contemporary look warmed with stylish lighting, crisp linen and polished country pieces (including winegrowers' chairs). The honeymoon suite has a private piece of garden. It's bliss to relax on the main terrace and gaze across vineyards to the ramparts of old Beaune before wandering down a wildflower path to a family-run restaurant.

| | |
|---|---|
| Rooms | 1 twin: €220.<br>4 suites for 2: €150–€270.<br>1 cottage for 4,<br>1 cottage for 4-6: €395–€510 per night. |
| Meals | Breakfast €13. Picnic available.<br>Restaurant 400m. |
| Closed | Rarely. |

Vincent, Christine & Jean-Louis Martin
La Terre d'Or,
Rue Izembart La Montagne,
21200 Beaune, Côte-d'Or

| | |
|---|---|
| Tel | +33 (0)3 80 25 90 90 |
| Email | jlmartin@laterredor.com |
| Web | www.laterredor.com |

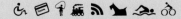

## Les Jardins de Loïs

This 200-year-old house once belonged to a wine broker. Now, under the connoisseurship of its charming, attentive owners, Philippe and Anne-Marie, it has returned to its roots; they are both wine buffs and their pride and joy is their cellar, open to guests. Details delight throughout. Bedrooms, reached by a splendid exterior staircase, are lavish, trad/modern, and beautiful: lilacs and suave creams offset polished limestone and black cabochon; antique armoires flatter oriental rugs; bathrooms (and a pretty steam room) are immaculate in russet-ochre marble with Italianate monsoon showers. The garden suite, 'Clos des Renards', is the most private, in its own outbuilding with a sitting room and huge bath. Enjoy a generous breakfast with homemade jams in the elegant, airy dining room, stroll Beaune's ancient cobbles, visit the famous Hospices, drink the fruits of the region's wine capital. Then retire with a bottle of their own fine burgundy to the gem of a garden – half a hectare, walled, teak-furnished, with neat beds, roses, shady magnolias and fruit trees – a stunning surprise in this city-central position.

| | |
|---|---|
| Rooms | 3 doubles: €160. |
| | 2 suites for 2: €185-€195. |
| Meals | Restaurant 150m. |
| Closed | Christmas & New Year. |

Anne-Marie & Philippe Dufouleur
Les Jardins de Loïs,
21200 Beaune, Côte-d'Or

| | |
|---|---|
| Tel | +33 (0)3 80 22 41 97 |
| Mobile | +33 (0)6 73 85 11 47 |
| Email | contact@jardinsdelois.com |
| Web | www.jardinsdelois.com |

## Hôtel de Vougeot

Rows of vines sweep down an incline, surround the Château de Clos de Vougeot, and then come to an abrupt halt at the back doorstep of this spotless place, whose 16 rooms inhabit three modest clusters of buildings; ask for a view of château and vines. For centuries, Clos de Vougeot was considered the finest of all burgundies; the Cistercian monks planted some of the vines in the 12th century and the cloister, cellar and vast presses are among the most interesting examples of architecture in Burgundy (it's fabulous at harvest time). Alain speaks excellent English and is a great host, but you are mostly on your own here with a key to come and go as you please. The staircase could be awkward for the very young or very old, and there's no sitting area; however, the terrace has marvellous views. Inside, everything has been kept simple and clean, the rough outlines of dark timbers contrasting with white walls, light coloured bedspreads, parquet floors and teak furniture. The buffet breakfasts and the cold supper platters are delicious – or splash out on a Michelin-starred table in the next village, the perfect end to a great day.

| Rooms | 12 doubles: €69–€133. |
| | 1 family room for 5: €156–€167. |
| | 1 triple: €88–€129. |
| | 2 quadruples: €137–€148. |
| | Extra bed/sofabed available €19 per person per night. |
| Meals | Buffet breakfast €12. |
| | Cold platter €22. Wine from €15. |
| Closed | 20 December to 20 January. |

Alain Senterre
Hôtel de Vougeot,
18 rue du Vieux Château,
21640 Vougeot, Côte-d'Or

| Tel | +33 (0)3 80 62 01 15 |
| Email | contact@hotel-vougeot.com |
| Web | www.hotel-vougeot.com |

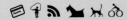

## Le Domaine des Prés Verts Spa

In a lovely rural hamlet, with cows for neighbours, find four interesting eco-builds, a spa and a shop. All are deeply modern and well-designed, a blend of natural materials and bang up to date ideas, right down to the iPad you need for ordering breakfast or getting ideas for excursions — no expense has been spared with really good beds, crisp white sheets, fluffy towels, thick fabrics, good lighting, a very contemporary bathroom divided from the bedroom by a heavy felt curtain (in the cabane so not for the less than intimate) and a tempting mini-bar (watch it!). Couples still in the dreamy stage can hunker down and enjoy each other, or enjoy a range of treatments in your room. The cabane has a calming private pond, the gardens and boules pitch are for all guests to enjoy. Just down the road the owners have applied their style to the classic French *roulotte* wagon with a modern garden. Breakfast is continental with excellent croissants, organic jam or honey, good restaurants abound and can be booked for you, there are 1950s solex scooters or 2CVs to hire and plenty of super places to visit, including fine vineyards and the National Park of Morvan. Swish.

| | |
|---|---|
| Rooms | Le Logis – 1 barn for 6: €140-€220. |
| | La Cabane – 1 cabin for 2: €180-€260. |
| | La Réserve – 1 cabin for 2: €180-€260 |
| | Le Refuge – 1 gypsy caravan for 2: €220. |
| | All prices per night. Extra bed/sofabed |
| | available €30 per person per night. |
| Meals | Restaurants 15-minute drive. |
| Closed | 14 December to 5 January. |

Jérémy Leleu
Le Domaine des Prés Verts Spa,
10 Impasse des Prés Verts, Hameau de
Pochey, 21230 Jouey, Côte-d'Or

| | |
|---|---|
| Tel | +33 (0)3 45 44 05 60 |
| Email | info@domainedespresverts.com |
| Web | www.domainedespresverts.fr |

## Les Deux Chèvres

In the privileged heart of Gevrey Chambertin, surrounded by vineyards and hills that stretch as far as the eye can see, is a splendid small hotel. The décor is delectable, the artwork is special, and the manageress and the owners (he Welsh, she Polish) look after you with warmth and discretion. There's tons of history too, with a most impressive ancient wine press and huge cellars for the café-to-be. In short, it's a wine-lover's dream. You'll find a formal salon with choice antique pieces, a sitting room for loungers, a library for readers, a dining room for breakfast (local, organic), two gravelled courtyards elegant with roses, and everywhere the most gorgeous, gilt-framed art. Bedrooms are serene, classical, traditional, one on the ground floor with a centuries-old fireplace and a flagstone floor, four more above, up a lovely dark wood staircase. A further two lie the other side of the courtyard; bathrooms, each luscious, are state-of-the-art. For culture and markets there's Dijon, 12km; for medieval history and wines, Beaune; for wine and champagne tastings, the cellars just beneath you.

| | |
|---|---|
| Rooms | 5 doubles: €175–€225. 2 suites for 2: €275. |
| Meals | Breakfast €12 per person. Restaurants 5-minute walk. |
| Closed | Rarely. |

Paul Thomas & Jolanta Bakalarz
Les Deux Chèvres,
23 rue de l'Eglise,
21220 Gevrey Chambertin, Côte-d'Or

| | |
|---|---|
| Tel | +33 (0)3 80 51 48 25 |
| Email | info@lesdeuxchevres.com |
| Web | www.lesdeuxchevres.com |

## Le Château de Courban

This ambitiously renovated 19th-century mansion – with a 17th-century dovecote bearing witness to an even older heritage – was transformed into its present incarnation by Jérôme and Frédéric's father, perfectionist Pierre Vandendriessche. Most of the rooms are in the original mansion and flaunt a wide variety of styles, from the bold and bright to the floral and cosy, all tastefully harmonised and generously comfortable: recessed bedheads, draped four-posters, crisp colour schemes and carefully chosen prints. Newer buildings vaunt more contemporary design; rustic chic comfort and their own verandas. Bathrooms feature claw-foot tubs in some, walk-in showers with monsoon heads in others. Cuisine here is in the hands of award-winning chef Ismail Yilmaz. Try the great things he does with truffles and lobster, inter alia, in the expansive restaurant, the orangery or the veranda; breakfast should be enjoyed in bed with the shutters wide open. There are relaxed, formal gardens to one side, and an inviting infinity pool (and thoroughly kitted-out spa) to the other. Take all the time you can.

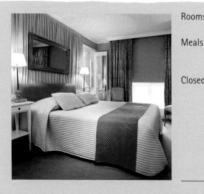

| | |
|---|---|
| Rooms | 14 twin/doubles: €130–€160. |
| | 10 suites for 2: €260–€320. |
| Meals | Breakfast €18. |
| | Dinner €45–€90. |
| | Wine €40–€295. |
| Closed | Christmas. |

Jérôme Vandendriessche
Le Château de Courban,
7 rue du Lavoir Courban,
21520 Courban, Côte-d'Or

Tel      +33 (0)3 80 93 78 69
Email   contact@chateaudecourban.com
Web    www.chateaudecourban.com

 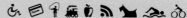

Région Parisienne

Photo: Hôtel de
Londres, entry 74

## Le Relais du Louvre

Look down the throats of gargoyles, soak up the history. The Revolutionaries printed their newsletter in the cellar; the place inspired Puccini's Café Momus in *Bohême*. It is utterly delightful and so are the charming young managers who greet you from the antique desk. Everywhere, antiques and oriental rugs complement the modernity of firm beds and perfect bathrooms. Front rooms look onto the church's Gothic flights of fancy and along to the austerely neo-classical Louvre; others give onto a light-filled patio. Top-floor suites have space for a sofabed, pastel walls, exuberant upholstery and heaps of light from mansard windows. One of the suites is big and beautiful with fireplace, books, music, old engravings and a superb veranda kitchen. Smaller rooms are luminous, fresh and restful – yellow, a favourite colour, brings sunny moods into small spaces. You feel softly secluded and coddled everywhere. The sense of service is highly developed and, as there is no dining room, breakfast comes to you. *On each floor 2 rooms can interconnect to make a family suite.*

| Rooms | 14 twin/doubles: €155–€250. |
| --- | --- |
| | 1 suite for 4, 1 suite for 3, |
| | 1 suite for 2: €235–€330. |
| | 5 singles: €135–€170. |
| Meals | Breakfast €13. |
| | Dinner €10–€30. |
| | Wine €7. |
| | All room service only. |
| Closed | Never. |

Sophie Aulnette
Le Relais du Louvre,
19 rue des Prêtres St Germain
l'Auxerrois, 75001 Paris
Tel        +33 (0)1 40 41 96 42
Email    contact@relaisdulouvre.com
Web      www.relaisdulouvre.com

## Hôtel Molière

This is an enchantingly French hotel. The big lobby/salon is smart and rather grand with its faux-marbre columns, potted palms and bucket chairs, and the staff at reception are hugely competent and friendly; the young owners infuse the place with their intelligent enthusiasm. The breakfast room is a delight, and deep red curtains frame the leafy, cobbled courtyard. There's also a small, deep-chaired salon round the corner for your quiet moments, perhaps with an old book. Brand new bedrooms are super modern and grand with plush, bold carpets, velvet sofas and bucket chairs, white linen, white walls, antique-look portraits and chandeliers. Bathrooms (some separated from the bedroom by a glass wall) vary in size but all are modern; those in the suites dazzle with rectangular double sinks, huge tubs and swish Italian showers. Interesting paintings, books and ornaments give the hotel a well-cared-for feel. You're in the heart of Paris and can walk to everything - soak your aching limbs in the spa when you return. Everyone loves the Molière.

| | |
|---|---|
| Rooms | 14 doubles, 8 twins: €215-€360. 10 twin/doubles: €295-€410. 3 suites for 4: €500-€610. 2 triples: €345-€410. |
| Meals | Breakfast €14. Restaurants 1-minute walk. |
| Closed | Never. |

Patricia & Rémy Perraud
Hôtel Molière,
21 rue Molière, 75001 Paris

| | |
|---|---|
| Tel | +33 (0)1 42 96 22 01 |
| Email | info@hotel-moliere.fr |
| Web | www.hotel-moliere.fr |

## Hôtel du Jeu de Paume

The Ile Saint Louis is the most exclusive 17th-century village in Paris and this renovated 'tennis court' – three storeys soar to the roof timbers – is one of its most exceptional sights. Add genuine care from family owners, fresh flowers, time for everyone and super staff. Regulars will be stunned – and delighted – by the recent revamp, which sees sleek designer furniture set under ancient beams, bright colours flung across stone walls, new large built-in cupboards and funky lighting to show off contemporary art. Some rooms feature beautiful beams, one gives onto a little garden; number 109's bed perches on a high platform. We love it – for its sense of history, eccentricities, aesthetic ironies, peaceful humour and feel of home; and for its unconventional attitudes and relaxed yet thoroughly efficient staff. The serene, spacious lounge has low armchairs in chocolate and red, modern art and Scoop the soft gold dog; breakfast is beneath magnificent timbers by faux Greek columns; work out or take a sauna in a new spa in the vaulted cellars. *Let Madame Heckel know if your stay spans a birthday or anniversary.*

| | |
|---|---|
| Rooms | 20 twin/doubles: €295-€360. |
| | 3 suites for 2: €560. |
| | 7 singles: €195-€255. |
| | 2 apartments for 4-6: €620-€900 per night. |
| Meals | Breakfast €20. Restaurants next door. |
| Closed | Never. |

Nathalie Heckel
Hôtel du Jeu de Paume,
54 rue St Louis en l'Ile,
75004 Paris

| | |
|---|---|
| Tel | +33 (0)1 43 26 14 18 |
| Email | info@jeudepaumehotel.com |
| Web | www.jeudepaumehotel.com |

## Hôtel Jeanne d'Arc

Make haste if you want to experience the last breath of that dying species, the two-star Parisian hotel. The Jeanne d'Arc, always one of the friendliest and best-placed of the bunch, has a talented new owner who will soon be wielding her design flair and filing for an upgrade. She has already lifted the façade with glorious torrents of geraniums – the neighbours love them too. Hurry if you want to enjoy fresh croissants beneath the extravagantly kitsch bling-before-bling mirror in the airy breakfast room, a landmark for generations of Paris-loving guests. The hallway has already been beautified with soft pinky-mushroom paint over a gleaming white dado, some shower rooms have been done up with smart white tiles and trendy strips of brown wafer slices while others await their turn in their spotless but fuddy-duddy dated garb of bubbly tiles and reedy pictures. The staircase will soon match the hallway, all bedding is to be renewed and the brocante-style furniture mix brought up to date, but not at the price of the essence of the place, its cosy friendliness and superb value for the lively, trend-conscious Marais quarter.

| | |
|---|---|
| Rooms | 17 doubles, 10 twin/doubles: €150–€250. 2 family rooms for 4: €220–€420. 5 singles: €90–€120. Extra bed €40. |
| Meals | Breakfast €8. Restaurants next door. |
| Closed | Never. |

**Terrence & Stéphane**
Hôtel Jeanne d'Arc,
3 rue de Jarente,
75004 Paris

| | |
|---|---|
| Tel | +33 (0)1 48 87 62 11 |
| Email | ingavernaz@gmail.com |
| Web | www.hoteljeannedarc.com |

## Hôtel Les Jardins du Luxembourg

Freud once trampled this still peaceful cul-de-sac when he stayed in 1885 – and we know that the curtains round his bed were yellow: his disciple Ernest Jones relates that he applied chemical tests to make sure they did not contain arsenic. Now there are curtains at the windows only, some falling nicely to the floor; original beams are still on view on the top floor. Rooms are small, balconies minute, furnishings immaculate. We can imagine Freud sitting with a coffee in the tiny salon; Art Deco chairs and brass lights over paintings give it an intimate feel, and daily papers come free. The reception area, by contrast, is a big open space, with a handsome mahogany desk that doubles as a bar. Facing it is a long wrought-iron park bench with colourful cushions to remind us that the Luxembourg Gardens – one of Paris' largest, loveliest green spaces – are just across the street. Keep your eye out for the delightful ochre and orange checkerboard tiles in the downstairs breakfast room and joyful trompe-l'oeil lizards and vine wreaths in the bathrooms, some of which have free-standing basins and four-legged tubs.

| | |
|---|---|
| Rooms | 18 doubles, 7 twins, 1 single: €169–€179. |
| Meals | Breakfast €15. Restaurants 1-minute walk. |
| Closed | Rarely. |

**Les Jardins du Luxembourg**
Hôtel Les Jardins du Luxembourg,
5 imp Royer Collard,
75005 Paris

| | |
|---|---|
| Tel | +33 (0)1 40 46 08 88 |
| Email | jardinslux@wanadoo.fr |
| Web | www.les-jardins-du-luxembourg.com |

## Grand Hôtel des Balcons

Les Balcons has the lot: an idea of service that produces tea on winter afternoons and a daily feast of a breakfast (cooked specials, organic yogurt, fruit salad, espresso), that's free on your birthday. Owners and staff appear to work with lightness and pleasure. Having decorated their Art Nouveau hotel by taking inspiration from the floral 1890s staircase windows, Jean-François and directrice Marie run the place with great charm. Rooms are simple yet pleasing and those that have already been updated are lovely. The five big family rooms have smart décor and modern lamps, parquet floors and two windows, decent bathrooms (slowly but surely being updated); singles have new walk-in showers. Some rooms are tiny but purpose-made table units use the space judiciously, amusing prints decorate the walls and front rooms have balconies with planted window boxes. At the back, you may be woken by the birds. An eagle eye is kept on maintenance, beds are firm, colours and fabrics simple and bright. Remarkable value, super people, and bang in the heart of the Latin Quarter.

| | |
|---|---|
| Rooms | 17 doubles, 13 twins: €125-€180. 5 family rooms for 4: €240. 15 singles: €98-€180. |
| Meals | Breakfast €12. Restaurants 1-minute walk. |
| Closed | Rarely. |

Jean-François André
Grand Hôtel des Balcons,
3 rue Casimir Delavigne,
75006 Paris,

| | |
|---|---|
| Tel | +33 (0)1 46 34 78 50 |
| Email | grandhoteldesbalcons@orange.fr |
| Web | www.balcons.com |

## Hôtel Relais Saint Sulpice

Smack on the back doorstep of Saint Sulpice church, tucked into one of those tiny magic streets untouched by time, this is the perfect hideaway for sleuthing around for Da Vinci Code clues or spotting the literati of Saint Germain des Prés. You might miss the entrance if you're not careful; it's more an entryway into an aristocratic 18th-century home than a door to a hotel. The womb-like salon continues the lived-in feeling with deep red papered walls, screened mahogany bookcases, a white faïence stove, Chinese jars and some bottles of French liqueur tempting guests to an evening apéritif; in the lobby, find trompe l'oeil bookshelves and a vast oriental frieze reflected in tall mirrors. No reception desk to speak of here, just a friendly spirit behind the table to hand out keys to your small but cosy room. The attention to detail is impressive: you may spot a fringe-like frieze along the walls or an elegant wrought-iron bed and bistro table; most bathrooms have colourful floor tiles. A huge glass roof and a bounty of greenery give the downstairs breakfast room a winter garden feel. An exceptional address. *Pets by arrangement.*

| Rooms | 19 doubles, 7 twins: €134–€325. |
|---|---|
| Meals | Breakfast €15. |
| | Restaurants 2-minute walk. |
| Closed | Never. |

**Relais Saint Sulpice**
Hôtel Relais Saint Sulpice,
3 rue Garancière,
75006 Paris

| | |
|---|---|
| Tel | +33 (0)1 46 33 99 00 |
| Email | relaisstsulpice@wanadoo.fr |
| Web | www.relais-saint-sulpice.com |

## Hôtel St Paul Rive Gauche

An exceptionally welcoming place with a flickering fire in the sitting room and a day-lit interior patio. With the Luxembourg Gardens a stroll away, bustling Saint Germain at the end of the street, and exceptional service and attention to detail (such as organic croissants at breakfast), it's a favourite of many guests. Expect crisp white duvets with a mohair throw for a splash of colour, a thick tiger-stripe carpet underfoot, spotless bathrooms with real shower heads, L'Occitane en Provence soaps and towel heaters. Bedrooms come in different sizes – and that includes small, as with most Paris hotels. Those at the back have handsome views onto the classical façade of the famous Lycée St Louis, an educational hothouse, those in front look onto the ever fascinating Rue Monsieur le Prince. There are beamed ceilings, sleigh beds, faux ostrich bedheads, clever corner armoires, family antiques, even two baldaquin beds beneath the high ceilings of the lower floors. The fourth generation of a Franco-British family has made the St Paul Rive Gauche a welcoming marriage of French elegance and English comfort. *Some rooms interconnect.*

| | |
|---|---|
| Rooms | 21 doubles, 7 twin/doubles: €178–€408. 3 family rooms for 3-4: €328–€478. Singles €158–€268. |
| Meals | Buffet breakfast €14, continental €8. Restaurants next door. |
| Closed | Never. |

Valérie Benigno
Hôtel St Paul Rive Gauche,
43 rue Monsieur le Prince,
75006 Paris

| | |
|---|---|
| Tel | +33 (0)1 43 26 98 64 |
| Email | contact@hotelsaintpaulparis.com |
| Web | www.hotelsaintpaulparis.com |

Entry 54   Map 5

## Hôtel Sainte Beuve

This beautifully decorated hotel, well-known and loved during the wilder days of Montparnasse, exudes an atmosphere of unstuffy designer luxury – quiet good taste in gentle tones and thick fabrics. The harmoniously hued lobby/salon, which doubles as a breakfast room, has superb silk curtains, a winter fire in the marble fireplace, modern paintings and old prints. It is all small and intimate and the attentive, efficient staff are a vital element in your sense of well-being. Bedrooms come in ancient and modern finery: lots of pale walls, soft colours and textured fabrics, colourful chintzes and paisleys, at least one antique per room – a leather-topped desk, a walnut dressing-table, a polished armoire – and 18th and 19th-century pictures in rich old frames. The Sainte Beuve room is the largest and it's dazzling. Bathrooms are superbly modern with bathrobes and fine toiletries. Start the day with a feast of croissants and brioches… then you can run it off in the Luxembourg Gardens. End the day with très tasty food at teensy Le Timbre, in the same street.

| Rooms | 7 doubles, 15 twins: €165-€370. 1 suite for 4: €355-€490. |
|---|---|
| Meals | Breakfast €16. Restaurants 1-minute walk. |
| Closed | Never. |

**Matthieu Croisiez**
Hôtel Sainte Beuve,
9 rue Ste Beuve,
75006 Paris

Tel      +33 (0)1 45 48 20 07
Email    reservation@hotelsaintebeuve.com
Web      www.hotelsaintebeuve.com

## L'Hôtel

A place of legend old and new, L'Hôtel is the dosshouse where Oscar Wilde died destitute in 1900, and where now the most famous celebs stay in the hope of remaining as nameless as this gem of a small luxury hotel. 'Oscar Wilde Suite', now draped in silk and velvet, has a green marble bath in a mahogany alcove. The remarkable circular six-floor atrium still astounds, original works of art hang in Jacques Garcia's new, award-winning décor in Napoleon III style of heavy hangings, rich colours, swags, furbelows and ornate mirrors that give depth to small spaces, and every detail is a study in luxury. Each bedroom, small or large, is a jewel box of style; even the smallest is a work of opulent art, the apotheosis being the top-floor 'Cardinal Suite' where a sweeping portrait of its namesake surveys the bedroom and the richest red brocade covers the walls. Julien Montbabut's cooking has earned the restaurant a Michelin star, his wife Joana makes delectable desserts and pastries for the tea room, all is indulgence and the service is as pleasant as it is efficient. L'Hôtel is a masterly marriage of discretion and glamour.

| | |
|---|---|
| Rooms | 6 doubles, 13 twin/doubles: €305–€850. 1 suite for 2: €1,150. |
| Meals | Dinner €35–€55; 5–7 courses, €95–€110. Restaurants 5-minute walk. |
| Closed | Never. |

Julien Révah
L'Hôtel,
13 rue Des Beaux-Arts,
75006 Paris

| | |
|---|---|
| Tel | +33 (0)1 44 41 99 00 |
| Email | stay@l-hotel.com |
| Web | www.l-hotel.com |

## Millésime Hôtel

'Our room had an impossible peacefulness – all we could hear was birdsong' writes a guest. Behind its imposing old doors, the Millésime is welcoming, cosy and friendly. The hotel is undergoing a bit of a transformation and you'll now find a Scandinavian, chic feel with blond wood, clean lines and calm colours. Smart, comfortable bedrooms vary in size but are never too tiny (a rarity in Paris): charcoal curtains and throws, sleek white linen, modern lighting; three rooms open onto the charming flower-filled, leafy patio. Splurge on the spacious top-floor suite, with its high-peaked ceilings and tall windows overlooking historic towers and domes; reach it via the cute lift or the 17th-century wooden staircase – a genuine piece of French heritage. Breakfast is served in the 16th-century vaulted breakfast room. In the heart of the Left Bank quarter with literary cafés, bookstores and art galleries a few minutes' walk away. One of our favourite city hotels, and decent value for Saint Germain.

| | |
|---|---|
| Rooms | 20 twin/doubles: €140–€325. 1 suite for 2: €290–€550. |
| Meals | Breakfast €13, buffet €16. Restaurants 1-minute walk. |
| Closed | Rarely. |

**Louis Troillard**
Millésime Hôtel,
15 rue Jacob,
75006 Paris

Tel      +33 (0)1 44 07 97 97
Email    reservation@millesimehotel.com
Web      www.millesimehotel.com

## La Villa Saint Germain

A showcase of contemporary French design that screams trendy Saint Germain. Step in to soberly studied forms and colours: a blocky black desk, soft silky chestnut curtains, a curvy steel stair rail, ochre-flecked stone floor slabs; gentle music too, and grey and café latte chairs on a teak floor by the bar. Staff are appropriately young, bright, attentive. Bedrooms reflect Saint Germain's split personality: the drama of wine red, brown, white; the gentleness of ivory, beige. Materials are rich and yielding – thick burgundy curtains folded back on silk linings, 'crocodile'-skin bedheads, fluffy white duvets against scarlet walls. (If you like your room with extra personality, ask for a newly redesigned one on the fourth floor, where shelves groan with modern white objets and funky lighting gleams on half-moon tables.) And the details: room numbers light-projected by the door, monogrammed linen, superb designer bathrooms in chrome and ground glass. The bar is peaceful, the lift speedy, and breakfast is down the 1930s-look stairs in a stylish rich red space. It all feels so good and the cool Left Bank laps at your feet.

| | |
|---|---|
| Rooms | 17 doubles, 10 twins: €280–€390. 4 suites for 2: €390–€480. |
| Meals | Buffet breakfast €22, continental €16. Restaurants next door. |
| Closed | Never. |

**Christine Horbette**
La Villa Saint Germain,
29 rue Jacob,
75006 Paris

| | |
|---|---|
| Tel | +33 (0)1 43 26 60 00 |
| Email | hotel@villa-saintgermain.com |
| Web | www.villa-saintgermain.com |

## Hôtel des Académies et des Arts

Poetry moves from the pavements of Paris into the cosiest new Left Bank hotel in town. Coming to hotellery from television, Laurent and Charlotte wanted to echo the rich history of Montparnasse. Modigliani's studio was on the top floor, each room has a fine art book for guests to peruse, décor themes are Art Deco, Man Ray, music hall, high fashion. They asked renowned street artist (and mainstream refusnik) Jérôme Mesnager if he would join their new venture. Beginners' luck: yes, he would. He came in from the cold bringing a small army of his emblematic "white bodies" to dance across, climb up and generally enliven this tiny box of contemporary luxury. There are sculptures, too, by Charlotte's well-known mother, video installations, lots of books; the salon de thé serves exquisite Hermé macarons. Bedrooms are small and perfectly formed. In the scarlet light well a white giant reaches for the stars; in the stair well, the lift shaft... The final flourish is on the façade. It is an inspirational place. Matthieu keeps a light but accomplished eye on the details of daily life here and the wheels turn smooth as velvet.

| | |
|---|---|
| Rooms | 15 doubles, 5 twins: €165-€370. |
| Meals | Breakfast €16. |
| | Restaurants 1-minute walk. |
| Closed | Never. |

Matthieu Croisiez
Hôtel des Académies et des Arts,
15 rue de la Grande Chaumière,
75006 Paris

| | |
|---|---|
| Tel | +33 (0)1 45 48 20 07 |
| Email | reservation@hoteldesacademies.com |
| Web | www.hotel-des-academies.com |

## Hôtel Dauphine Saint Germain

You will find food for mind and body here, a superb breakfast buffet (or brought to your room), a thoughtful academic atmosphere in the bar later in the day, a youthful joie-de-vivre at all times; the new owner's family photographs help create this vibe. There are some interesting contemporary drawings, prints and photographs as well as traditional baroque-style lamps and furnishings. Under the guidance of the delightful and efficient manager, Inga, the staff are young, dynamic and welcoming. The bedrooms, all different, feel both elegant and personal with their 17th century beams and many-splendoured fabrics. Snuggle into the softness of timeless Jouy-cloth walls and moulded mahogany alcoves, admire the harmony of grey and pink with swags and tassels to match, rejoice in your luxurious marble-topped bathroom. The top-floor junior suite has, of course, the best view over Paris's renowned rooftops to Notre Dame on one side and St Germain des Prés on the other. You will be happy to return after a day's work or museum-tramping to this utterly Parisian hotel in the heart of the fashion and café-life district. *Well behaved dogs welcome.*

| | |
|---|---|
| Rooms | 29 twin/doubles: €100–€350. |
| | 1 suite for 2: €250–€450. |
| | Extra bed €25. |
| Meals | Breakfast €12, children under 12 €6. |
| | Restaurants next door. |
| Closed | Never. |

Adrien
Hôtel Dauphine Saint Germain,
36 rue Dauphine,
75006 Paris

| | |
|---|---|
| Tel | +33 (0)1 56 81 10 10 |
| Email | ingavernaz@gmail.com |
| Web | www.dauphine-st-germain.com |

## Hôtel Le Clément

This cute little hotel has been in the same family for 100 years and Madame Charrade, should you be lucky enough to meet her, is the gentlest hotelier you could hope to meet (her staff are less personal). More living room than lobby is the inviting sitting area off the new breakfast room, with fireplace, gleaming wood panelling and bookshelves. From the higher floors, the view across the St Germain marketplace to the towers of St Sulpice church is super. These rooms at the top have loads of character with their sloping ceilings, though little space and thin walls, and access is by narrow stairwell or even narrower lift! Back rooms have no view, of course, except over the pretty planting at the bottom of one of the lightwells (the hotel occupies two connecting buildings), but peace is guaranteed. Madame's decorative style is southern cottage: small spriggy or floral prints, harmonious fabrics, good colour combinations – midnight-blue and ivory, Provençal red and orange – and crisp, white piqué bedcovers; bathrooms are often tiled in colourful mosaic. A hotel of good value – from which reaching all the sights is a breeze.

| | |
|---|---|
| Rooms | 12 doubles, 6 twins: €136–€175. 5 triples: €193. |
| Meals | Buffet breakfast €13. Restaurants next door. |
| Closed | Never. |

**Patricia & Rémy Perraud**
Hôtel Le Clément,
6 rue Clément,
75006 Paris
Tel          +33 (0)1 43 26 53 60
Email     info@hotel-clement.fr
Web       www.hotel-clement.fr

## Pension Les Marronniers

It's an honest-to-goodness *pension de famille*, one of the very last, so if you're young and penniless or old and nostalgic, head for Marie's quintessentially French family place overlooking the Luxembourg Gardens. It's been in her family since the 1930s and is as personal and cluttered as anything in Balzac. There are countless pictures, portraits and photographs, statues and plants galore, notices from guests on flower pots and mantelpieces, a cuckoo clock that was silenced 20 years ago and a superbly carved, grass-green armoire topped with candlesticks – plus a motley crew of friendly dogs. Marie coddles her guests (some return year after year) and loves cooking for them: she clearly enjoys food herself, especially vegetarian, and makes sure others do too. She is also down-to-earth, compassionate, perceptive and hard-working – a remarkable woman. The bedrooms for short-stayers have less personality than the drawing-dining room, rather as if they have been furnished with what was left over, and some share washing facilities. But what counts is the wonderful welcome, the tradition and the food.

| | |
|---|---|
| Rooms | 6 twin/doubles: €97.<br>5 singles sharing bathroom: €71.<br>Breakfast & dinner included. Singles'<br>surcharge for double room €23. |
| Meals | Full board, except Saturdays &<br>Sundays (breakfast on Saturdays<br>included). |
| Closed | Rarely. |

Marie Poirier
Pension Les Marronniers,
78 rue d'Assas,
75006 Paris

| | |
|---|---|
| Tel | +33 (0)1 43 26 37 71 |
| Email | o_marro@club-internet.fr |
| Web | www.pension-marronniers.com |

Entry 62   Map 5

## Le Petit Chomel

Owners Georges and Charlotte Ferrero cleverly create a private house vibe in their boutique hotels – Le Petit Chomel is a delight, and manager Mathieu Renaudin and team are warmly helpful. Style and elegance are their trademarks, and contemporary touches mix with lovely old things in an effortless way. Mme Ferrero hunts out flea market pieces and has a great eye for colour and comfort. Sink into a big sofa or bright orange chair in reception, relax by glowing lamps and vases of flowers; coffee tables invite lingering. The breakfast lounge is a wonderful space to sit in too – shelves of books and sculptures, china and vibrant art. There's something beautiful in every corner. Bedrooms vary in size, but all have beds with bright throws and more eclectic fun; find bathrobes in bigger rooms. Suites, on the sixth floor, have sitting rooms with paintings, a purple, cushion-strewn sofa perhaps, a dumpy china bird here and there; some have balconies with rooftop views. You're in the heart of Montparnasse, next door to Les Botanistes, named best bistro in 2014, and steps from luxurious department store Bon Marché.

| Rooms | 11 doubles, 10 twin/doubles: €175–€350. 2 suites for 2: €270–€390. Extra bed €40. |
|---|---|
| Meals | Breakfast €14. Restaurants 1-minute walk. |
| Closed | Never. |

**Mathieu Renaudin**
Le Petit Chomel,
15 rue Chomel, 75007 Paris

| Tel | +33 (0)1 45 48 55 52 |
| Mobile | +33 (0)6 11 02 61 15 |
| Email | chambre414@hotmail.com |
| Web | www.lepetitchomel.com |

## Hôtel de Varenne

Step into the little green cul-de-sac with its ivy covered walls, hidden fountain and exquisite canopy over the entrance door and you will feel like Alice in Wonderland; you have tumbled into an oasis of peace and calm, far from the hustle bustle of the city streets. The front doors slide open, the reception desk is a friendly antique writing table, two bronze statues grace antique chests of drawers and a handsome gilt-studded balustrade leads you upstairs. There's a traditional hotel feel to the bedrooms and most of them (the quietest) look onto the courtyard where breakfast or an evening drink is a delight. Most are a reasonable size for Paris and all have a desk and a chair. Monsieur Pommier is a man of detail and classic taste: green, gold, blue or wine red are the classic figured bedspreads while curtains repeat the colour schemes – certainly no design surprises. There are framed prints of Parisian monuments and well-kept bathrooms with plenty of shelf space. Four bigger rooms give onto the street; slightly less quiet than the rest. The charming staff will always go out of their way to make your stay special.

| | |
|---|---|
| Rooms | 16 doubles, 10 twins: €182–€500. Extra bed/sofabed available €40 per person per night. |
| Meals | Breakfast €12. Restaurants 1-minute walk. |
| Closed | Never. |

Jean-Marc Pommier
Hôtel de Varenne,
44 rue de Bourgogne,
75007 Paris

| | |
|---|---|
| Tel | +33 (0)1 45 51 45 55 |
| Email | varennehotel@gmail.com |
| Web | www.hoteldevarenne.com |

## Hôtel La Sanguine

Through a little lobby and up one flight to a house of flowers and easy friendliness. You will be welcomed by delightful, energetic people – family or long-standing staff – and Tokyo, the sausage dog. The atmosphere is one of quiet country-style comfort; find a desk and a couple of classical statues overlooking the floral breakfast tables and the view through to a little green patio. Carpets are thick, rooms are fresh and bright with good designer fabrics, upholstered chairs to complement colourful bedcovers, discreet personality, well-equipped marble bathrooms and umpteen red-chalk drawings to lend gentle interest; family rooms have just been updated and the little singles take one back to childhood and Beatrix Potter. Service here is infinitely human and attentive: in season, the owners make your breakfast jam with fruit from their orchard; Monsieur bakes your breakfast croissant; Madame is full of good advice on what to see and do. Hard to believe that the powers of this world – ministers, fashion gurus, ambassadors – live just around the corner.

| | |
|---|---|
| Rooms | 17 doubles, 5 twins: €141–€183. |
| | 1 family room for 3: €219–€384. |
| | 8 singles: €105–€130. |
| Meals | Breakfast €10–€13. |
| | Restaurants next door. |
| Closed | Rarely. |

**Monsieur & Madame Plumerand**
Hôtel La Sanguine,
6 rue de Surène,
75008 Paris

| | |
|---|---|
| Tel | +33 (0)1 42 65 71 61 |
| Email | info@hotel-la-sanguine.com |
| Web | www.hotel-la-sanguine.com |

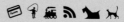

## Hôtel de la Paix

A calm retreat in the heart of zippy Montparnasse. The avenue is leafy, and owner Georges Ferrero's  manager, Mathieu Renaudin, and team are especially agreeable; step out of the bustle and into a foyer full of natural light with a view on the street, comfortable armchairs and a big sofa topped with jaunty cushions. The clever blend of old and new gives an individual, warm atmosphere throughout: attractive flea market finds, antiques, characterful dark or honey-coloured wood furniture and headboards – all chosen with Mme Ferrero's good eye. Bedrooms have sleekly made up beds, art, flowers in glass vases, splashes of colour from stylish fabrics, lamps dotted about; bathrooms are tip-top gleaming. Families and groups can choose the communicating rooms; if you don't want to tackle the lifts one room is on the ground floor next to reception. Have breakfast in your room, or join the buffet in the dining room. Montparnasse is still a place where people live and work; St Germain des Prés – heaps of shops and well-known restaurants – is within a stone's throw and Luxembourg Gardens are a 5-minute walk.

| | |
|---|---|
| Rooms | 27 doubles, 10 twin/doubles: €100–€210. 3 suites for 3: €170–€230. Extra bed/sofabed available €20 per person per night. |
| Meals | Breakfast €10. Restaurants 10-minute walk. |
| Closed | Never. |

**Mathieu Renaudin**
Hôtel de la Paix,
225 bd Raspail, 75014 Paris

| | |
|---|---|
| Tel | +33 (0)1 43 20 35 82 |
| Mobile | +33 (0)6 11 02 61 15 |
| Email | chambre414@hotmail.com |
| Web | www.paris-montparnasse-hotel.com |

## Hôtel Passy Eiffel

The first owner was a passionate bee-keeper so he perhaps picked a place with a bit of nature as a centrepiece. When you step off the smart shopping street you can certainly believe that Passy was just a little country village a hundred years ago. Breathe deeply in this calm atmosphere, a restful mix of old-fashioned and contemporary styles where nothing is overdone. Lounge in the glassed-in veranda where you can see a darling gardener's cottage across the tiny cobbled yard. There is a comfortable salon and an inviting breakfast room off the panelled hall which give onto the street through arching windows. Rooms are decorated in firm but unaggressive colours with floral quilts and curtains. The family rooms have large windows, some of which provide an excellent view of the Eiffel Tower. Beams and timbers frame the upper floors; furniture is cane and wood; storage space behind mirrored folding doors is good. On the courtyard side, you look down onto the hotel's green patio and the next-door neighbour's very well-kept garden. Lovely staff, too.

| Rooms | 46 twin/doubles: €99–€155. |
| | 3 family rooms for 3: €199–€250. |
| Meals | Breakfast €14. Restaurants next door. |
| Closed | Never. |

Christine Horbette
Hôtel Passy Eiffel,
10 rue de Passy,
75016 Paris

| Tel | +33 (0)1 45 25 55 66 |
| Email | contact@passyeiffel.com |
| Web | www.passyeiffel.com |

## Villa du Square

Return from museum or shopping pleasures to a gorgeous Parisian guesthouse that rubs shoulders with Le Corbusier's Villa Jeanneret. Revel in fine arts and antiques, ancient and modern all beautifully put together by your warm, friendly and super-chic hosts; they live on the top floor with three well-behaved teenagers and a small dog. Bedrooms are sumptuous in their fine objets and fabrics and superbly comfortable beds (the largest has its own garden door); indulge in the wonderful walk-in mosaic showers, lotions and towels de-luxe and fabulous washbasins. The street is peaceful, and the garden a haven with seating places, box topiary and ivy-covered walls. Breakfast is fresh and delicious and there's a grand piano among the family portraits. Vintage clothes shops on the rue de la Pompe, beautiful gardens and a host of authentic restaurants (and Michelin stars) in this tourist-free quarter will keep you busy and happy; Versailles is a ten-minute drive, the metro a three-minute walk. *Minimum stay: 3 nights in high season. Children over 10 welcome.*

| | |
|---|---|
| Rooms | 5 doubles: €175–€305. |
| Meals | Restaurant 2-minute walk. |
| Closed | Rarely. |

Marie-Victoire Gicqueau
Villa du Square,
26 rue Raffet, 75016 Paris

| | |
|---|---|
| Tel | +33 (0)1 71 72 91 33 |
| Mobile | +33 (0)6 10 11 83 42 |
| Email | contact@villadusquare.com |
| Web | villadusquare.com |

## Hôtel Gavarni

The neat little Gavarni has heaved itself up the hotel ladder on ropes of rich draperies, smart bathrooms and (mostly) refurbished bedrooms; it's also growing more eco-friendly by the year. Bedrooms are slowly being done up – so ask for one that's had a makeover – they are light and airy, painted in pastel colours, have original artwork on the walls and look very modern. Suites are big and traditional with jacuzzis and massage shower panels, fine canopies and beautiful furniture – supremely French with Eiffel Tower views – yet never overdone. The first-floor rooms are less luxurious but the quality is the same: thick lovely carpets, finely stitched quilts, heavy curtains and good little pieces of furniture. The triumph is those little bathrooms which have gained so much space with their utterly ingenious made-to-measure red 'granite' basin, shower and loo. Xavier, the dynamic young manager, is dedicated to making the Gavarni as 'green' as possible and a terrific organic, fairtrade breakfast is served in the conservatory; energy is renewable and all cleaning is done with eco-friendly ingredients.

| Rooms | 10 doubles, 6 twins: €160–€190. |
| | 3 suites for 2, 1 suite for 4: €220–€450. |
| | 4 family rooms for 3-4: €400–€520. |
| | Singles €110–€160. |
| Meals | Breakfast €15. |
| | Restaurants 1-minute walk. |
| Closed | Never. |

Xavier Moraga
Hôtel Gavarni,
5 rue Gavarni,
75116 Paris

| Tel | +33 (0)1 45 24 52 82 |
| Email | reservation@gavarni.com |
| Web | www.gavarni.com |

## Hôtel Eiffel Trocadéro

Paris's latest eco hotel, sister to the Gavarni, is a gem with Eiffel Tower views, beautiful new rooms and impressive water, energy and materials-saving credentials. Under Xavier Moraga's committed baton, there is inventive use of led lighting, intelligent fittings in small spaces and a fun choice of décor – he's even bought an electric van so guests can take a green tour of the city. Landing walls, done in metallised limewash, glow softly under hand and eye. Choose a soberly chic modern-classic room in quiet grey, brown or caramel stripes with a sensuously padded wall behind the bed, or a joyous, hand-painted backdrop of giant flowers – fuchsia, mimosa – matching velvet curtains and floor-level lighting; take the Eiffel suite and you'll feel you are sitting on top of the tower. Many rooms are connected to the latest in eco-friendly air treatment and have recycling showers or jacuzzi baths in their excellent (unchanged) marble bathrooms. Organic breakfast is in the jaunty black and white basement, fine French food with oriental tinges in the stunning ground-floor restaurant with its variegated seating and living walls. A delight.

| | |
|---|---|
| Rooms | 11 doubles, 5 twin/doubles: €220–€350. 1 suite for 4: €500–€650. Family apartment €400–€520 per night. |
| Meals | Breakfast €8–€18 (included for Sawday's guests). Child's breakfast €9–€12. Lunch from €23; dinner à la carte. Wines €20–€200. |
| Closed | Never. |

Xavier Moraga
Hôtel Eiffel Trocadéro,
35 rue Benjamin Franklin,
75116 Paris

| | |
|---|---|
| Tel | +33 (0)1 53 70 17 70 |
| Email | reservation@hoteleiffeltrocadero.com |
| Web | www.hoteleiffeltrocadero.com |

## Hôtel le Relais Montmartre

There are good reasons why artists still live in this village, tucked in behind the Sacré Coeur, that giant marshmallow of a church. It could be the views over the rooftops of Paris, or the meandering little streets, or Montmartre's transformation at dusk as bistros, bars and clubs come into their own. It deserves much more than an afternoon visit so book into this little jewel and the secrets of this rediscovered neighbourhood will be revealed. Just up from Amélie's celebrated café, tucked into a sweet side street, the entrance is discreet. Elegance and intimacy blend in the lobby with fireplace and antique desk; the sofa, the period chairs and the curtains are an extraordinary mix of rich fabrics; the small trellised patio set with sunny yellow garden furniture is the cherry on the cake. It feels like someone's home and anglophone Vincent knows every café and gallery by heart. In the rooms, find deep armchairs, quilted headboards and curtains in quiet pastels or reds, pinks and greens, mixed and matched with care. The mattresses are dreamy, the staff are delightful; this is simple luxury at its best.

| Rooms | 26 doubles: €139–€249. Extra bed/sofabed available at no charge. |
| --- | --- |
| Meals | Breakfast €15. Restaurants 1-minute walk. |
| Closed | Never. |

Samia Mobarek
Hôtel le Relais Montmartre,
6 rue Constance,
75018 Paris

| Tel | +33 (0)1 70 64 25 25 |
| --- | --- |
| Email | contact@relaismontmartre.fr |
| Web | www.relaismontmartre.fr |

## Hostellerie du Prieuré

Medieval Saint Prix, on the edge of the forest, feels delightfully rural but from the village church you can see the Sacré Coeur: Paris is 15 minutes by train. This is an immaculate small hotel in a beautiful village, with bedrooms that are really quite something. Decorated with a flourish and a theme, from boudoir chic to eastern exotica, all have Middle Eastern carpets, gorgeous textiles, crisp sheets. There's purple-walled 'Aladdin' with an octagonal Syrian table and a silver hand basin and mirror, and lovely 'Coloniale', with a bamboo four-poster and magnificent long views – to Paris, of course. Bathrooms are worth a wallow, thanks to scented oils and fine soaps. Yves and Frédérique are a warmly professional couple and breakfast is worth getting up for, served in the creamy-walled Café de la Côte with a long velvet banquette and 1900s-style bar. Reservations for dinner are essential as there are only a handful of tables. You will find gourmet dishes and an organic wine list is as long as your arm plus a choice of nine champagnes. All this on the edge of fine forest; head off and explore. *Secure parking available.*

| | |
|---|---|
| Rooms | 3 doubles: €125. |
| | 4 suites for 2: €148. |
| | 1 family room for 4: €190. |
| | Dinner, B&B €220–€250 for 2. |
| | Extra bed/sofabed available €18 per person per night. |
| Meals | Breakfast €15. |
| | Dinner €35–€50. Wine €22–€50. |
| | Restaurant closed Sundays. |
| Closed | Rarely. |

**Frédérique & Yves Farouze**
Hostellerie du Prieuré,
74 rue Auguste Rey,
95390 St Prix, Val-d'Oise

| | |
|---|---|
| Tel | +33 (0)1 34 27 51 51 |
| Email | contact@hostelduprieure.com |
| Web | www.hostelduprieure.com |

## Pavillon Henri IV

The historic and artistic credentials are impeccable. Louis XIV was born here, Dumas, Offenbach and George Sand stayed here. There's a fascinating mix of styles, too – Renaissance domed roof, Art Nouveau porch – and materials – ivory limestone, rosy brick. As for the views, the panorama sweeps across the valley of the Seine to Paris and La Défense; the city centre is 20 minutes away. Relish it all from the rooms, the restaurant, the terrace: feel on top of the world. Bedrooms are filled with luxury and charm while reception rooms are big and beautiful – white walls, shining parquet and mellow rugs, gilded antiques, moulded cornices, marble busts, sumptuous chandeliers and striking flowers; there's even a self-playing piano. The dining is unquestionably lavish (you can choose to eat in two fabulous dining rooms), and should you wish to walk off your indulgence afterwards, a wrought-iron gateway allows you into the vast walled and terraced gardens of Château de St Germain en Laye next door. Supremely enjoyable, wonderfully French.

| | |
|---|---|
| Rooms | 42 twin/doubles: €139-€390. Singles €99-€340. Extra bed/sofabed available €25 per person per night. |
| Meals | Breakfast €19. Lunch €49. Dinner à la carte, approx. €90. |
| Closed | Rarely. |

**Charles Eric Hoffmann**
Pavillon Henri IV,
19-21 rue Thiers,
78100 St Germain en Laye, Yvelines
Tel      +33 (0)1 39 10 15 15
Email    reservation@pavillonhenri4.fr
Web      www.pavillonhenri4.fr

Entry 73   Map 5

## Hôtel de Londres

Gaze on the Château de Fontainebleau, one of France's loveliest buildings, from your room in this 18th-century hostelry; it lies opposite. The hotel has been in the family for three generations; Philippe runs it quietly and considerately, with occasional help from his brother. The sitting room has an 18th-century classical look, also rich colours, comfy armchairs, plump cushions, grand flowers. The breakfast room – for simple breakfasts – has the feel of a small brasserie; both rooms have views to Fontainebleau. Bedrooms, on the upper floors, are similarly classical in style – smart, spotless and traditional; colours are bold, fabrics floral. A sense of timelessness pervades this peaceful place. You are also brilliantly placed for exploring the Forest of Fontainebleau, the hunting grounds of kings. As for the Château, it was built around the keep of a smaller medieval building, completed in 1550 and has been added to over the years; the gallery of François I is considered one of the finest in Europe. You can visit for free on Sundays and it's magnificently floodlit at night.

| | |
|---|---|
| Rooms | 5 doubles: €128-€188. |
| | 8 suites for 2: €158-€210. |
| | 2 triples: €200-€228. |
| | 1 single: €98-€168. |
| Meals | Breakfast €14. |
| | Restaurants 1-minute walk. |
| Closed | 12 to 18 August & 23 December to |
| | 9 January. |

**Philippe Colombier**
Hôtel de Londres,
1 place du Général de Gaulle,
77300 Fontainebleau, Seine-et-Marne

Tel       +33 (0)1 64 22 20 21
Email    hdelondres1850@aol.com
Web      www.hoteldelondres.com

## Château de Bourron

Surrounded by perfectly clipped yew and box topiary, the early 17th-century château built on fortress foundations is hugely warm and inviting. Louis XV and his regal in-laws once met here; now it is owned by a charming young family. Inside is a feast of original Versailles parquet, oriental rugs and period pieces, exquisite fabrics and elegant tapestries. Breakfast tables are laid in a fine big ground-floor room that leads to the cosy guest sitting room. Upstairs, bedrooms in perfectly chosen bold colours display pale marble bathrooms – some with draped free-standing tubs – handsome fabrics and fitting period-style furniture: five-star stylishness in a château setting. On the first floor is the library, with panelled walls and shelves laden with leather-bound tomes. Outside, there are more treasures to uncover. The 80 acres of walled gardens and woodland are extraordinary… statues of Ceres and St Joseph, a chapel in one of two small pavilions, and the St Sévère spring supplying moat, canal and village wash-house. Your friendly hosts will tell the stories. Beyond lie the pretty village and the great forest. *Free shuttle service between Bourron train station and Château.*

| Rooms | 8 twin/doubles: €199–€520. Twin room service charge of €25 per room per night. Extra bed/sofabed available €25 per person per night. |
|---|---|
| Meals | Breakfast €16. Dinner €33. |
| Closed | Rarely. |

Comte & Comtesse Guy de Cordon
Château de Bourron,
14 bis rue du Maréchal Foch,
77780 Bourron Marlotte, Seine-et-Marne
Tel     +33 (0)1 64 78 39 39
Email   bourron@bourron.fr
Web     www.bourron.fr

Normandy

Photo: Le Petit Coq
aux Champs, entry 97

## La Ramade

La Ramade, half a century old, was built in golden granite by a livestock merchant. Véronique took it on in 2001 and transformed it from B&B into charming hotel, fulfilling a long-held dream. Her individual interiors are a pleasing mix of modern and brocante finds, with her own Breton cradle displayed on the second floor. Bedrooms feel feminine and are named after flowers; the newest (with a modern theme) are in the handsome 'sister villa' behind, spread across three floors – Véronique has an exceptional eye for detail. Green-carpeted 'Laurier' has white-painted furniture and steps to a bathroom with a sunken bath, 'Coquelicot' has a poppy theme and matching curtains and towels, pretty 'Eglantine' a canopied bed and afternoon sun streaming through large windows. The grounds are filled with mature trees that give privacy from the road, and you are near Mont St Michel and the sea; children would enjoy a guided tour across the bay at low tide. Véronique has added a smart glassed-in conservatory for breakfast, and a tea room and a bar for sampling the local pommeau, or a calvados before tucking into bed.

| | |
|---|---|
| Rooms | 2 doubles, 14 twin/doubles: €78-€150. 1 suite for 2-5: €165-€250. 3 triples: €127-€165. 1 quadruple: €142-€180. Extra bed €20. |
| Meals | Breakfast €12.50. Restaurants 500m. Caterer available on request. |
| Closed | 19 December to 25 December & 4 January to 24 January. |

Véronique Morvan Gilbert
La Ramade,
2 rue de la Côte, Marcey les Grèves,
50300 Avranches, Manche

| | |
|---|---|
| Tel | +33 (0)2 33 58 27 40 |
| Email | hotel@laramade.fr |
| Web | www.laramade.fr |

## Le Manoir de l'Acherie

A short way from the motorway is this hotel, deep in the Norman countryside, a lovely, oh-so-French discovery: an old granite house with immaculately tended gardens and an ancient granite cider press sunk into the lawn brimming over with red roses. At one side is a chapel, now bedrooms; on the other is an extension providing a sort of *cour d'honneur* entrance. Some of the furniture is authentically old though most is solid quality repro in the rustic Norman style; rooms are carpeted, bed covers are patterned, curtains are frilly. Mother and daughter Cécile handle the hotel and restaurant service, Stéphane runs the kitchen and continues to win prizes for his robust cuisine. Charcuterie is homemade, cider and calvados comes from the locality. The tables are dressed in prim, cream tablecloths; dark wooden beams, well worn floor tiles and a giant stone fireplace create a pleasant, cosy feel. The small number of people running this establishment and the quiet unstressed, unhurried but efficient way they do so, is admirable. Note that last orders in the restaurant are at 8.30pm.

| | |
|---|---|
| Rooms | 10 doubles, 4 twins: €70–€120. 4 suites for 2: €120. |
| Meals | Breakfast €10. Lunch & dinner €21–€43. Restaurant closed Mondays (September–June); Sunday eve (mid-October to week before Easter). |
| Closed | 3 weeks in November & 2 weeks in February. |

**Stéphane & Cécile Poignavant**
Le Manoir de l'Acherie,
37 rue Michel de l'Epinay,
50800 Ste Cécile, Manche

| | |
|---|---|
| Tel | +33 (0)2 33 51 13 87 |
| Email | manoir@manoir-acherie.fr |
| Web | www.manoir-acherie.fr |

## Château de Canisy

They say it is the oldest bed and breakfast in France. Well, few would argue – one of William the Conqueror's barons built the original castle and his descendants are your charming hosts. Medieval towers rise from misty swan-graced lakes, tapestries hang in 16th-century galleries and rococo ceilings float above a collection of oils. The architecture is breathtaking, but this is no museum-piece stately home – Canisy is home to the Comte and Comtesse de Kergorlay, and they keep their château pristine and cosy. Logs cut from the forest glow in marble fireplaces, silverware flickers in the candlelight, and every sumptuous bedroom is stuffed with family heirlooms. Beds are big; bathrooms too – bathe in a handmade copper tub or douse yourself in a huge Italian shower. Fifty hectares of parkland will lure those in search of tranquillity and flora. Billiards and boules, archery and fishing will keep others busy. Walkers can promenade for miles, and you're only an hour's drive from Mont Saint Michel and the D-Day beaches. Hot buffet breakfasts and the chef's gourmet dinners in the elegant dining room are a must.

| | |
|---|---|
| Rooms | 10 twin/doubles: €210–€300. |
| | 3 suites for 3, 1 suite for 4: €230–€300. |
| | Singles €165. |
| Meals | Dinner, 3 courses with wine, €65. |
| | Gastronomic menu with fine wine, €80. |
| | Restaurants 10km. |
| Closed | Rarely. |

Patrick Hilyer
Château de Canisy,
6-8 rue de Kergorlay,
50750 Canisy, Manche

| | |
|---|---|
| Tel | +33 (0)2 33 56 61 06 |
| Email | manager@chateaudecanisy.com |
| Web | www.chateaudecanisy.com |

## Manoir de Coutainville

Secluded rooms with views over rooftops and (from many windows) sparkling seas are a traveller's joy. Add a cultured hostess, a 15th-century manoir, delectable dining and a fire in the grate and you have a dash of French magic. Through pale stone arches serenity awaits, genteel apéritifs ushering in five-course dinners that showcase local lobster, sea bass or oysters. Sophie Véron provides spare wellies and captivating conversation, her fashion career informs her calm interiors — a rare mix of charm and luxury — and history resonates through every room, be they in the house or across the courtyard. Try Sénéchal's Japanese zinc shower or linger in the roll-top bath of the three-bedroom'd Seigneurie; then snuggle into fluffy robes and watch the waves. In white tranquillity, Mahogany links with sweet Prairie, the twin — but note that, when taken separately, the latter is reached via a steep ladder stair from its private shower on the ground floor. Downstairs, library armchairs and a scullery kitchen offer rest and refreshment. Stroll to Coutainville and look at the boats.

| Rooms | 2 doubles; 1 twin with separate shower: €170–€260. 1 suite for 2-5: €240–€370. Courtyard annexe – 1 suite for 2-4: €240–€370. |
| --- | --- |
| Meals | Breakfast included. Dinner with wine, €56. |
| Closed | Rarely. |

Sophie Véron
Manoir de Coutainville, 2 rue de la
Maugerie, 50230 Agon Coutainville, Manche

| Tel | +33 (0)2 33 47 05 90 |
| --- | --- |
| Mobile | +33 (0)6 07 55 29 77 |
| Email | sophie-veron@manoir-de-coutainville.com |
| Web | www.manoir-de-coutainville.com |

## Pavillon du Château de Tocqueville

The family live in Paris so charming manager Danielle will walk you through your wing of this historic building. With its tapestries, plush and brocade, its panelling and French antiques it is deliciously château-esque. The big red salon has a vast stone fireplace, ancestral portraits, deep sofas, fresh flowers — and a magical Alice in Wonderland sized door to a stone spiral staircase which leads to the next three floors. Don't panic if you're less than keen on stairs — there's a concealed lift to the great-timbered third-floor bedroom, the home cinema and the telescope. All bedrooms, done with style and elegance, rejoice in a regal atmosphere that oozes from canopies, fine wallpapers and noble fabrics — the triple has the original Napoleon style bed of Alexis de Tocqueville himself and the bathrooms are bang up to date. All bedrooms have high windows which overlook the great park — fourteen acres you are free to explore. Discover the suntrap walled garden with its exotic palm trees, wildflower meadows, woodland, and in late winter, thousands of delicate snowdrops. Strut your aristocratic stuff for a spell, it is magical. *The château can be rented for self-catering.*

| | |
|---|---|
| Rooms | 2 twin/doubles, 1 twin, 2 four-posters: €200. |
| Meals | Caterer available on request. Restaurants 4km. |
| Closed | Rarely. |

Stéphanie de Tocqueville
Pavillon du Château de Tocqueville,
40 rue Alexis de Tocqueville,
50330 Tocqueville, Manche

| | |
|---|---|
| Tel | +33 (0)6 83 17 22 67 |
| Email | s.detocqueville@gmail.com |
| Web | www.chateaudetocqueville.com |

## Ferme-Manoir de la Rivière

How romantic! Breakfast by the massive fireplace (lit of course, summer and winter when needed) may be oil lamp-lit on dark winter mornings in this 13th-century fortress of a former dairy farm, with its ancient tithe barn and little watchtower. Isabelle, friendly and fun, is proud of her family home, its flagstones worn smooth with age, its high vaulted stone living-room ceiling, its second-floor rooms, one narrow with a shower in a tower, another with exposed beams and ciel de lit drapes. Her energy boundless, she is ever improving her rooms and gives you great breakfasts. Feast on homemade brioche, homemade jams, cream from the farm, chocolate cream flan! Make sure you have dinner too (Madame is aided here by Gérard) – perhaps bacon and mushroom flan, followed by fresh cod steak with whole grain mustard cream sauce, served with saffron rice and baked cherry tomatoes. Polish it off with ripe Normandy camembert, local cider or herb tea. Delicious, all local and organic. The garden is large with swathes of lawn, mature trees to find shade under and swings for energetic children. A real taste of France.

| | |
|---|---|
| Rooms | 1 double, 2 triples: €70–€75. |
| Meals | Dinner with cider or wine, €27–€30; book ahead. |
| Closed | Rarely. |

**Gérard & Isabelle Leharivel**
Ferme-Manoir de la Rivière,
14230 Géfosse Fontenay, Calvados

| | |
|---|---|
| Tel | +33 (0)2 31 22 64 45 |
| Mobile | +33 (0)6 81 58 25 21 |
| Email | leharivel@wanadoo.fr |
| Web | www.lemanoirdelariviere.net |

## Le Château

Close to the little fishing port of Grandcamp, the château dates proudly from 1580. Charming stone buildings wrap themselves around a big central courtyard, restored to tremendous shape and character as a garden area for guests, with a chestnut tree standing central stage. In the ancient arched barn are two beamy bedrooms (admire astounding roof timbers through a trap window) and a two-storey suite for five, its three loft-room beds up a spiral wood stair. Just beyond the flowering stone steps: a fourth room in a tiny cottage. These are country bedrooms, simple, elegant, traditional with toile fabrics and sweet antiques, restful and private with views to courtyard and fields. Wake to the call of the rooster and the quacking of ducks, then settle down to a fresh home-produced breakfast served at pretty tables in the dining room. Madame is a vibrantly warm, well-read and discreet person who loves having guests and can discourse at fascinating length about the Vikings, the Dukes of Normandy, the history of the farm during WWII. As for dinner, it's home-grown, delicious and washed down by pommeau, wine and calvados.

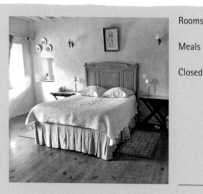

| | |
|---|---|
| Rooms | 2 doubles, 1 twin, 1 suite for 5: €70-€85. |
| Meals | Dinner with wine or cider, €35; children's menu €20. Restaurants 2km. |
| Closed | December to mid-January. |

Dominique Bernières
Le Château,
14450 Grandcamp Maisy,
Calvados

Tel     +33 (0)2 31 22 66 22
Email   dominiquebernieres@orange.fr
Web    alain.marion.pagesperso-orange.fr

## Hôtel Tardif

A mid 18th-century house in the centre of Bayeux, this is an architectural jewel. It was built for a botanist who worked at Versailles and specimen trees still stand in the grounds. In those days, carriages would rumble through the archway and enter the central 'cour d'honneur'; still cobbled, the yard is an exquisite spot from which to glimpse a fascinating range of building styles. Delighted to share all he knows about this house and its history, Anthony, with impeccable English, is an exceptionally generous young host. Inside are white walls, parquet étoile floors and a curved and suspended staircase, one of only two in France. And such beautiful things: antiques and tapestries, brocade chairs and gilt-framed mirrors, a grand piano and a chandelier from Compiègne where the Empress Josephine lived. Bedrooms are elegant, spacious and sober, in keeping with the history. One bedroom, on the first floor, is a listed 'monument historique', its panelling immaculately revived in regulation browns and golds. Other rooms have pale stone walls; all are uncluttered and serene. What value!

| | |
|---|---|
| Rooms | 6 doubles: €50–€160.<br>1 suite for 4: €150–€200.<br>Extra bed €20. |
| Meals | Breakfast €10.<br>Restaurants 2-minute walk. |
| Closed | Christmas. |

**Anthony Voidie**
Hôtel Tardif,
16 rue de Nesmond, 14400 Bayeux,
Calvados

Tel     +33 (0)2 31 92 67 72
Email   hoteltardif@orange.fr
Web     www.hoteltardif.com

Entry 83   Map 4

## Ferme de la Rançonnière

Drive through the narrow arch into the vast courtyard and history leaps out to grab you. This was originally a fortified stronghold – the tower is 13th century – to protect against English reprisals after Duke William of Normandy conquered England.... exposed timbers and limestone floors announce the Norman heritage. Each courtyard building houses eight to ten rooms. One amazing suite has stone steps down to a double bedroom then up a spiral stair to a children's room in the tower with tiny windows. Handsome, solid furniture combines with pieces that are plainer, and rustic-medieval is the look: a butter churn in the corridor, an awe-inspiring armoire, a well-worn kneading trough: reminders that this was a working farm. Off the huge breakfast room and restaurant is a vaulted, stone-flagged sitting area with a log fire at one end: great spot for after-dinner coffee. The bright breakfast room and terrace face south to catch the morning sun. Young, friendly, professional Isabelle Sileghem and her husband keep this place humming, with help from a devoted staff. It's big and rooms vary: book ahead for the best.

| Rooms | 21 twin/doubles: €70–€170. |
|---|---|
| | 1 suite for 2: €180–€215. |
| | 13 triples: €128–€198. |
| | Extra bed/sofabed available €28 per person per night. |
| Meals | Breakfast €12. Lunch €24. |
| | Dinner €30.80–€42.80. Wine €15–€40. |
| | Restaurant closed 3-25 January. |
| Closed | Rarely. |

Isabelle & Koen Sileghem
Ferme de la Rançonnière,
Route de Creully Arromanches,
14480 Crépon, Calvados
Tel        +33 (0)2 31 22 21 73
Email    ranconniere@wanadoo.fr
Web      www.ranconniere.fr

## Château La Cour

Your hosts are warm and charming and their attention to detail is impressive. Not everyone can take a 13th-century castle, once owned by the Ducs d'Harcourt, and so successfully blend history with comfort. Expect some subtly bold décor and subdued luxury: Lloyd Loom chairs, marble fireplaces, Egyptian cotton. One bedroom has a curved wooden stair up to a superb bathroom; the apartment is stunning; all face south over the garden. Breakfast includes home-grown fruit, homemade yogurt and eggs from the château's happy hens. A house for fine dining, too: English china, damask and candelabra set the table in the lovely dining room. David grows – beautifully – for Lesley to cook – deliciously – and his organic potager is a delightful diversion (seven varieties of potato, 50 of vegetable); high stone walls shelter it from unkind winds, fruit trees shade the lawn, long narrow beds make for easy harvesting. The Cravens are keen conservationists, too; barn owls nest in the end wall and there is good bird-watching. The Normandy beaches, Bayeux and its tapestry are within easy reach. *No credit cards. Children over 12 welcome.*

| | |
|---|---|
| Rooms | 3 doubles, 1 twin: €160. |
| Meals | Hosted dinner with wine, €35-€50; book ahead. |
| Closed | November – February. |

David & Lesley Craven
Château La Cour,
14220 Culey le Patry,
Calvados

| | |
|---|---|
| Tel | +33 (0)2 31 79 19 37 |
| Email | info@chateaulacour.com |
| Web | www.chateaulacour.com |

## Château des Riffets

The square-set château stands handsome still as the park recovers from the 1999 storm and beyond the pretty flowered and shrubbed parts, huge expanses of grass are dotted with venerable beeches, horse chestnuts, conifers and limes. Period ceilings and parkland views make Riffets a gracious château experience, a place in which you may admire yourself in myriad mirrors, luxuriate in a jacuzzi, bare your chest to a supersonic shower (two bathrooms have them!) and lie, at last, in an antique bed in one of the great, cherished and recently updated bedrooms. The walls of the huge entrance hall and the galleried landing have been repainted pastel grey, an elegant foil for tapestries, plants, mirrors and austere antique pieces. Wry Monsieur was a psychologist, gentle Madame an English teacher, and a fine breakfast is served at one big table. Take a stroll in the park – all 15 hectares of it – hire a nearby horse or a canoe, hone your carriage-driving skills, enjoy a lap in the pool. Caen's historic treasures are a ten-minute drive, Bayeux and Mont St Michel are an hour away.

| | |
|---|---|
| Rooms | 2 doubles, 2 suites for 2: €125–€175. |
| Meals | Restaurant 1km. |
| Closed | Rarely. |

**Anne-Marie & Alain Cantel**
Château des Riffets,
14680 Bretteville sur Laize, Calvados

| | |
|---|---|
| Tel | +33 (0)2 31 23 53 21 |
| Mobile | +33 (0)6 14 09 74 93 |
| Email | chateau.riffets@wanadoo.fr |
| Web | www.chateau-des-riffets.com |

## Château du Mesnil d'O

The approach to this 18th-century château lifts the spirit. Stone pillars and tall iron gates mark the entrance from the road, a tree-lined avenue set in five hectares of garden and parkland rolls you to the front door: the setting is enchanting. The four bedrooms, one with listed wallpaper from 1905, are on the first floor up a beautiful staircase in white Caen stone with (listed) wrought-iron handrail and balustrade. A square landing with a long view over the park is the perfect place to spread your newspaper on a lovely old dining table; bookshelves bursting with literature line the length of one wall. Family portraits bring the corridor to life, along with the odd antique; fresh flowers are placed in bedrooms and on landings. A feast for the eye: blue velvet chairs, chevron parquet floor, panelled walls with painted scenes above the doors and a wonderful Louis XVI buffet displaying its collection of old plates — that is the backdrop for buffet breakfast. One might feel overawed by such splendour but the welcome makes the visitor feel instantly at home. *No credit cards.*

| | |
|---|---|
| Rooms | 3 doubles: €110. |
| | 1 suite for 4: €170. |
| Meals | Restaurants 5km. |
| Closed | Rarely. |

**Guy de Chabaneix**
Château du Mesnil d'O,
14270 Vieux Fumé,
Calvados

| | |
|---|---|
| Tel | +33 (0)2 31 20 01 47 |
| Email | lemesnildo@wanadoo.fr |
| Web | www.lemesnildo.com |

Entry 87  Map 4

## Château de Bénéauville

Down the plane-flanked drive to an immaculate Renaissance château in 50 acres of harmonious grounds. Find painted 17th-century beams in perfect condition, a panelled library, a powder-blue dining room, and fireplaces imposing and theatrical – panache, elegance and a huge amount of fine château character. There's more: heads of antelope and oryx jumping out of the walls, a curled up fox on a sitting room sofa, a cheetah on a branch hitched up high on the library wall: the unmissable presence of the hunter's passion. Here live the Augais family (she gentle and artistic, he ruler of the roost, both great travellers) with horse, hens and handsome gundogs. In big peaceful bedrooms with tall windows are chestnut floors and grey-washed beams, oriental carpets, quilted bedspreads, boudoir armchairs, deep baths (with shower attachments) and exquisite curtain tassels. Take a dip in the discreet pool; set off for culture in Caen. Super breakfasts come with homemade jams; there's no table d'hôtes but restaurants all around. Marvellous.

| | |
|---|---|
| Rooms | 3 doubles (2 doubles join to form a suite), 1 twin (extends into suite): €190–€270. |
| Meals | Restaurants 5km. |
| Closed | 1 October to 1 June. |

Philippe Augais
Château de Bénéauville,
Bénéauville,
14860 Bavent, Calvados

| | |
|---|---|
| Tel | +33 (0)2 31 72 56 49 |
| Email | reservation@chateaudebeneauville.fr |
| Web | www.chateaudebeneauville.fr |

## Hôtel Maison de Lucie

Named after the poet Lucie Delarue Mardrus, who was born here, the 1850 house in the heart of Honfleur is shielded by a high wall. Sunshine illuminates panelled walls and leather sofas, the parquet'd salon has an Edwardian air and bedrooms, elegantly colour-themed, now expand into an adjoining house; those on the second floor overlook the estuary. Furnishings are immaculate – plum taffeta, burgundy velvet – beds are big and reading lamps won't spoil your eyes. Bathrooms are awash with potions and lotions, there are fresh orchids and vivid rugs, roll top baths and antique chests of drawers, and wide views over rooftops to the sea. Our favourite room is under the eaves, but they're all lovely. In the courtyard, the old caretaker's house is now a suite, its ground-floor sitting area furnished in a deliciously decadent 1930s manner; another room has a small new terraced courtyard area. Soak away your cares in the brick-walled jacuzzi spa; take your time over a great homemade breakfast of bacon, eggs, fruits, cheese, in bed or in the sun. Muriel's welcome is the cherry on the cake. *Parking €15 per night (4 spaces).*

| Rooms | 9 doubles: €170-€200. |
|---|---|
| | 3 suites for 2: €250-€330. |
| Meals | Breakfast €12-€18. Restaurants 300m. |
| Closed | Early to mid-December. |

**Muriel Daridon**
Hôtel Maison de Lucie,
44 rue Capucins,
14600 Honfleur, Calvados

| Tel | +33 (0)2 31 14 40 40 |
|---|---|
| Email | info@lamaisondelucie.com |
| Web | www.lamaisondelucie.com |

Entry 89  Map 4

## Hôtel-Restaurant & Spa Les Maisons de Léa

You could almost do with a guide, to steer you round the passageways, narrow stairs and twists and turns of this intriguing 16th-century building — once three fishermen's houses and a salt warehouse. Each of the bedrooms has its own decorative style — romantic, nautical, Baltimore, country; the attention to detail is exquisite. Imagine dreamy fabrics, limewashed walls, cushions on painted wicker, toys and chairs for children and a booklet for each guest on the treasures of Honfleur. Sample gourmet food in the hotel's new restaurant with blazing log fire in winter, or delicious home-made scones for afternoon tea. Breakfast is laid out in a red-walled room with views to the big square and the church of Sainte Catherine; on Saturdays, the food market leaps into action. Relax in the salon, spoil yourself in the spa or the (free) hammam, self-cater in the delicious Petite Maison. No lift — that would spoil the charm — and a car park a few minutes' walk away, but staff will happily ferry bags to the upper floors. A total gem.

| | |
|---|---|
| Rooms | 24 twin/doubles: €160–€205. 5 suites for 2: €260–€285. 1 cottage for 5: €295 per night. |
| Meals | Buffet breakfast €15. Lunch €22. Dinner €28-56. Restaurant closed Wednesday & Thursday out of season. |
| Closed | Rarely. |

Didier Lassarat
Hôtel-Restaurant & Spa Les Maisons de Léa, Place Ste Catherine, 14600 Honfleur, Calvados

| | |
|---|---|
| Tel | +33 (0)2 31 14 49 49 |
| Email | contact@lesmaisonsdelea.com |
| Web | www.lesmaisonsdelea.com |

## La Petite Folie

Fabulously sited for exploring Honfleur, just steps from the old harbour, these three townhouses are havens from the artistic bustle. The commanding main house (B&B), built for a sea captain in the 1830s, has heavy shutters over grand mansard windows. Its more modest but older neighbour, a gorgeous 14th-century house, contains three double-aspect apartments that march up three floors. Up the street are two more superb apartments with views onto a beautiful listed garden. American-born Penny married Frenchman Thierry and they set out to tailor bedrooms lavishly and beautifully, each an enchanting mix of handsome bedsteads, plump duvets, lacquered armchairs, mahogany chests of drawers and whirls of different tones. The ground-floor sitting room, as wide as the house, offers red suede sofas at one end and a leather chesterfield at the other. The garden is a compact, neatly planted square of charm, its focal point a summerhouse with a Byzantine flourish and belvedere views out to sea. Breakfast is a daily treat. All this, free WiFi, and delightful hosts. *Minimum stay: 2 nights. Over 12s welcome (except for one apartment where under-12s are also welcome).*

| Rooms | 4 doubles, 1 twin: €145–€175. |
|---|---|
| | 3 apartments for 2, |
| | 2 apartments for 1-4: |
| | €195–€295 per night. |
| Meals | Breakfast to apartments on request. |
| | Restaurants 1-minute walk. |
| Closed | Early January to mid–February. |

Penny & Thierry Vincent
La Petite Folie,
44 rue Haute, 14600 Honfleur,
Calvados

| Mobile | +33 (0)6 74 39 46 46 |
| Email | lapetitefoliehonfleur@gmail.com |
| Web | www.lapetitefolie-honfleur.com |

## Le Manoir des Impressionnistes

As you watch the sun set over the Seine estuary, revel in the comfort and serenity of this charming 18th-century manor house, in the green embrace of a wooded hillside. There are bedrooms on all three floors; some peep from beneath the gables of the stone-tiled roof, others gaze boldly from the half-timbered façade and you can choose between sea and garden views. Each room is individually decorated with simplicity and taste, unmistakably French, with snowy bed linen and oriental rugs on warm-hued floors; bathrooms are a riot of thoroughly modern marble. In the terracotta-tiled breakfast room, a buffet table loaded with organic local produce is a welcome start to the day, but your evenings belong to the spectacular dining room. Beneath ancient wooden beams, in the flickering light of the gothic limestone fireplace, crisp linen and white china frame gourmet meals of Gallic splendour. English owner Bridget is thoughtful, warm and friendly, and leaves a welcome note and fresh fruit and flowers in your room. The name? You're a mile from the picturesque port of Honfleur, cradle of Impressionism. *Minimum stay: 2 nights at weekends.*

| | |
|---|---|
| Rooms | 2 doubles, 7 twin/doubles: €180–€395. 1 family room for 3: €485. Extra bed/sofabed available €20 per person per night. |
| Meals | Breakfast €20–€25. Dinner €45–€89. Wine from €28. Restaurants 1.5km. |
| Closed | Never. |

Bridget Boelen
Le Manoir des Impressionnistes,
Phare du Butin, Route Adolphe Marais,
14600 Honfleur, Calvados

| | |
|---|---|
| Tel | +33 (0)2 31 81 63 00 |
| Email | contact@le-manoir.com |
| Web | www.manoirdesimpressionnistes.eu |

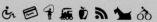

## La Grange des Marettes

In pure, peaceful countryside, an impeccably renovated hay barn and luxurious B&B. From the car park it's a sprint to the wide raised terrace, behind which lie four lovely bedrooms. (The fifth – cosy pine-clad 'Noisette' – rests below.) A steel corkscrew stair leads to the family suites on the first floor, sinfully comfortable and inviting. Each has a romantically draped bed and a further single on the mezzanine reached by ladder (perfect for a nimble child). The décor is mix-and-match in contemporary style, the walls are clad in white wood, the furniture is pastel-washed and each room is different. Feel spoiled by big square French pillows, pristine hand basins, fat duvets, and a couple of saunas to steam up in. Accomplished paintings and engravings add colour and depth and from every upper room there's a beautiful view. Look forward to buffet breakfast in the day room, served until 11; glimpse the owner's manor house through the sheltering trees. Riverside Rouen is a 20-minute drive; the pretty Château de Clères – with gibbons, geese and exotic birds – is just down the road.

| | |
|---|---|
| Rooms | 1 double: €150.<br>2 suites for 2,<br>2 suites for 2-3: €150-€180.<br>Singles €130. Extra bed/sofabed<br>available €30 per person per night. |
| Meals | Breakfast included. Guest kitchen.<br>Restaurant 3km. |
| Closed | Rarely. |

Jacques Lernon
La Grange des Marettes, Lieu-dit Le Bois Hébert,
Les Marettes, 76690 Clères, Seine-Maritime

| | |
|---|---|
| Tel | +33 (0)2 35 33 24 44 |
| Mobile | +33 (0)6 84 77 21 42 |
| Email | la-grange@les-marettes.fr |
| Web | www.les-marettes.fr |

## Château de Bonnemare

You could almost imagine the Vicomte de Valmont and the Marquise de Merteuil plotting in the *grand salon*! A Renaissance gatehouse leads to a remarkable 16th-century *brique de St Jean* façade as you enter the grounds of this enticing 'monument historique'. Alain and Sylvie, generous and charming, have restored two elegant ground-floor rooms in the north wing, and two with listed decoration on the first floor. Breathtaking 'La Parade' announces a velvet swagged four-poster in an ornate alcove, a monumental fireplace and a single-bedded nursery; 'Louis XVI', decorated in 1777, reveals a pure French classical elegance, its exquisitely furnished yellow salon adjoining a vast bedroom with chandeliers and intricate mouldings. Bathrooms are pleasingly lavish – and modern. Breakfast in the vaulted Great Kitchen, its vast fireplace replete with a turbine-driven spit designed by da Vinci, means embroidered napkins, fresh fruits and flowers, pâtisserie and homemade jams. The estate walls enclose a small kingdom: chapel, farm, cider press, bakery, barns and 44 acres of park and woodland. Amazing.

| Rooms | 1 double: €112–€145. |
| | 3 suites for 2-3: €202–€235. |
| | Singles €112. |
| Meals | Shared guest kitchen. Restaurant 6km. |
| Closed | 1 December to 15 February. |

**Sylvie Vandecandelaere**
Château de Bonnemare, 990 route de
Bacqueville, 27380 Radepont, Eure

| Tel | +33 (0)2 32 49 03 73 |
| Mobile | +33 (0)6 03 96 36 53 |
| Email | sarlbonnemare@nordnet.fr |
| Web | www.bonnemare.com |

## Le Moulin de Connelles

Bring your boater, hop in a green and red-trimmed flatboat right out of a Monet painting and punt along a quiet arm of the Seine after a morning at Monet's garden (Giverny is 30 minutes). Watery greens, pinks and that scintillating veil of haze that is particular to this part of Normandy intensify the Impressionist mood. Then look up at the extraordinary half-timbered, chequer-boarded, turreted manor house and you will have to pinch yourself, hard. Part of the house is on an island; hidden paths lead through flowering bushes to a private pool; Karine keeps up her father's tradition of quiet hospitality and has refined the park, its flowerbeds and furniture. Bedrooms and restaurant have been renovated with fine materials: oak, mosaics, weathered marble, granite and limestone. Step around to the garden and peek through the kitchen windows at rows of copper pots, reflections of the lovely meals served in the restaurant. Reserve a room with a balcony overlooking the river and its water-kissing willows or splurge on a suite: one has a jacuzzi for two in the tower. Bring your paintbrushes.

| | |
|---|---|
| Rooms | 6 doubles: €90–€160. |
| | 6 suites for 2: €230–€340. |
| | Dinner, B&B €125–€230 per person. |
| | Extra bed/sofabed available €27 per |
| | person per night. |
| Meals | Breakfast €17–€25. |
| | Dinner €35–€75; |
| | children's menu €16–€25. |
| | Wine from €6.50. |
| Closed | Rarely. |

**Karine Petiteau**
Le Moulin de Connelles,
40 route d'Amfreville sous les Monts,
27430 Connelles, Eure

| | |
|---|---|
| Tel | +33 (0)2 32 59 53 33 |
| Email | moulindeconnelles@wanadoo.fr |
| Web | www.moulin-de-connelles.fr |

## Manoir de Surville

The estate's handsome buildings span the 16th to the 19th centuries, and sit amid lush lawns and trees in bucolic Normandy countryside. The old stones and wood beams breathe elegance and a light-filled reception room, with its fireplace, books and chessboard, sets the welcoming tone. You'll be well looked after by gentle, multilingual hosts Hugues and Camille – and by talented chef Magalie, who serves creative four-course menus if booked in advance. The French concept of 'cocooning' floats through eleven fresh rooms and suites spread over two buildings and themed in imaginative colours like rose pink, honey orange and mimosa yellow. Accessible 'lime green' room has a suntrap terrace, while others are upstairs, with two cute 'cocoon' rooms with open baths under steeply sloping eaves. You can pamper yourself in modern granite bathrooms, and make full use of the basement wellness area with its steam and sauna cabins, and showers enhanced by light and music. The surrounding forested countryside offers walking, cycling and horse-riding, 18-hole golf courses and an aquatic complex in Louviers.

| Rooms | Main house – 9 doubles: €180-€240. Exterior building – 2 suites for 3: €240-€300. |
| --- | --- |
| Meals | Dinner €35-€39 (Thurs, Fri & Sat eve only; July/August Tues-Sun eve). Restaurants 6km. |
| Closed | 20 December to 31 December. |

**Camille & Hugues Oeyen**
Manoir de Surville,
82 rue Bernard Petel,
Surville 27400, Eure

| Tel | +33 (0)2 32 50 99 89 |
| --- | --- |
| Email | contact@manoirdesurville.com |
| Web | www.manoirdesurville.com |

## Le Petit Coq aux Champs

The thick thatch roof of this Norman-style farmhouse is a fitting end to your journey into the countryside to find it. Only after a trek down a long village lane and parking among the azaleas and rhododendrons do you really catch sight of the elusive hotel itself. Extensions to the original timbered building give it an eclectic air despite the ubiquity of the thatch; the motif of the eponymous cockerel is represented in every form from sculpture to tapestry. The bedrooms are simpler, with understated comfort and modern bathrooms enhanced by the occasional antique and most rooms sport balconies where the lush vegetation gives shade and privacy. The garden, as with most of the hotel, is centred around providing for the restaurant. Here you find a menu as diverse as the décor is constant. The rustic, cosy dining room serves up not just fowl but foie gras, lobster, veal sweetbreads, beef fillet and more. If the occasionally hefty prices make you head for town, then historic Rouen and coastal Deauville, both around 40 minutes away, will sate all your senses on any budget.

| | |
|---|---|
| Rooms | 10 doubles, 6 twin/doubles: €119-€180. |
| Meals | Dinner €35-€73. Restaurants 7km. |
| Closed | Rarely. |

Fabienne Huard
Le Petit Coq aux Champs, 400 chemin
du Petit Coq, La Pommeraie Sud,
27500 Campigny, Eure

| | |
|---|---|
| Tel | +33 (0)2 32 41 04 19 |
| Email | info@lepetitcoqauxchamps.fr |
| Web | www.lepetitcoqauxchamps.fr |

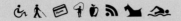

## Château de la Puisaye

Cats, dogs, horses, sheep and a fleet of farmyard fowl in 27 acres of countryside heaven. Delightful ex-solicitor Diana moved to France with her French husband to indulge her love of horses. With its scattering of shuttered windows and classically pale façade, this fine château oozes 19th-century elegance. Large airy bedrooms, where genuine English wallpapers are artfully mixed with French antiques, huge mantelpiece mirrors and glass-panelled doors that flood spaces with light; ivory paintwork, marble fireplaces and snowy linen create an ordered calm. The salon and library have elaborate woodwork and the dining room, with its gleaming table and silver candlesticks, invites you to linger over breakfast, a feast of homemade pastries, jams and cooked dishes. Diana, a stylish cook, will prepare a light supper or dinner on request, perhaps foie gras then truffle-stuffed guinea fowl; fruit and veg come from the potager, the 19th-century greenhouse and local markets. Lounge in the library over books, games, WiFi; borrow a bike and pedal the grounds; relax in the infra-red sauna among delicious aromatherapy oils.

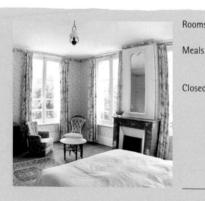

| | |
|---|---|
| Rooms | 3 doubles, 1 twin: €98–€128. 1 suite for 2-4: €185. |
| Meals | Dinner with wine €35; menu gourmand €55; Normandy platter with cider, €17. |
| Closed | Rarely. |

Bruno & Diana Costes
Château de la Puisaye,
Lieu-dit La Puisaye,
27130 Verneuil sur Avre, Eure

| | |
|---|---|
| Tel | +33 (0)2 32 58 65 35 |
| Email | info@chateaudelapuisaye.com |
| Web | www.chateaudelapuisaye.com |

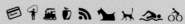

## Domaine de la Louveterie

From the forested road, the drive descends to glorious views over the hills of the Perche. And there is the house, a 17th-century *longère* in 32 acres of peacefulness, rescued and restored by Carol and Pietro. A charming ex-Parisian couple, well travelled and fluent in several languages, they are enchanted with the slow pace of life here. A gravelled courtyard sets the scene, beyond are two gîtes. Inside is a mixture of rustic and antique with a few exotic notes and no ostentation, simply an overwhelming feeling of comfort and well-being. Pietro oversees pasture and woodland, potager and pool; Carol, a food photographer, stars in the kitchen. Good wines and food are ferried to a room where logs smoulder; hosts join guests for after-dinner coffee and digestifs. And so to bed... the Fifties room is caught in a cosy time warp (in spite of the flat-screen TV), 'Chinoise' and 'Voyage' lie warmly under the eaves, and the suites spread themselves impressively over two floors, the grandest with wooden panelling, choice antiques and a real fire. *No credit cards.*

| | |
|---|---|
| Rooms | 3 doubles: €100–€115. |
| | 2 suites for 2: €140–€165. |
| | 1 cottage for 3, |
| | 1 cottage for 2: €640 per week. |
| Meals | Dinner, 3-5 courses with wine, |
| | €39–€75. |
| Closed | Rarely. |

|  | |
|---|---|
| | Pietro Cossu |
| | Domaine de la Louveterie, |
| | 61110 Moutiers au Perche, Orne |
| Tel | +33 (0)2 33 73 11 63 |
| Mobile | +33 (0)6 22 47 42 71 |
| Email | domainedelalouveterie@wanadoo.fr |
| Web | www.domainedelalouveterie.com |

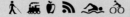

## Villa Fol Avril

Once a stopover for travellers passing on this peaceful road, the 19th-century staging post became a petrol station some years ago; now it's been rescued by the Sicres. Since leaving Paris, this energetic couple have added modern touches to authentic features and created a beautiful, bright hotel. Sunshine pours in through windows overlooking the pretty village's rosy-coloured roofs, and handcrafted furnishings pop up everywhere. Bedrooms are bold and individual, all with elaborately carved key fobs and something to make you go "ooh!" In one, an oak ladder leads to a high mezzanine – great fun for kids. The exposed timbers upstairs are magnificent and some remnants from the coach house's old life have been given a new lease of life: an ancient hayrack and shutters have become quirky headboards. Bathrooms are equally distinctive, with yellow tiles. Fresh local produce is served in the restaurant or on the garden terrace; look out for snails from the local 'escargotière'. Venture into the Perche for plenty of surprises: forested walking tracks, fairy-tale manoirs and the famous Percheron horses.

| Rooms | 4 doubles, 2 twins: €90–€130. |
| | 6 suites for 2: €120–€180. |
| | 1 triple: €125–€170. |
| Meals | Breakfast €13. Dinner €25–€45. |
| | Wine €20–€60. Restaurants 8km. |
| Closed | Never. |

Monsieur & Madame Sicre
Villa Fol Avril,
2 rue des Fers Chauds,
61110 Moutiers au Perche, Orne

| Tel | +33 (0)2 33 83 22 67 |
| Email | contact@villafolavril.fr |
| Web | www.villafolavril.fr |

## Château de la Mouchère

Art Deco enthusiasts will happily splash out on a stay at this 18th-century château. Step through an impressive hall lined with books, and discover bold tiling and fabrics, muted colours on the walls, stained glass lamps, wallpapers and art. The sitting and dining rooms have stunning parkland views, a huge Alsace wood-burning stove, delicate 1840s watercolours, parquet floors and rugs; some bedrooms have fireplaces and all have elegant shuttered windows. Lucky dogs are treated to their own towel and biscuits on arrival – the laundry room with washing and sewing facilities is an added plus – while the sunny south-facing terrace is a birdwatcher's dream. Charming, cultured, generous Roger and Marie-Monique give you homemade jams at breakfast, and join you for an apéritif before a dinner of home-grown and the best local produce. They keep parkland, gardens and outbuildings pristine too; vegetable and herb gardens are in tip-top order and leafy strolls through the magnificent trees are a delight. The area is famous for Percheron horses, there are heaps of local markets and Le Mans race track isn't far.

| Rooms | 3 doubles: €110-€150. |
| | 2 suites for 2-4: €160-€190. |
| Meals | Dinner with wine, €30-€40. |
| | Restaurant 5km. |
| Closed | Rarely. |

|  | Marie-Monique Huss |
| | Château de la Mouchère, |
| | 61130 St Cyr la Rosière, Orne |
| Tel | +33 (0)2 33 83 02 99 |
| Mobile | +33 (0)6 32 35 92 66 |
| Email | lamouchere@gmail.com |
| Web | www.lamouchere.com |

## Château de Sarceaux

Up its long sweeping drive there's a pleasing informality to this traditional château with its huge rambling estate, lake and mature trees – heaven for a roam or a run-around. Your courteous, unstuffy hosts' ancestry goes back some 400 years, the place is full of period treasures, and Madame la Marquise is an outstanding cook; her four course dinners in the elegant dining room – with silver, family porcelain, ancient, faded black and white frescoes – are a huge treat. So too is relaxing afterwards – perhaps to a tune on the grand piano – by the immense open fire in the sitting room. A family-friendly variety of view-filled rooms have polished wooden floors, marble fireplaces, good mattresses, heavy silk drapes – all very French and authentic, as are the immaculate and happily retro bathrooms. Just three kilometres away is Alençon, with its medieval centre, its lace and fine arts museum, shops and restaurants. There are good riding stables nearby, bikes for hire and a 'Voie Verte' cycling and walking trail. All very rural and peaceful yet not far from the motorway and only 120km from the ferry at Caen.

| Rooms | 2 doubles: €135–€150. |
| --- | --- |
| | 1 family room for 4: €135–€170. |
| | 2 twin/doubles: €150–€180. |
| | Extra bed €35. |
| Meals | Dinner, 4 courses with wine, €54. |
| Closed | Rarely. |

Marquis & Marquise Gicquel des Touches
Château de Sarceaux, Rue des Fourneaux,
Valframbert, 61250 Alençon, Orne

| Tel | +33 (0)2 33 28 85 11 |
| --- | --- |
| Mobile | +33 (0)6 07 49 52 58 |
| Email | chateaudesarceaux@yahoo.fr |
| Web | www.chateau-de-sarceaux.com |

Entry 102   Map 4

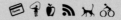

## La Louvière

It's a joy to discover this 18th-century manor house, a classic gentilhommière encircled by divine grounds. Drive up an avenue of lime trees, step under the clematis-strewn pergolas, enter the hall. Charming hostess Isabelle Groult says the old house has "une ambiance de soie": a chandelier sparkles above lace tablecloths in the dining room, pale chintz frames elegant windows in the *grand salon*, and the *petit salon*'s fireplace is flanked by charming chairs. Colours and fabrics harmonise beautifully. Take an apéritif on the terrace, get sporty on the tennis court, and relish the gardens, scented with roses and buzzing with bees. Patterned paving leads to an old-style potager, source of dinner's vegetables. Inside, an oak staircase curves up to bedrooms on the first floor: exquisitely romantic with exceedingly fine fabrics and antiques; up again is 'Chambre d'Aurélie' tucked into the beautiful 'charpente'. 'Chambre d'Alexandre' is equally striking – and discreet. Everything you could want for a weekend is here: a heated pool, a tennis court, a small fishing lake, happiness, peace.

| | |
|---|---|
| Rooms | 3 doubles; 1 double with separate private bathroom: €95-€160. 1 suite for 4: €190. |
| Meals | Dinner with wine & coffee, €39. |
| Closed | Rarely. |

Isabelle & Alain Groult
La Louvière,
Le Fault,
61420 St Denis sur Sarthon, Orne

| | |
|---|---|
| Tel | +33 (0)2 33 29 25 61 |
| Email | isabelle@louviere.fr |
| Web | www.louviere.fr |

Entry 103   Map 4

## Bois Joli

In the middle of a pretty, fashionable and traditional spa town whose waters rise at 24° and whose original boating lake, casino and spa remain intact, Bois Joli was a *pension* built in the mid-1800s for those taking the waters. It sits at the edge of the Andaines Forest in a neat, railing'd acre of lawn, shrubs and sequoias. Décor is traditional classic French, understated and elegant. In the salon are good chairs, books, newspapers, flowers in pewter vases and a piano you may play; in the dining room, fine rush-seated chairs and white napery. The food is good-looking and delicious: fresh bread and squeezed orange for breakfast; oysters, pigeon breast and apricot tart for dinner. Slip off your shoes in a carpeted bedroom, immaculate with matching toile de Jouy or pale spriggy wallpaper and fabrics, perhaps an old country wardrobe to add character. That lovely lake is a minute away and the hotel arranges mushroom-picking weekends in the woods. Owners and staff are friendly, discreet and helpful, and you are surrounded by all the benefits of civilisation – golf, swimming, tennis and restaurants aplenty.

| Rooms | 20 twin/doubles: €80–€168. |
|-------|----------------------------|
| Meals | Breakfast €11. |
|       | Lunch & dinner €21–€69. |
| Closed | Rarely. |

Yvette & Daniel Mariette
Bois Joli, 12 av Philippe du Rozier,
61140 Bagnoles de l'Orne, Orne

| Tel | +33 (0)2 33 37 92 77 |
|-----|----------------------|
| Email | boisjoli@wanadoo.fr |
| Web | www.hotelboisjoli.com |

## Le Pavillon de Gouffern

More mansion than lodge, Gouffern was built 200 years ago by a wealthy gentleman with plenty of fellow hunters to entertain. But the scale of this elegant 'pavilion' is perfect for today's traveller. It stands in an estate of over 60 hectares and guests can walk, cycle or ride in the private forest in peace and seclusion. Big windows let in lots of soft light to illuminate the newly renovated décor: hunting themes, an Edwardian salon with leather chairs and oak floors, an unfussy elegance that gives a sense of the quiet, comfortable, class of a good country house. Recently renovated bedrooms, some of them in the well-converted outbuildings, are big and eminently striking (smaller on the top floor), new bathrooms have all the necessary bits and meals are served in the handsome dining room – the food has been much praised. In the grounds, the delightful Doll's House, built for children of another age, is now an idyllic suite (honeymoon specials arranged). A nearby stable delivers horses to the door and, if you are lucky, the chef will cook your freshly caught trout.

| | |
|---|---|
| Rooms | 18 doubles, 1 single: €75-€200. 1 suite for 2-4: €150-€200. |
| Meals | Breakfast €12. Picnic available. Lunch & dinner €28-€55. |
| Closed | Christmas. |

**Karelle Jouaux & Vincent Thomas**
Le Pavillon de Gouffern,
61310 Silly en Gouffern, Orne

| | |
|---|---|
| Tel | +33 (0)2 33 36 64 26 |
| Email | pavillondegouffern@wanadoo.fr |
| Web | www.pavillondegouffern.com |

## Manoir de Bénédicte

A really wonderful house, bursting with history and beautiful architecture, surrounded by a stunning National Park. The owner, Bénédicte, is warm, engaging and a delight to stay with, opening her home and also the impressive grounds in an informal, relaxed way. Light floods in to a rich red dining room with oak parquet floor and picture windows overlooking lawns and river; the salon is calming and has equally fine views; upstairs are lofty-ceilinged bedrooms with Persian rugs and family antiques. Breakfast is round the large table in front of a grand fireplace: freshly-squeezed orange juice, local cheeses, bread from the local bakery, homemade cakes and jams. Energetic walks abound – or just stroll the garden to find vast lawns, pasture, woodland and the river Noireau on the boundary. There's a small lake fed by the river, enchanting little wooden bridges for you to cross and even a secret passage between the lake and the river where soldiers from the allied forces hid during the war. You can hang around here all day in fine weather, or take a romantic evening picnic to the lake – Bénédicte will even give you glasses and a corkscrew.

| | |
|---|---|
| Rooms | 3 doubles: €110–€150. Extra bed €25. |
| Meals | Restaurants 3km. |
| Closed | End October to April. |

Bénédicte de Saint Pol
Manoir de Bénédicte,
Les Planches, 61430 Cahan, Orne

Tel      +33 (0)6 74 13 17 49
Email    xb.desaintpol@club-internet.fr

## Le Vieux Chateau, Le Renouard

Down a lane below the old village church, a 1,000-year-old fortified manor house replete with history set between two lakes and surrounded by lawns, paddocks and mature trees. Australian owner Donna is on site to greet you. Her renovations, decoration and furnishings have created exquisite spaces, imposing but welcoming, with the grandeur of large public rooms, pale stone walls, monumental fireplaces and tall windows enhanced by capacious sofas, old prints and paintings, oriental rugs and heavy fabrics. Bedrooms are large, three with four-posters, one with a handsome brass bed and its own dressing room: sink into comfortable mattresses and silken quilts, and enjoy bucolic views. Bathrooms, with fluffy robes, are state of the art. Continental breakfasts and five-course dinners are served at the large table in the elegant dining room looking out to the gardens. While away the days in country pastimes: walk, cycle (bikes provided), fish. Browse markets and meet producers of local cheese, cider and calvados. See the Bayeux tapestry, visit the Normandy beaches. Wrap yourself in the comfort of French provincial life.

| Rooms | 4 doubles: €165–€185. |
| Meals | Restaurants 10km. |
| | Dinner, 5 courses with wine, €50. |
| Closed | January/February. |

Donna McDougall
Le Vieux Chateau,
61120 Le Renouard, Orne

| Tel | +33 (0)2 33 12 88 16 |
| Email | donna.mcdougall@virgin.net |
| Web | www.levieuxchateaulerenouard.com |

Brittany

## Le Manoir du Rodoir

You can drift in a heated pool as the breeze rustles through ancient oaks, and chat with charming owners over a pre-dinner cocktail on the terrace. Then slip into the brasserie for inventive cuisine that matches the conservatory dining room's contemporary décor. Built in 1875, the ivy-clad mansion sits in lush parkland overlooking a lake. It's as peaceful as can be, and bedrooms feel as natural and calm as the surroundings. Solid wood furniture, original lamps, soft carpets, colourful fabrics... If you'd like a cup of tea, just ask helpful staff. Guests and locals compliment the chef for his modern twist on regional cuisine. You may have fresh oysters, magret de canard, mille-feuille of apple crêpes. Fresh fruit salad appears at breakfast, served buffet-style with mini pastries, hams and cheeses. There's also good eating a 10-minute walk away in La Roche-Bernard, a thousand-year-old town with a buzzing harbour and boat trips down La Vilaine. Long-distance hikers can pick up the GR39 to Mont St Michel or Brière Natural Park, and families will find beaches, boating and golf within a short drive.

| | |
|---|---|
| Rooms | 17 doubles, 5 twins: €85–€130. |
| | 2 triples: €115–€160. |
| Meals | Breakfast €12. |
| | Lunch €16 |
| | (Mon–Fri, September–June). |
| | Dinner €16–€60. |
| | Restaurants 1km. |
| Closed | December/January. |

| | |
|---|---|
| | **Alain De Sousa Reis** |
| | Le Manoir du Rodoir, |
| | Route de Nantes, |
| | 56130 La Roche Bernard, Morbihan |
| Tel | +33 (0)2 99 90 89 68 |
| Email | lemanoirdurodoir@wanadoo.fr |
| Web | www.lemanoirdurodoir.com |

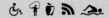

## Le Parc er Gréo

Fields, woods, sea and the coastal path are just yards away – all feels lovely and rural yet Vannes is a short drive. Owners Éric and Sophie built the neat modern building in the 1990s, but it's so well designed and decorated it feels like it's been in the family for ages. Warm colours, oriental rugs and fine family pieces sit easily in the smallish salon and dining room; these open onto terrace, garden and pool (heated and open all year round and sheltered by a high wall) – great places to relax or play with the children on the big lawn. Éric (who speaks excellent English) attentively prepares itineraries for guests: boating, swimming in the sea or inland exploration. His father's watercolours lend personality to all the rooms and the unusual candlesticks in the hall and ancestral portraits, including a large Velazquez–style child in a great gilt frame, are most appealing. Snug bedrooms, with a good mix of old and modern, are attractive in shades of red, green and salmon; nearly all have brand new bathrooms with spacious showers. Come by electric car and charge up at this easy, friendly place to stay.

| Rooms | 11 doubles: €99-€174. |
| | 1 suite for 4: €198-€278. |
| | 1 triple: €169-€209. |
| Meals | Breakfast €15. Restaurants 3km. |
| Closed | 3 January to 11 February. |

Éric & Sophie Bermond
Le Parc er Gréo,
9 rue Mané Guen Le Gréo,
56610 Arradon, Morbihan

| Tel | +33 (0)2 97 44 73 03 |
| Email | contact@parcergreo.com |
| Web | www.parcergreo.com |

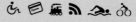

## Hôtel La Désirade

Everyone loves an island and this one, with its wild windswept coast, is especially enticing. Battered by storms in winter, it is hot and gorse-scented in summer and the roads are silent. La Désirade, sheltered in its parkland, is made up of a new village of colourwashed houses round a pool. If leafy gardens, comfortable hotelly bedrooms and super bathrooms (white bathrobes, lashings of hot water) don't bring instant relaxation, the spa and massages surely will. Breakfast is served buffet-style in the breakfast room or by the pool; dinner, formal but excellent, is in the hotel restaurant across the lane. The young chef specialises in local dishes and the presentation is impeccable; wines are first-class too. Research the island's possibilities curled up in a wicker chair in the reception salon with its unexpectedly blue fireplace: there are lots of illustrated books. You have 104 kilometres of coastal paths and cycle routes to choose from, while the beaches are a 20-minute walk away. Take your paintbox and you'll be in good company: Monet and Matisse both came to the island to paint. *Minimum stay: 2 nights in high season.*

| | |
|---|---|
| Rooms | 14 doubles, 14 twins: €109–€249. 4 family rooms for 4: €250–€370. Dinner, B&B €49 extra per person. Extra bed/sofabed available €30 per person per night. |
| Meals | Breakfast €17. Picnic available. Dinner from €27. Wine €24–€99. |
| Closed | Early November to early April. |

Pierre & Bénédicte Rebour
Hôtel La Désirade,
Le Petit Cosquet, Bangor,
56360 Belle Ile en Mer, Morbihan

| | |
|---|---|
| Tel | +33 (0)2 97 31 70 70 |
| Email | hotel-la-desirade@wanadoo.fr |
| Web | www.hotel-la-desirade.com |

Entry 110  Map 2

## Château de Penfrat

You can horse-ride or hike freely around 100 hectares of forested parkland, and watch birds on the banks of the Odet estuary, which flows into the Atlantic eight kilometres away. It's relaxing and peaceful, as is the château – a tall, handsome hunting lodge built by eccentric nobles, now owned by easy-going Patrick and Barbora. Here you can appreciate the simple pleasures of a good book, an easy chair and light jazz, and an apéro with your hosts and other guests. There's a retro feel to the salons and dining room, with their black and white photos and 50s brocante, and a fresh, sunny feel to the south-facing bedrooms: tall windows, low beds, colourful linen. (If you tend to quibble over the tap end, 'South Suite' has two candlelit baths.) The estate is a lovely bubble – but burst out and explore: the winding lanes and fish markets of Quimper; the tall ships of Douarnenez; the artists' village of Pont-Aven; and a string of quaint ports, beaches and seafood restaurants. In the morning, perhaps a Breton crêpe with chèvre frais and honey from Barbora's native Lithuania. Massages are available.

| Rooms | 1 double: €95–€115. |
| | 1 suite for 3, 1 suite for 4: €130–€180. |
| Meals | Dinner, €35, by arrangement |
| | (not in summer). |
| | Wine €8–€20. Restaurant 5km. |
| Closed | 1 December to 15 January. |

**Barbora Kairyte & Patrick Viossat**
Château de Penfrat,
25 chemin de Penfrat,
29950 Gouesnach, Finistère
Tel      +33 (0)6 33 33 37 63
Email    info@penfrat.fr
Web      www.penfrat.fr

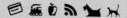

## La Vinotière

Mature elegance meets modern chic at the 'end of the earth' – that's the feel at this 16th-century merchant's house teetering on the Finistère coast. Around it, Le Conquet bustles: fishermen and ferries sail from the port, boutiques cluster, the market confabs every Tuesday. Inside lies innovation: squeezing bathrooms into all ten bedrooms has required a clever use of light and space and some bathrooms are sectioned from the bedroom by half-glazed walls or low panels. Quirky perhaps, but stylish to a fault: La Vinotière is part-owned by an interior decorator. Exposed stone, customised furniture, neutral colours and oak shutters convey class; bright oil paintings (for sale) add a splash. Most fun is for kids: bunk-bedded 'Petite Vinotière' is like a ship's cabin so little ones can sleep like sailors before paddling on the local beach. You can walk the Kermorvan Peninsula or have fishy fun at Brest's Océanopolis, a shortish drive. No outdoor space but adults can retire to the hotel's Salon de Thé whose comfy confines offer cakes and organic teas – the perfect pick-me-up before more exploring.

| | |
|---|---|
| Rooms | 7 doubles, 1 twin/double: €60–€135. 1 family room for 4: €60–€200. 1 bunk room for 2: €60–€135. |
| Meals | Breakfast €10. Light lunch available. Restaurants 2-minute walk. |
| Closed | Rarely. |

Joëlle Tromeur
La Vinotière,
1 rue Lieutenant Jourden,
29217 Le Conquet, Finistère

| | |
|---|---|
| Tel | +33 (0)2 98 89 17 79 |
| Email | info@lavinotiere.fr |
| Web | www.lavinotiere.fr |

## Grand Hôtel des Bains

Marine purity on the north Brittany coast: it's like a slightly snobby yacht club where you are an old member. The minimalist magician has cast natural spells of cotton, cane, wood, wool, seagrass: nothing synthetic or pompous. Sober lines, little ornamentation and restful colours leave space for the scenery, the sky pours in through walls of glass, the peaceful garden flows into rocks, beach and sea. Moss-green panelling lines the deep-chaired bar where a fire leaps in winter. Smallish, pale grey-panelled bedrooms have dark mushroom carpets and thick cotton stripes and checks, a four-poster here, a balcony there, nearly all have the ever-changing sea view. Bathrooms are due for refurbishment but bathrobes give you that four-star look on your way to the indoor seawater pool and treatment spa. Staff are smiling and easy, the ivory-panelled dining room with its sand-coloured tablecloths is deeply tempting. Spectacular coastal paths, a choice of beaches, yoga and spa retreats, even a writer's workshop – the luxury of space, pure elegant simplicity and personal attention are yours.

| | |
|---|---|
| Rooms | 36 twin/doubles: €201-€337. Singles €183-€317. Extra bed/sofabed available €40-€69 per person per night. |
| Meals | Dinner €37-€50. |
| Closed | Rarely. |

Madame Nicol
Grand Hôtel des Bains,
15 bis rue de l'Église,
29241 Locquirec, Finistère
Tel        +33 (0)2 98 67 41 02
Email    reception@grand-hotel-des-bains.com
Web      www.grand-hotel-des-bains.com

## Ti al Lannec

Heaps of English antiques yet it is superbly French and fulsome: an Edwardian seaside residence perched on the cliff, its gardens tumbling down to rocky coves and sandy beaches; fall asleep to the sound of waves and wind in the pines. (The beach club closes at midnight.) Inside, a mellow warmth envelops you in armfuls of drapes, swags and sprigs. Each room is a different shape and size, individually decorated as if in a private country mansion, with a sitting space, a writing table, a pretty bathroom and a view to the cypresses or, most wonderful, the sea. Expect florals, stripes, oriental rugs, white linen. Some bedrooms are big, with well-furnished white loggias, some are made for families with convertible bunk-bed sofas. Salons are cosily arranged with little lamps, mirrors, ornaments, old prints; the restaurant faces the sea and serves some pretty fancy and decorative food. The genuinely charming Jouanny family, immersed in the community and very mindful of their guests' welfare, have created a smart but human hotel with a lovely intimate spa by the indoor pool. Walk, swim, or just lounge in this stunning setting.

| Rooms | 24 twin/doubles: €244–€395. |
|---|---|
| | 7 family rooms for 3-5: €280–€540. |
| | 2 singles: €167–€192. |
| | Extra bed/sofabed available €48–€65 per person per night. |
| Meals | Breakfast €18. |
| | Lunch & dinner €28–€78; children's menu €17–€25. |
| Closed | Mid-November to March. |

**Jouanny Family**
Ti al Lannec,
14 allée de Mezo Guen,
22560 Trébeurden, Côtes-d'Armor

| Tel | +33 (0)2 96 15 01 01 |
|---|---|
| Email | contact@tiallannec.com |
| Web | www.tiallannec.com |

Entry 114  Map 2

## Manoir de Kergrec'h

Come for genuine château life. The elegant place has seen battles under the monarchy, the French Revolution, two Empires... until in modern times it became a château B&B. After a sweeping refurbishment, the charming new owner continues the tradition of hospitality and knows the best eateries, the area's hidden art treasures, the locals who will take you fishing, beach-hopping, sailing. A 15th-century stone staircase winds up to big, elegantly simple bedrooms full of fine period pieces; superb new bathrooms are in perfect contrast. Sophisticated furnishings are in plain soft-hued high-quality fabrics, there's just the occasional splash of coloured wall, bold wallpaper or tartan cushions. A huge double, with views across the garden to the sea, has one fabulous blue wall, blue striped curtains and an equally vast bathroom; even the wardrobe is enormous. It's not overpowering, just deliciously luxurious. Giant trees line the drive, great lawns disappear into the distance, the sea sparkles beyond the shrubs: there is much to explore so try to resist the appeal of the two club-like sitting rooms with their big windows and log fires. *Minimum stay: 2 nights in high season.*

| Rooms | 5 doubles: €99–€178 |
|---|---|
| | 2 suites for 4, 1 suite for 5: €225–€285. |
| | 3 family rooms for 3: €180–€195. |
| Meals | Breakfast €15. Restaurants 3km. |
| Closed | November & January/February. |

**Pierre-Louis Enriore**
Manoir de Kergrec'h,
22820 Plougrescant,
Côtes-d'Armor

Tel     +33 (0)2 96 92 59 13
Email   kergrec.h@wanadoo.fr
Web    www.manoirdekergrech.com

### Hôtel le Manoir St Michel

On a hillside overlooking wide white sands and wild coves is a 400-year-old sturdy stone 'manoir' with a long and varied history. Ducks wander the peaceful gardens, there's a small lake stocked with fish, wooden loungers dot the lawns and there are fine sea views from every angle. Inside, fresh flowers pretty up the reception and Monsieur and Madame greet you warmly: your hosts could not be nicer. Bedrooms vary in size and shape, not luxurious but comfortable and cosy, some traditional with floral fabrics and patterned carpets, others more contemporary. Bathrooms are spotless and small. Exposed stone walls add rusticity, antique armoires add character and there are 20 rooms to choose from so let the website guide you. Some are in the converted stables, some have sea views, some are on the ground floor. Take a ferry between St Malo and Dinard, visit the ancient, unspoilt Château de la Hunaudaye, come home to cakes and tea by the great log fire, and walk to dinner (take a torch!). Breakfasts are to die for: homemade croissants, yogurts and jams: Monsieur was once a pâtissier.

| | |
|---|---|
| Rooms | 9 doubles, 2 twins: €55–€95. |
| | 3 triples: €75–€135. |
| | 1 quadruple: €93–€163. |
| | 2 cottages for 2, 1 cottage for 3, |
| | 1 cottage for 5, 1 cottage for 6: |
| | €63–€188 per night. |
| Meals | Breakfast €10; children's menu €5. |
| | Restaurant 800m. |
| Closed | November – March. |

Jérôme Fournel
Hôtel le Manoir St Michel, 38 rue de la
Carquois, 22240 Fréhel, Côtes-d'Armor

| | |
|---|---|
| Tel | +33 (0)2 96 41 48 87 |
| Mobile | +33 (0)6 26 87 54 05 |
| Email | contact@manoirstmichel.com |
| Web | www.manoirstmichel.com |

## Hôtel Manoir de Rigourdaine

At the end of the lane, firm on its hillside, Rigourdaine breathes space, sky, permanence. The square-yarded manor farm, originally a stronghold with moat and all requisite towers, now looks serenely out over estuary and rolling pastures, and offers a sheltering embrace. The reception/bar in the converted barn is a good place to meet the friendly, attentive master of the manor, properly pleased with his excellent conversion. A high open fireplace warms a sunken sitting well; the courtyard, a gravelled enclosure overlooking the estuary, is made for lounging in the sun; breakfast is at long tables laid with bright mats. Refurbished (or in the process) rooms are attractive and comfortable: Iranian rugs on plain carpets, coordinated contemporary-chic fabrics in pleasing colours, some fine old furniture, pale bathrooms with all essentials. Six ground-floor rooms have private terraces onto the garden – ideal for sundowners. Everywhere, atmosphere is lent by old timbers and antiques, and always the long limpid view. Great for families, cyclists, sailors, walkers. *Minimum stay: 2 nights at weekends, 2 nights in high season. Children over 2 welcome.*

| | |
|---|---|
| Rooms | 10 doubles, 4 twins: €97-€105. 3 triples: €117-€125. 2 quadruples: €137-€145. Singles €89-€97. |
| Meals | Breakfast €9.50. Restaurants 4km. |
| Closed | 1 November to 1 April. |

Patrick Van Valenberg
Hôtel Manoir de Rigourdaine,
Rigourdaine,
22490 Plouër sur Rance, Côtes-d'Armor

| | |
|---|---|
| Tel | +33 (0)2 96 86 89 96 |
| Email | hotel.rigourdaine@wanadoo.fr |
| Web | www.hotel-rigourdaine.fr |

## Malouinière le Valmarin

The graceful *malouinière* was built in the early 18th century by a wealthy shipowner. Very near the ferry terminal, and in the centre of town, whence the urban buzz, this hotel has an unexpectedly large rose-filled garden with loungers and tables beneath mature cedars and the copper beech. Most bedrooms – light-filled with high ceilings, tall windows carefully draped to match the bedcovers – overlook the garden. Second-floor rooms have sloping ceilings and a cosier feel, with exposed beams, white walls and pale blue carpets. The indefatigable and cheerful Françoise and Bertrand refurbish a couple of rooms each winter. There are lavender bags in the wardrobes, plenty of books in French and English, and breakfast at the small yellow and blue dining tables. Or have your café-au-lait in bed and laze a bit before exploring the fabulous ramparts of the city or sunning on the nearby beaches. There's riding nearby and excellent thalassotherapy spas, or take an ocean ride to one of the Channel Islands (Sark is fascinating). Dinard, the 'Nice of the North', is a very short drive. Great value. *Secure parking available.*

| Rooms | 8 twin/doubles: €95–€165. |
|---|---|
| | 4 family rooms for 2-5: €139–€215. |
| Meals | Breakfast €12. |
| | Restaurants 5-minute walk. |
| Closed | Never. |

**Françoise Nicolas-Quéric**
Malouinière le Valmarin,
7 rue Jean XXIII, St Servan,
35400 St Malo, Ille-et-Vilaine

| Tel | +33 (0)2 99 81 94 76 |
| Email | levalmarin@wanadoo.fr |
| Web | www.levalmarin.com |

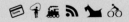

## Hôtel de l'Abbaye

Owned by the Saget Family, famous winemakers of the Loire, this former Benedictine monastery is now a contemporary, stylish hotel. It's set on the edge of a quiet Bretagne village, by the Forest de Mesnil (great for walking and cycling) and overlooking St Malo golf course. Modern furniture sits happily with exposed stone walls, beams and monumental granite fireplaces – a reminder of the monastic past. Light and views flood in through huge windows – ask for a room with lake or garden view – some have French windows to the garden. Bedrooms are all similar with impressive oak beamed ceilings and comfortable king-sized beds; bright, white bathrooms are smart and warm, most with showers rather than baths. Buffet breakfasts are hearty; evening menus are filled with local and seasonal delights, and washed down with their own very good wine. On balmy evenings it's lovely to eat out on the terrace. Explore the Abbey next door or, further afield, St Malo, Mont St Michel and the beautiful Côte d'Emeraude. A handy spot to stop off if you're travelling south.

| Rooms | 40 doubles: €129–€159. |
| | 5 suites for 2: €189–€239. |
| | Extra bed €35. |
| Meals | Breakfast €15–€25. Lunch €18–€22. |
| | Dinner €28–€34. Restaurants 1km. |
| Closed | November – March. |

François-Xavier Hastings
Hôtel de l'Abbaye,
35540 Le Tronchet, Ille-et-Vilaine

| Tel | +33 (0)2 99 16 94 41 |
| Mobile | +33 (0)6 80 13 92 19 |
| Email | direction@hotel-de-labbaye.com |
| Web | www.hotel-de-labbaye.com |

## Château de la Ballue

Artists say this 1620s château inspires creativity; spot its graceful two-winged façade and fall under its spell. The formal gardens are so wonderfully recreated they are listed and open to the public – a French reverie of bosquets and paths sprinkled with modern sculptures, gazing over Mont St Michel. Now they are joined by a hidden spa, zen garden and pool. Baroque recitals may ring in the courtyard; inside, Purcell odes may float through elegant wood-panelled rooms, over marble fireplaces, antique paintings, gilded mirrors and orchids. This is no museum, however, but a family home enlivened by three sons; your spirited hosts are passionate about the place. Drift off on dreamy canopied beds in bedrooms that are all different but all fabulous – from bold red 'Victor Hugo' to 'Florence' with blue fern patterns and feathery toile. Three have tented *cabinets de toilette* rather than separate bathrooms – a fascinating period feature. Silver cutlery tinkles over a fine continental spread in the blue-panelled breakfast room; birds sing a glorious hymn in the *bosquet de musique*.

| | |
|---|---|
| Rooms | 3 doubles: €210–€250.<br>1 suite for 2-4: €260–€385.<br>1 triple: €270–€290.<br>Extra bed €40. |
| Meals | Breakfast €20. Restaurants 15km. |
| Closed | Rarely. |

**Marie-Françoise Mathiot-Mathon**
Château de la Ballue,
35560 Bazouges la Pérouse,
Ille-et-Vilaine

| | |
|---|---|
| Tel | +33 (0)2 99 97 47 86 |
| Email | chateau@la-ballue.com |
| Web | www.la-ballue.com |

Entry 120   Map 3

## Château du Quengo

Anne, descendant of an ancient Breton family, and Alfred, who is Swiss, are passionate about animals, gardens, music, life! They welcome you open-armed to their inimitable house: a private chapel, a bio garden, rare trees, 1800s wallpapers, a carved staircase, a mosaic'd floor. She runs willow-weaving classes and plies you with homemade delights; he builds organs; both love the slow life. Down corridors, through doors, up stairs, bedrooms in this sprawling, many-winged place are properly old-fashioned with a mix of furniture old and new, faded wallpapers and vintage radiators, our favourite being the family room. No pomp, no ceremony, just books and papers strewn around and friendly animals to meet in the grounds: dogs and cats, a donkey, a Shetland pony. As you discover Anne's jams at breakfast (everything is home-produced and/or organic) she will entertain you with château stories and exciting tales, and advise you where to go (such as the book town of Bécherel). No plastic anything, few mod cons, just intelligent, humorous hosts and a house steeped in atmosphere, beauty and peace.

| Rooms | 1 double: €82. |
| | 1 family room for 5: €87. |
| Meals | Guest kitchen. |
| | Restaurants 1.5km. |
| Closed | Rarely. |

Anne & Alfred du Crest de Lorgerie
Château du Quengo,
35850 Irodouër,
Ille-et-Vilaine

| Tel | +33 (0)2 99 39 81 47 |
| Email | lequengo@laposte.net |
| Web | chateauduquengo.free.fr |

## Château du Pin

The small château with its pretty faded shutters is now inhabited by the Josses. They have neatened the lawns but the swagged roses remain, as do the previous owners' beautiful artistic interiors. A strong red on the walls is a bold statement of welcome in the salon where breakfast is served, modern furniture rubs shoulders with brocante finds, bookshelves burst with books and art. The late 18th-century staircase clambers up to soft-hued bedrooms above, their swathes of ruched silk clasped by tassels, their beds delicious with hand-painted headboards and luxurious covers; spotless bathrooms squeeze ingeniously behind rafters. Outside: masses of park and woodland for children to roam, fields for ponies, a small terrace overlooking the paddock and, should you choose to self-cater, a simple gîte in one of the courtyard's barns. A light supper is available at separate tables: a platter of smoked salmon, a hot gratin – ideal for the first night. This is a land of legends: King Arthur's Brocéliande forest is within easy reach… as are the Emerald coast, the gulf of Morbihan, Dinard and St Malo. *Helipad available.*

| Rooms | 1 double, 2 twin/doubles: €88–€163. |
| --- | --- |
| | 2 family rooms for 4: €88–€163. |
| | 1 cottage for 3-4: €140. |
| | Extra person €29. |
| Meals | Breakfast €14. |
| | Dinner €29 on request. Wine €10–€30. |
| | Restaurant 5km. |
| Closed | Rarely. |

**Marie France & Jean-Luc Josse**
Château du Pin, Route départementale 125,
La Veronnière, 35750 Iffendic,
Ille-et-Vilaine

| Tel | +33 (0)2 99 09 34 05 |
| --- | --- |
| Email | josse.jeanluc@free.fr |
| Web | www.chateau-pin.fr |

## Château de Bézyl

Rescued from ruin in 2001 by the Dutch Roest family, this late 19th-century country manor has been transformed with unabashed indulgence by Dutch designer Bert Strik, who has created a magnificent homage to a bygone era with a flair for all things Art Deco: décor, furnishings, light fittings, bespoke wallpapers, nature-inspired frescoes and stained glass ooze with a passion for the period. Set at the end of a long drive on a 230-acre estate, Aly welcomes you to a grand entrance hall and gracious public spaces, from dining room to oak-panelled fumoir. Three huge double rooms each come with a mix of bold colours, period and contemporary furnishings and views of the surrounding estate. Bathrooms are modern and luxurious with mosaic tiled walls, walk-in shower and claw-foot baths. Meals are taken with Aly in either the dining room or at the big kitchen table. Tuck in to breakfasts of homemade jams, fruit, smoked salmon and eggs cooked to order. Explore the grounds, visit Rennes, take a trip to the beach or the Vallée de l'Oust. Return to the peace of the estate and a four-course dinner. *Well behaved dogs welcome.*

| | |
|---|---|
| Rooms | 3 doubles: €140–€180. Extra bed €30. |
| Meals | Dinner €33; children's menu €18. Restaurants 7km. |
| Closed | November – March |

Aly Roos
Château de Bézyl,
35550 Sixt Sur Aff, Ille-et-Vilaine

| | |
|---|---|
| Tel | +33 (0)2 99 70 10 31 |
| Mobile | +33 (0)6 32 48 11 07 |
| Email | info@chateaudebezyl35.com |
| Web | www.chateaudebezyl35.com |

Western Loire

Photo: Château de la
Flocellière, entry 126

## Le Château de l'Abbaye

In wide flat countryside, set back from the main road in its own walled grounds, this *castel romantique* had been graciously managed by Danielle Renard for 25 years; now she, her son Renaud-Pierre and daughter-in-law Korakot make a delightful, welcoming trio. Visual enticements greet you as you arrive: bibelots and boxes, photographs and fresh flowers, Korakot's little embroideries, furniture antique and new, even a vintage Belgian stove. Roosters, a family passion, can be found in every medium, shape and size; don't miss the bulging scrapbooks of drawings by guests and their children. Continental breakfast is on the veranda in summer; dinner at candlelit tables reflects the best seasonal produce (French menus by Danielle, Thai by Korakot). In the château, bedrooms, not huge, are decorated to create cocoon-like spaces; extras include children's books and embroidered needlework, typical touches from these thoughtful hosts. Five big rooms in an outbuilding are more modern-oriental with fabulous ceiling lights. All have electronic extras, suites have their own garden and jacuzzi bath. There's a wellness space, too.

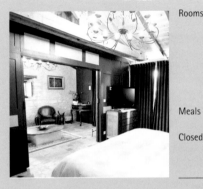

| Rooms | Château – 3 twin/doubles, Le Portal – 1 twin/double: €79–€149. Château – 2 suites for 2, Le Portal – 3 suites for 2: €99–€299. 1 apartment for 2-4: €159–€189. Dinner, B&B €95-€195 per person. Extra bed/sofabed available €25 per person per night. |
|---|---|
| Meals | Breakfast €15. Dinner €38. Wine €15–€54. |
| Closed | Rarely. |

**Family Renard**
Le Château de l'Abbaye,
85450 Moreilles,
Vendée
Tel        +33 (0)2 51 56 17 56
Email     chateau-moreilles@orange.fr
Web       www.chateau-moreilles.com

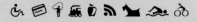

## Manoir de Ponsay

The family manor, a listed building, goes back to 1492: note the coat of arms over the door. Now both castle and hotel are run generously, and singlehandedly, by charming young Laurent, who was born here, and his Romanian wife Orelia. Outside is one of the oldest dovecotes in France, a peaceful pool and a hot tub, a tiny sauna, table tennis and bikes; the grounds are open and safe, the meadows stretch to the horizon. Inside, a dignified room for candlelit feasts, a sitting room with billiards and a tapestry or two, a priest's hole for hiding revolutionaries, should any lurk, and a massive stone stair. This sweeps you up to five characterful suites, historic, traditional, their long windows overlooking the park, their armoires polished to perfection, their chintz bright, their fireplaces lit (when required); the 'Chambre à Baldequin' has an exquisite four-poster and there's fine new Italian-style shower in the largest room. Dinner is prepared, served and hosted by Laurent and Orelia; special wines can be ordered from the cellar. Beyond, the summer extravaganzas at Puy de Fou draw a million spectators a year.

| | |
|---|---|
| Rooms | 1 suite for 4, 1 suite for 3, 3 suites for 2: €65-€125. |
| Meals | Breakfast €9. Dinner €34. |
| Closed | November – April (except by arrangement). |

Laurent de Ponsay
Manoir de Ponsay,
85110 Chantonnay,
Vendée

| | |
|---|---|
| Tel | +33 (0)2 51 46 96 71 |
| Email | manoirdeponsay@gmail.com |
| Web | www.manoirdeponsay.com |

## Château de la Flocellière

You really need to see La Flocellière from a helicopter. The aerial view is the most striking; the battlement'd castle was built around 1090 and is listed. Guests stay in the château, where bedrooms are vast, gracious and opulent, with huge windows on two sides onto the gardens and park. Overseeing this vast dominion is the Vicomtesse and her meticulous eye misses nothing, from the topiary in the grounds to the maids' attire. All is opulence and beauty and beeswax infuses every room. You can lounge around in the sitting room in the gallery, play a game of billiards, admire the magnificent potager below the ruined walls, visit the library or be taken on a full tour. This is living at its most sedate and children are welcome providing they behave impeccably! The heated pool area (saltwater pool open April to October) is secluded and as smart as the rest ("a terrace, not a beach"). If you choose to dine, tables d'hôtes for ten takes place two to three times a week: your chance to meet the hosts. It's a fabulous place to have a big party and the setting is sensational. Historic, magnificent, hospitable. *Pets by arrangement.*

| Rooms | 3 twin/doubles: €175-€235. |
| --- | --- |
| | 2 suites for 2-4: €235-€295. |
| | Singles €150-€175. |
| | Dinner, B&B €140-€170 per person. |
| | Extra bed/sofabed available €30 per person per night. |
| Meals | Breakfast included. |
| | Dinner with wine, €55; book ahead. |
| | Restaurant 500m. |
| Closed | January/February. |

Patrice Vignial
Château de la Flocellière,
85700 La Flocellière,
Vendée

| Tel | +33 (0)2 51 57 22 03 |
| --- | --- |
| Email | flocelliere.chateau@gmail.com |
| Web | www.chateaudelaflocelliere.com |

## Château de la Maronnière

The approach is down a small, winding road fringed by ancient, elegant trees which mask the house until you are in front of it. Friendly Marie and François, who have excelled in restoring their luxurious, 18th-century château, have the needs of their visitors at heart and are always on hand. Inside, the beautiful circular hall is painted in a rich yellow, the oak parquet is warm underfoot, copper leaf chandeliers light the circular hall and a stuffed fox surprises on the spiral staircase. Many rambling acres of green-fingered Eden await; take a wildlife walk or pluck cherries by the pool. Stylish shared spaces are immaculate with a baby grand (yes, you can play it if the urge strikes) in residence: Le Petit Bois has carved antique furniture; La Rotonde is marble grey with unusual panelling. Textiles and trimmings are sumptuous, bath robes fluffy; throw open the shutters for views. Breakfast is served in the guest dining room at one large, convivial table; much of it is home grown, with fresh eggs from their hens and home baked cakes. Walk, or bike, it off with a brisk stroll into Aizenay, visit sandy beaches and museums.

| Rooms | 1 double, 2 twin/doubles: €110–€120. 1 suite for 2: €195. Extra child bed €25. |
|---|---|
| Meals | Dinner with wine, €35. Restaurants 500m. |
| Closed | Never. |

François-Xavier & Marie-Hélène d'Halluin
Château de la Maronnière,
Route des Sables,
85190 Aizenay, Vendée

| Tel | +33 (0)6 25 02 00 55 |
| Email | dhalluinmh@gmail.com |
| Web | www.chateauvendee.com |

## Hôtel Fleur de Sel

Noirmoutier has a personality all its own: this group of simple white buildings in its Mediterranean garden is typical, sitting tranquilly between sea and salt marsh, long sandy beach and little yachting harbour. Perfect for family holidays, it has a tennis court, golf driving range, big pool and hot tub. Bedrooms are good too, some in classic cosy style with country fabrics and teak and pine, others more bracing with ship-shape yew furniture and yachting motifs; several have little ground-floor terraces. The delightful, caring owners have humour and intelligence and their daughter's paintings sit well in several of the rooms. The chef has worked with the very best in Paris and meals are served by courteous waiters in the airy, raftered dining room or on the oleander-lined terrace. It is all clean-cut, sun-warmed, impeccable and welcoming: you will feel sheltered. There is a bridge but try and come by the Passage du Gois causeway, open for three hours at low tide: an unforgettable four-kilometre drive 'through the sea' where shellfish-diggers cluster. The island is naturally very popular in summer. *Min. stay: 2 nights, 3 in high season. Pets by arrangement.*

| | |
|---|---|
| Rooms | 30 doubles, |
| | 5 family rooms for 4: €100–€220. |
| | Singles €86–€160. |
| | Dinner, B&B €84–€140 per person. |
| | Extra bed/sofabed available €15–€50 |
| | per person per night. |
| Meals | Lunch €20. |
| | Dinner €31–€41. Wine €16. |
| Closed | Early November to mid-March. |

**Pierrick Wattecamps**
Hôtel Fleur de Sel,
10 rue des Saulniers, 85330
Noirmoutier en l'Ile, Vendée
Tel      +33 (0)2 51 39 09 07
Email    contact@fleurdesel.fr
Web      www.fleurdesel.fr

## Château de Coët Caret

Come for a taste of life with the French country aristocracy – it's getting hard to find; the family have lived here for 13 generations. Gwénaël greets you on arrival and is helpfully on hand when needed. The château is tucked into the woods and 100 hectares of parkland with beautiful trees and plants and plenty of paths for wandering: serenity and relaxation are guaranteed. Bedrooms are faded but comfortable and traditional; all have coordinated bed covers and curtains, antiques, lamps and vases of fresh flowers; Saumon, under the eaves, comes with binoculars for the birds. Start the day with excellent bread, jams and coffee in the large, sunny breakfast room: painted panelling, china plates on the walls, more in glass cabinets and tables set with candles, napkins and more flowers. Gwénaël is full of tips for outings and places to eat – there are some excellent restaurants nearby, and you are in the Brière Regional Park where water and land are inextricably mingled and wildlife abounds.

| Rooms | 3 doubles: €100–€120. |
| | 1 twin: €85. |
| Meals | Restaurants 2km. |
| Closed | Rarely. |

**Gwénaël de La Monneraye**
Château de Coët Caret,
44410, Loire-Atlantique

| Tel | +33 (0)2 40 91 41 20 |
| Mobile | +33 (0)6 98 40 20 74 |
| Email | coetcaret@gmail.com |
| Web | www.coetcaret.com |

## Château de Cop Choux

The name, from 'couper la chaux' (cutting lime), refers to the old lime kilns: nothing to do with cabbages. Where to start: the elegant house built just before the French Revolution with towers added in the early 20th century, the 18 hectares of park, the pool, the rolling lawns and ancient trees? Or the 17 marble fireplaces and your friendly hosts? Patrick took over a Dutch-renovated château and has been developing the 'events market' (weddings are held in a distant building) ever since. The park is huge, chestnut trees line the approach, a river runs through the grounds, there are lakes and woods for ramblers, rare ferns for plant buffs, farm animals, even dromedaries in summer. The house is full of light, several bedrooms have windows on three sides and all are spacious. Filmy fabric floats at tall windows in 'Violette', 'Romarin' has carved twin beds and an interconnecting room. Bathrooms are still good. Breakfast comes with a selection of teas in a pretty panelled room or on the terrace; dinner is at separate tables.

| Rooms | 4 twin/doubles: €95-€120. |
| --- | --- |
| | 1 suite for 4: €160-€240. |
| | Extra bed/sofabed available €15-€20 per person per night. |
| Meals | Breakfast €9. |
| | Dinner with wine €39. |
| | Restaurants 12km. |
| Closed | Christmas & 15 November to 28 November. |

Patrick Moreau
Château de Cop Choux,
44850 Mouzeil,
Loire-Atlantique

| Tel | +33 (0)2 40 97 28 52 |
| --- | --- |
| Email | contact@copchoux.fr |
| Web | www.chateau-cop-choux.com |

## Château de la Frogerie

It's not often you can pretend to be medieval royalty but ascending the fabulous spiral staircase to your turret bedroom presents the ideal opportunity! Overlooking glorious Loire countryside, this petite château dates back to the fifteenth-century. Panelled walls, a moat and parquet floors create historical atmosphere but dynamic and charming owners, Jean-Christophe and Raymond-Pierre, have ensured that it co-exists with modern comfort. Antique beds are dressed in fine linen; cosy leather armchairs surround the fireplace in the elegant sitting room and there's a pool shaded by ancient walls and fine old cedars and oaks in the pretty garden. You breakfast like a king at separate tables in the dining room: bread and croissants from the local baker, yogurt and milk from the Jersey cows on the organic farm next door, honey from their own bee hives and homemade cake. Walk it off in the garden here, drive to Maulévrier for the wonderful and renowned Japanese garden, or visit Le Puy du Fou where there is a spectacular theme park and show every summer. Return to peace and quiet by the fire – this is a grown up sort of place. *Parking on-site.*

| Rooms | 3 doubles: €80-€144. |
|---|---|
| | 1 family room for 4-5 with sofabed: €140-€240. |
| | Singles €65-€126. |
| Meals | Restaurant 6km. |
| Closed | Rarely. |

**Jean-Christophe Robert**
Château de la Frogerie,
49360 Maulévrier,
Maine-et-Loire

| Tel | +33 (0)2 41 30 60 67 |
|---|---|
| Email | contact@chateau-frogerie.fr |
| Web | www.chateau-frogerie.fr |

## Château du Beugnon

Gasp with delight as you turn off the country road and glimpse the house, its luscious lake and lawns peeping through the trees. It is run by an irresistible pair, she gently discreet, he a retired restaurateur with a twinkle in his eye, passionate about beautiful food. Masses comes from the potager and if you stay for sociable dinner, you're in for a treat. The setting couldn't be more lovely: a fine landscaped park shaded by plane trees, an imperious swan gliding across the lake, charming outbuildings in the back courtyard, once used for making wine (the owners still make a few bottles of sauvignon). Bedrooms in the château have the old-world charm of a family home: wooden floors, pale colours, much-loved antiques. Those in the barn, on the ground floor, are more rustic-chic than traditional, with exposed stone walls and terracotta floors. All have immaculate en suites, some have handsome 1930s basins. Hire bikes and pedal off to explore the villages, plan a Layon Valley wine tour, visit Angers for its Apocalypse tapestries. And don't miss the wonderful Château de Brissac.

| Rooms | 4 doubles: €95. |
| | 1 suite for 5: €105. |
| Meals | Dinner with wine, €38. |
| | Restaurant 5km. |
| Closed | Never. |

Jean-Yves Bauchart
Château du Beugnon,
49540 La Fosse de Tigne,
Maine-et-Loire

| Tel | +33 (0)2 41 38 32 05 |
| Email | reservation@chateaudubeugnon.fr |
| Web | www.chateaudubeugnon.fr |

## Manoir de Boisairault

Our inspector had an Alice Through The Looking Glass moment as she stepped off the street, through the unremarkable gate and into the wonderful gardens – a series of secret 'rooms' – that surround this elegant, 18th-century, cloistered manor. Find masses of roses and colour, clambering wisteria and box parterres. There's a labyrinth of caves too, typical of the region – atmospheric and rustic, guests sometimes dine here with Jean-Pierre and Béatrice, your cultured, interesting hosts. Pray for the camembert sprinkled with pastis, cooked in the fire's embers – it's divine. Inside there's an attractive dining room, and immaculate bedrooms decorated and furnished with charm and taste: pretty bedheads and fabrics, beams against a white wall, antiques and flowers; the ground-floor one – all Louis XV – is particularly enchanting. Historic Saumur, between the Loire and Thouet rivers and surrounded by vineyards, is a few minutes away – visit the turretted château and the magnificent Fontevraud Abbey.

| Rooms | 2 doubles: €125-€140. |
| | 1 family room for 4: €180-€240. |
| Meals | Hosted dinner with wine, €35; |
| | children's menu €15. |
| | Restaurants 10km. |
| Closed | Rarely. |

Jean-Pierre Delmas
Manoir de Boisairault, 8 rue de Pas
d'Aubigné, 49260 Le Coudray
Macouard, Maine-et-Loire
Tel      +33 (0)6 08 93 85 61
Email    contact@manoir-de-boisairault.com
Web      www.manoir-de-boisairault.com

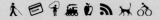

Entry 133  Map 4

### Château de Verrières

Guests are full of praise for this elegant château, built in 1890 to host balls and grand soirées. In recent years it has been passionately, authentically, lavishly restored. The house stands in huge grounds – unusual since it is right in the heart of old Saumur – and the charming new owners, Sükrü and Louise, could not be more welcoming or more helpful. Bedrooms are lofty, lovely and filled with light. Every trace of modern updating – central heating, rewiring – has been artfully concealed, and generous curtains hang at huge windows overlooking the private park. Other rooms overlook the elegant Ecole de Cavalerie, where aristocratic officers used to hone their equestrian skills, or Château de Saumur. The décor is classic French at its finest, apart from the contemporary and zen-like top-floor suite. Bathrooms are as luxurious, each one unique. Swim in the heated pool or step into town – don't miss the Saturday market! Breakfasts include homemade cakes and pancakes; good restaurants are on the doorstep. Worth every penny. *Minimum stay: 2 nights on weekdays.*

| Rooms | 8 doubles, 1 twin: €180–€295. 1 suite for 2: €345. Extra bed/sofabed available €35 per person per night. |
|---|---|
| Meals | Breakfast €19. Restaurant 400m. |
| Closed | Christmas, New Year & 12 January to 28 February. |

**Sükrü & Louise Karaca**
Château de Verrières,
53 rue d'Alsace, 49400 Saumur,
Maine-et-Loire

| Tel | +33 (0)2 41 38 05 15 |
| Email | contact@chateau-verrieres.com |
| Web | www.chateau-verrieres.com |

## Château de Beaulieu

Set back from the banks of the river Loire lies a château of character and charm, a perfect reflection of its owners. The Coady-Maguires are Irish, animated, delightful, and have many interests. Architect Jean Drapeau built the château in 1727 and the décor, traditional, authentic, captures the romance of that earlier age. Five bedrooms lead off an oak-beamed corridor and range from the dramatic ('Louis XIII' comes with a four-poster bed and bold colours) to the cosy and intimate. Antique armoires, ornate fireplaces and spotless bathrooms are yours, along with dreamy views of the large, enticing, tree-brimmed garden – note the lily-covered pond full of fish, the heated swimming pool, and the small, prospering vineyard. Snuggle down into deep-seated sofas with a book from the library or try your hand at billiards – it's all super relaxed. There's wine tasting next door, the market town of Saumur is a short jaunt up the river and the treasures of the Loire valley are legendary – you can visit the châteaux on horseback! We'd stay for the atmosphere and company alone.

| Rooms | 4 doubles: €120. |
| | 1 suite for 2-4: €160–€200. |
| Meals | Breakfast included. |
| | Restaurants 1km. |
| Closed | November – Easter. |

**Conor & Mary Coady-Maguire**
Château de Beaulieu,
98 route de Montsoreau,
49400 Saumur, Maine-et-Loire

| Tel | +33 (0)2 41 50 83 52 |
| Email | info@chateaudebeaulieu.fr |
| Web | www.chateaudebeaulieu.fr |

Entry 135   Map 4

## Demeure de la Vignole

To sleep in hand-carved ancient caves is rare indeed, especially when they're so luxurious. Several rooms in this tree-hugged hotel are literally set into the rock: spacious and airy, they have comfy beds cocooned in rock, state-of-the-art bathrooms and chandeliers dangling from bumpy limestone. Other rooms are in a 17th-century house, jazzed up with colourful rafters, chequered tiles and quirky furnishings that reflect your Parisian hosts' sense of style: a Chinese table, a stained-glass window, Murano-tiled bathrooms with vintage basins and baths. And a treat for swimmers – there's a heated pool like a secret lagoon in a rocky cave. You can sit out on the terrace for a generous French breakfast or a glass of wine from the vineyard in the next valley, or (on advance booking) Madame's home-cooked dinners fresh from the market. Or wander into arty Turquant, where there's a good restaurant, craft studios and caves hosting everything from mushroom farms to wine cellars. Pack a picnic and pedal west along the Loire cycle route to Saumur and Angers. For a cave room, specify on booking. *Minimum stay in cave rooms: 2 nights, 7 nights in July/August.*

| | |
|---|---|
| Rooms | 5 doubles, 2 twins: €130–€155. Cave rooms – 1 suite for 4 with sitting room, 3 suites for 2: €155–€270. Cave room – 1 apartment for 4 with kitchen, sitting room & 2 bathrooms: €290 per night. |
| Meals | Breakfast €12–€17. Dinner €25–€35; book ahead. Wine €5–€30. Restaurants 1km. |
| Closed | 15 November to 18 March. |

M Bartholeyns
Demeure de la Vignole,
3 imp Marguerite d'Anjou,
49730 Turquant, Maine-et-Loire

| | |
|---|---|
| Tel | +33 (0)2 41 53 67 00 |
| Email | demeure@demeure-vignole.com |
| Web | www.demeure-vignole.com |

## Domaine de Mestré

History oozes from every corner of Mestré. A Roman road; a cockleshell for the pilgrims en route to Compostela; the remnants of a 12th-century chapel; the mill and tithe barn to remind us that monks farmed here when Mestré was part of Fontevraud Abbey. Most of the present building is 18th century and the family have farmed here for 200 years, keeping the traditions of French country hospitality alive. Monsieur (the grandfather) runs the eco-conscious farm, milking by hand; one daughter makes fine natural soaps by sustainable methods (there's a spa too), the other manages the estate with its ancient, efficient drainage system. All take pride in their delicious home-grown food (including dairy and meat) and elegant service. Big bedrooms are furnished with lovely family antiques – huge sleigh or brass beds with wool mattresses, fluffy eiderdowns – and no TV; some have views over the wooded valley. The sitting room is a 'Victorian parlour' with dark panelling and red wallpaper; the dining room is simply delightful. A sense of timeless welcome and class enfolds guests of the family. Popular with cyclists. *Cash or euro travellers' cheque only.*

| | |
|---|---|
| Rooms | 7 doubles: €118. <br> 2 suites for 4, 1 suite for 5: €189–€221. <br> 1 triple: €139. <br> 2 singles: €79. <br> Extra bed/sofabed available €16 per person per night. |
| Meals | Breakfast €12; children under 7 €6. <br> Lunch €19. Dinner €29 (book ahead). <br> Restaurant closed Sunday eve & Monday. |
| Closed | January. |

Marie-Amelie & Benoit de Courcy
Domaine de Mestré,
49590 Fontevraud l'Abbaye,
Maine-et-Loire

| | |
|---|---|
| Tel | +33 (0)2 41 51 72 32 |
| Email | contact@domaine-de-mestre.com |
| Web | www.domaine-de-mestre.com |

## Hostellerie La Croix Blanche

A soothing, relaxing place to stay, which is not surprising; the building's creamy, stone façade is bang opposite the Royal Abbey, which has been a beacon to pilgrims since the 17th century. Today, run by French Christophe and Dutch/English Mieke, the emphasis is still on good food and relaxation. Menus are fresh, local and inventive and meals are served in the smart, wood-floored dining room with its exposed stone walls and bright red and purple velvet chairs; in the summer you can dine on the terrace. Standard rooms are crisp and minimalist but genuinely 'standard', so it's worth paying the extra for the boldly designed bedrooms in the historic part of the inn with their beams, fireplaces, antique furnishings, good views and more space; find a wall with a blown-up 18th-century map of France, a large red faux-leather bedhead, a splash of tartan or a hunting theme. All have sleek bathrooms. Explore the abbey, Loire châteaux and pretty hollyhock villages. Return to a dip in the pool and an aperitif on the terrace while you watch the world go by. *Parking on-site.*

| | |
|---|---|
| Rooms | 24 doubles: €75–€170. Singles €75–€145. Dinner, B&B €82–€125 per person. Extra bed/sofabed available €30 per person per night. |
| Meals | Lunch €18. Dinner €27. |
| Closed | Christmas. |

Christophe & Mieke Chabenat
Hostellerie La Croix Blanche,
5-7 place des Plantagenêts, 49590
Fontevraud l'Abbaye, Maine-et-Loire
Tel        +33 (0)2 41 51 71 11
Email    bonjour@hotel-croixblanche.com
Web      www.hotel-croixblanche.com

## Hôtel & Spa La Marine de Loire

In a pretty little town on the banks of the Loire, this lovely hotel is casual, stylish and run with superb efficiency. Friendly, elegant Caroline bought the building five years ago and gave it a fabulous new look. With her flair for interior decoration she's clearly had fun: 'Sous la Lune' has glittering stars, 'Reflet' has a floaty airy feel, while driftwood and pebbles adorn others, decorated in chalky colours. There are super bathrooms and many have views over the river or the handsome courtyard. Suites are big and mostly come with mezzanine sleeping areas, although access to one is up some tricky stairs – check before you go. In the large salon you'll find comfy sofas, fresh flowers, lots of plants and a relaxed homy feel. In a long sunny room that gazes over the garden, on the second Sunday of the month, brunch includes heavenly terrine and sweet French treats from the local brocante market. Then off to explore narrow winding streets that take you up to the cliff face for stunning views. You're well placed for cycling, gardens and châteaux, cocktails at the bar will tempt you back.

| Rooms | 7 doubles: €150–€190. |
|---|---|
| | 4 suites for 2: €250. |
| Meals | Breakfast €13–€16. Dinner €35. |
| | Restaurant 1km. |
| Closed | Rarely. |

Caroline Chagnaud
Hôtel & Spa La Marine de Loire,
9 av de la Loire, 49730 Montsoreau,
Maine-et-Loire
Tel     +33 (0)2 41 50 18 21
Email   resa@hotel-lamarinedeloire.com
Web    www.hotel-lamarinedeloire.com

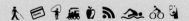

## Château de Salvert

This highly sculpted and vast neo-gothic folly on the edge of a forest is home to a couple of grand aristocrats. Madame, an aficionado on diets based on unrefined grains, cooked fruits and vegetables, is also a pianist and occasionally holds concerts. Monsieur is jovial and utterly delightful… somewhat in contrast to the baronial hall, properly dark and spooky. The dining room and the grand salon are elegant and plush with gilt chairs and ancestral paintings, and the two guest rooms are smartly decorated and rather swanky; imagine striped wallpapers, French antique pieces, large rugs and floral fabrics. Both overlook the grounds through huge windows, and the suite itself is vast, with two double bedrooms and its own sitting area, a library in an alcove and a bathroom you could waltz in. As for the park, it's magnificent; watch wild boar roam and spring boarlets scamper. After a breakfast of fresh croissants and homemade conserves, you can set off and discover more Loire Valley châteaux and vineyards. Come home to a modern heated pool set about with clumps of flowers and plastic loungers. *Arrival after 4pm.*

| Rooms | 1 suite for 4: €120–€200. |
|---|---|
| Meals | Dinner with wine, €55. |
| Closed | Rarely. |

**Monica Le Pelletier de Glatigny**
Château de Salvert,
Salvert, 49680 Neuillé, Maine-et-Loire

| Tel | +33 (0)2 41 52 55 89 |
|---|---|
| Mobile | +33 (0)6 15 12 03 11 |
| Email | info@salvert.com |
| Web | www.chateau-de-salvert.fr |

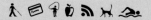

## Le Château des Forges

Arrive in style, through wrought-iron gates and along a tree-lined drive, passing through six handsome hectares of sloping lawns shaded by cedars. The château, grand yet welcoming, has been renovated to a high standard by easygoing owner Philippe Dufresne; he meets and greets in a large hall bathed in light slanting through original arched windows, some with stained glass. Refurbished bedrooms mix styles in keeping with the building's age – silk bedspreads, four-posters, glass chandeliers, elegant wallpaper... Situated at the back of the château, all rooms enjoy splendid views, and 'Plantagenet' has two small balconies. Downstairs, enjoy the sumptuous sitting room with double aspect windows, Blüthner half-grand piano and old pictures; doors and parquet floor are original, comfy new chairs upholstered in rich fabrics. Relax here or in the adjoining dining room, where a French home-style meal can be served if four or more guests request it – or chill out by the pool with great views across the park. In charming Angers see the medieval château with its 14th-century tapestry, then strike out to Saumur and Chinon.

| Rooms | 3 doubles, 2 twins: €100–€160. |
| Meals | Dinner with wine, €40, on request. |
| Closed | Never. |

Philippe Dufresne
Le Château des Forges,
Chemin du port de l'Ile, 49100 Angers,
Maine-et-Loire

| Tel | +33 (0)9 54 25 71 27, +33 (0)2 41 88 16 |
| Email | contact@lechateaudesforges.com |
| Web | www.lechateaudesforges.com |

## Château de Montriou

The park will explode your senses – and once the visitors have gone home, what a treat to have it to yourselves: the lake, the famous sequoia, the waves of crocuses in spring, the centuries-old chapel with three statues of Mary. All this and an Enchanted Forest (with special paths for children to follow), a Squash Garden, the Italian Garden, the Princess Garden, the vegetable garden and a collection of outstanding dahlias and Italian cyclamen – plantsmen will adore it here. And now for the house. This 15th-century château has been lived in and tended by the same family for 300 years and Monsieur and Madame know exactly how to put you at your ease in truly endearing aristocratic style. A spiral stone staircase leads to homely, old-fashioned bedrooms whose bold colours were design flavour of the period; wooden floors, thick rugs and antiques are only slightly younger. Bathrooms are a bit dated, but clean as a whistle. And the venerable library is now a guest sitting room – a lovely quiet space to explore so many interesting books. Special for its sense of history, and the gardens, but not for those expecting modern luxury.

| | |
|---|---|
| Rooms | 2 doubles, 1 double with kitchen: €95–€130. 1 suite for 4 with kitchen: €175. Singles €85–€115. |
| Meals | Restaurant 6km. |
| Closed | 1 April to 30 November. |

Régis & Nicole de Loture
Château de Montriou,
49460 Feneu,
Maine-et-Loire

| | |
|---|---|
| Tel | +33 (0)2 41 93 30 11 |
| Email | chateau-de-montriou@wanadoo.fr |
| Web | www.chateau-de-montriou.com |

## Château de Chambiers

An exquisite family château, surrounded by deep forest and rhododendrons. Smiling Madame (a good cook, and wonderful with children) speaks perfect English and is a talented designer. She's proud of her gardens and her big, beautiful rooms, and it's a huge treat to stay here if you appreciate history. There's a panelled salon de thé, a billiards room, a playhouse and heaps of books. Bedrooms brim with rich fabrics, flowers and stunning antiques; some have four-posters with colourful drapes, one has a French-Caribbean mahogany bed; floors are 18th-century oak with antique terre cuit borders; the views over the gardens are glorious. Bathrooms are grand and big enough to dance in, and some of the baths, washstands and fittings are period originals. Wander the grounds and admire roses, camellias, magnolias, herbs and a 400-year-old oak tree; children can hunt for the treehouse and the organic potager provides vegetables and fruits for dinner. *Un coin de paradis*!

| | |
|---|---|
| Rooms | 1 double: €167.<br>4 family rooms for 3: €137–€206.<br>Extra bed/sofabed available €28 per person per night. Well-behaved pets welcome €12.50 per night. |
| Meals | Dinner, 3 courses, €36.50;<br>4 courses, €49.50;<br>children's menu €14.50. |
| Closed | Rarely. |

**Anne & Élie Crouan**
Château de Chambiers,
49430 Durtal,
Maine-et-Loire

| | |
|---|---|
| Tel | +33 (0)2 41 76 07 31 |
| Email | info@chateauchambiers.com |
| Web | www.chateauchambiers.com |

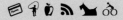

## Château des Briottières

Deep in the Loire valley countryside, this 18th-century château, in the family for six generations, is an experience of opulence and splendour. It is now occupied by your host, the relaxed and endearing Monsieur de Valbray, his wife and children (most of them grown and flown), rightfully proud of their extraordinary home. A charming and laid-back place to stay, in spite of the grandiose surroundings, it has handsome interiors decorated in fine traditional French style. The grand drawing room is a symphony of rich red velvet with swathes of fine silk floating elegantly to the ground; sweep up the marble staircase to bedrooms beautifully adorned; many beds are canopied; many windows have sweeping estate views; there are candles everywhere. A local Crémant de Loire, served by Monsieur, is the perfect apéritif before a three-course meal, prepared by Madame (an exquisite cook) and served in the dining room by candlelight. A digestif can, on cool nights, be sipped in the drawing room where the log fire roars delightfully. In the grounds is a country-style Orangery with extra rooms in a more rustic style.

| Rooms | 7 doubles: €129–€196. |
| | 3 suites for 2, 1 family suite for 4: €270–€350. |
| | 1 triple: €130–€164. |
| | 1 apartment for 6 (no WiFi available): €389–€420 per night. |
| | 1 chalet for 2 (sofabed available): €259–€280 per night. |
| Meals | Breakfast €18. |
| | Dinner €50; book ahead. |
| | Wine from €18. Restaurants 10km. |
| Closed | 10 November to 31 March. |

François de Valbray
Château des Briottières,
49330 Champigné,
Maine-et-Loire

| Tel | +33 (0)2 41 42 00 02 |
| Email | briottieres@gmail.com |
| Web | www.briottieres.com |

## Château du Plessis Anjou

You can lift off from the grounds in a balloon; some of the finest châteaux and wineries of the Loire are within easy reach. Built in the 16th century, Le Plessis has always been in the family and has been welcoming guests for years. Though large and very elegant, the château, set in 21 hectares of wooded park, is inviting not imposing, with Anjou slate roofs, white walls and creeper-covered shutters. One bedroom is striking with oriental rugs and the bed in a deep alcove; others have lofty beamed ceilings; beds are turned down at night: water and chocolates placed on bedside tables. Dinner, at a long table in a rather ornate dining room with scenes from the Roman Empire, could include salmon, duck with apricots, cheese and a crisp fruit tart. Fruit (masses of raspberries) and vegetables come directly from the walled potager. Children are welcome: the Renouls have two of their own, hence the playground and trampoline as well as rabbits and a goat. There's a small pond brimming with fish and lilies, and a hen house – Madame invites children to gather the eggs. Terra Botanica is a 15-minute drive.

| Rooms | 3 doubles: €105–€180. |
|---|---|
| | 2 suites for 2: €220–€250. |
| | Singles €95–€220. |
| | Extra bed/sofabed available €25–€35 |
| | per person per night. |
| Meals | Hosted dinner €48; book ahead. |
| | Wine €20–€240. |
| Closed | Rarely. |

**Valérie & Laurent Renoul**
Château du Plessis Anjou,
49220 La Jaille Yvon,
Maine-et-Loire
Tel      +33 (0)2 41 95 12 75
Email    plessis.anjou@wanadoo.fr
Web      www.chateau-du-plessis.com

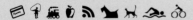

## Hôtel Haras de la Potardière

François, an architect specialising in restoring old buildings, Marie-Yvonne, relaxed and efficient, and their children live in a creeper-covered wing of this grand château. The entertaining brochure tells the family's story: François' grandfather built up a successful centre for training show jumpers alongside an established thoroughbred stud; then, in the nineties, after ten years of empty stables, La Potardière began taking in stallions for the summer. Now, horse-loving guests ride up on their own mounts from all over France… the fine approach includes mares and foals grazing beneath the oaks. Château bedrooms are a graceful mix of prettiness and elegance, polished parquet and fresh flowers; rooms in the stables are less formal, cosier and have their own wicker-furnished terrace. A glorious place for a horse-mad child – though all children love it here: fields, a safe and secluded pool, billiards, table football, a Wendy house full of toys. There's an honesty bar and relaxed seating, a piano you may play and sociable apéritifs on Saturdays. The welcome is superb.

| Rooms | Château – 3 twin/doubles: €100–€120. Stable – 2 suites for 4–5: €180. |
|---|---|
| Meals | Breakfast €12. Cold platter €25; book ahead. Wine €28. Group dinners by arrangement. |
| Closed | Rarely. |

**François & Marie-Yvonne Benoist**
Hôtel Haras de la Potardière,
Route de Bazouges,
72200 Crosmières, Sarthe

| | |
|---|---|
| Tel | +33 (0)2 43 45 83 47 |
| Email | haras-de-la-potardiere@wanadoo.fr |
| Web | www.potardiere.com |

## Auberge du Port des Roches

If you like the idea of idling with an evening drink by the slow green water, watching out for the odd fish, looking forward to an exceptionally good dinner, this is the place for you. Not grand, not the Loire – the Loir is a sweet, lovely and unsung river – but we can hear you saying: "Oh, what a pretty spot". Valérie and Thierry, who have been here for almost two decades, are young, very friendly, though a touch shy, and full of enthusiasm for their auberge. The lively little restaurant, which seats about 50 people in two rooms, and the riverside terrace heavy with roses and sweet-smelling climbers, are the star turns here, though Valérie is also justly proud of the effort she has put into the bedrooms and the way everything sparkles. Rooms are not large but done up in fresh colours with white bedcovers. Those at the back overlook the courtyard, those at the front face the Loir, double glazing separates you from the small road that runs past and peace reigns at night. This is a quiet, very French place to stay, within easy reach of the châteaux. All round superb value – and plenty of choice for vegetarians.

| | |
|---|---|
| Rooms | 9 doubles, 2 twins: €58–€70. 1 family room for 3: €80. |
| Meals | Breakfast €8. Picnic available. Lunch & dinner €25–€54. Wine €16–€72. Restaurant closed Sunday eve, Monday, & Tuesday lunchtime. |
| Closed | February & 1 week in autumn. |

**Valérie & Thierry Lesiourd**
Auberge du Port des Roches,
Le Port des Roches,
72800 Luché Pringé, Sarthe
Tel      +33 (0)2 43 45 44 48
Email    leportdesroches@orange.fr

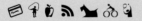

## Hôtel de France

Beloved of motor racing buffs, this charming hotel has been part of the Le Mans 24-hours story for ever. The nostalgia is spread by a history of champion drivers, film stars and world leaders, as well as some glorious old cars that have roared up to the front door. Its creeper-clothed face looks over the lovely town square, its bar clients spill onto the convivial pavement. An English classic-car enthusiast fell in love with the hotel years ago and… finally it was his. He renovated the Art Deco dining room, built a pretty pool beside the river and kept the head chef and barman whom everyone loved. Bedrooms have been beautifully refurbished: some have famous racing names, four-posters and damask wall fabric, all have brand-new bathrooms and fine attention to detail, all are excellent value. But motor racing isn't all: the châteaux of the Loire are an hour away; the bucolic valley has some fine historic buildings of its own, including Le Lude with its glorious furniture and gardens. Vineyard tours in an eccentric pre-war bus can be arranged; or bicycle trips, or hot-air ballooning… Then back for a high-class dinner. *Parking on-site.*

| | |
|---|---|
| Rooms | 11 doubles: €78–€140. |
| | 8 suites for 4: €118–€140. |
| Meals | Lunch menu découverte €35. |
| | Dinner, 4 courses, €35. |
| | Restaurants 1-minute walk. |
| Closed | Never. |

Sally Carpenter
Hôtel de France,
72340 La Chartre sur le Loir, Sarthe

| | |
|---|---|
| Tel | +33 (0)2 43 44 40 16 |
| Email | welcome@hoteldefrance.com |
| Web | www.lhoteldefrance.fr |

## Château de Montaupin

Outside, a virginia creeper has the façade in its clutches – to pretty effect! Inside, wine and conversation flow. Mme David is friendly and welcoming and adores her house, family and guests. There's a laid-back feel, a cluttered elegance, a faded décor; the atmosphere is that of a happy household with plenty of interesting history. A suspended spiral staircase leads to the upper floors and the best suite is right at the top, its roof timbers exposed. Families will feel at home. Breakfasts are robust and table d'hôtes is classic French: homemade terrine with mayonnaise, chicken cooked in cider and cream, cheese and salad, fresh seasonal fruit tart, and much produce from the garden, which is worth strolling around. Find a rosebush tunnel, a 15th-century tower converted for self-catering guests, and a pool for cooling off. You're deep in the heart of the Loire valley so there's plenty to do in this pretty part of France: canoeing, wine tasting, cycling (for people who don't like hills!), day hikes and long distance trails. Return to ease and comfort and be sure you try the family wines!

| | |
|---|---|
| Rooms | 2 doubles, 2 suites for 4, 1 triple: €75–€80. Extra person €20. |
| Meals | Dinner with wine, €22.50. |
| Closed | Occasionally. |

**Marie David**
Château de Montaupin,
Montaupin, 72330 Oizé, Sarthe
Tel       +33 (0)2 43 87 81 70
Mobile    +33 (0)6 83 56 60 40
Email     chateaudemontaupin@wanadoo.fr

## Château de Vaulogé

A fairy-tale place! The Radinis, from Milan, wanted their children to have an international education, eventually finding Vaulogé. Marisa and her delightful, amusing daughter Micol now run the place, Marisa devoting herself to the garden, her latest project being the horseshoe-shaped potager for fresh dinner produce. The original part of the château, where the family lives, was built in the 15th century. Vaulogé was later remodelled in troubadour style, giving it two circular pepperpot towers; when the shock waves of the Revolution had faded, the aristocracy reclaimed their houses. If it's space you're after, stay in 'Casanova': a huge round tower room, with terracotta floor and amazing, near-vertical beams – excellent for propping books on. (There are plenty of books: Marisa feels a house is not properly furnished without them.) There are other round rooms – 'La Grande Tour' is smaller, and ravishingly pretty. The whole place is enticing with flowers and little nooks and crannies, often put to good use as wardrobes or cupboards. The grounds are lovely, with lilies on the moat and a delicate stone chapel. *Pets by arrangement.*

| | |
|---|---|
| Rooms | 1 double: €230–€280.<br>4 suites for 2: €260–€310.<br>Extra bed/sofabed available €40–€70 per person per night. |
| Meals | Dinner with wine, €70; book ahead. |
| Closed | 2 January to 31 March. |

**Marisa Radini & Micol Tassan Din**
Château de Vaulogé,
72430 Fercé sur Sarthe, Sarthe

| | |
|---|---|
| Tel | +33 (0)2 43 77 32 81 |
| Email | vauloge@mail.com |
| Web | www.vauloge.com |

## Château d'Eporcé

Grand and pure 17th century with a moat and a magnificent, perfectly straight avenue of trees leading to the door. Yet you arrive to discover a laid-back, lived-in atmosphere with three salons for guests and little change for the past 50 years. Find lofty beamed ceilings, antiques, books, pictures, engravings and butterfly collections galore. The downstairs dining and sitting rooms have tapestries, polished wood and flowers; meals are easy-going (not gourmet, family silver and Wedgwood) with drinks before, and tea in the lounge afterwards. Bedrooms are charmingly faded; all face the sunny south and have lovely views of the park and rather eccentric, ancient bathrooms. First-floor rooms are the ones to go for — proper château stuff. Anglophile Rémy is kind and gentle — a charming host. His gardens are handsome, formal, wonderful — with fantastic spring flowers and autumn colours; there's a pool in the kitchen garden, seating places and fish to spot in the moat. Visit traditional bastide Realmont, beautiful little Brousse-le-Chateau; Le Mans is a 15-kilometre drive. Pack a woolly jumper or two in the winter…

| Rooms | 2 doubles, 1 twin/double: €90-€150. |
|---|---|
| Meals | Dinner with wine, €40. |
| Closed | Rarely. |

Rémy de Scitivaux
Château d'Eporcé,
Eporcé, 72550 La Quinte, Sarthe
Tel      +33 (0)2 43 27 70 22
Email    eporce@wanadoo.fr
Web      www.chateau-eporce.com

## Château de Saint Paterne

A marvellous mix of the Renaissance and the 18th century, a château abandoned for 30 years then rediscovered by an heir who gave up Provence for lovely Perche pastures. He and his wife, a charming couple, have redecorated with spirit, respecting the style and history of the building, adding a zest of southern colour to panelled, antique-filled rooms, pretty country furniture before ancient fireplaces and rough, hand-rendered finishes. Sitting, dining and first-floor bedrooms are in château-style, the Henri IV room (he had a mistress here, of course) has thrillingly painted beams; ancestors and objets adorn but don't clutter. The theatrical new tower room is worth every one of the 52 steps up and the attic floor is a fantasy among the rafters. Now there's a spectacular new room on the ground floor awash with Indian silks, and a dreamy Datcha in the forest, heaven for two. Your host creates classic cuisine nuanced with contemporary flavours and exotic vegetables from his potager and calls his cookery courses *Liaisons Délicieuses*. A fine mixture of past and present values and superb high-energy hosts.

| | |
|---|---|
| Rooms | 5 doubles: €145–€175. |
| | 5 suites for 2: €220–€260. |
| | Dinner, B&B €208–€386 per person. |
| | Extra bed/sofabed available €20 per person per night. |
| Meals | Breakfast €14. |
| | Dinner, with aperitif & coffee, €49; book ahead. Wine €15–€49. |
| Closed | January – March & Christmas week. |

Charles-Henry & Ségolène de Valbray
Château de Saint Paterne,
72610 St Paterne,
Sarthe

| | |
|---|---|
| Tel | +33 (0)2 33 27 54 71 |
| Email | chateaudesaintpaterne@wanadoo.fr |
| Web | www.chateau-saintpaterne.com |

## Hôtel Oasis

Efficient anglophile Steve and his young wife Emilie run a happy ship. You couldn't fail to feel well cared for: spotless and well-equipped bedrooms, leather sofas in the bar and a personal trainer in the gym. The cosy, woody reception sets the tone, flaunting all the beams, joists, exposed stones and wafer-brick walls you'd expect from a restored farmhouse with outbuildings. Bedrooms are in the stable wing, some off a raftered corridor upstairs, some at ground level. All have old timbers, attractive repro country furniture, comfy armchairs, writing desks and immaculate bathrooms. The bar, which has an English pubby feel, serves very decent food (there's also a super pizzeria/grill in the courtyard), the lounge is snug with plants, piano and pool table and the breakfast room is a treat: red-clothed tables on a stone floor and a big stone fireplace crackling with logs. A shame to stay just a night, there's so much to see in the area, from the 24-hour race at Le Mans to the 14th-century château at Carrouges. And you could squeeze in a round of mini-golf before breakfast. Friendly people, excellent value.

| | |
|---|---|
| Rooms | 8 doubles, 3 twins: €62–€140. 1 family room for 6, 2 family rooms for 4: €85–€140. Singles €50–€80. Extra bed/sofabed available at no charge. |
| Meals | Breakfast €7.80. Light meals available. |
| Closed | Never. |

**Steve & Emilie Chedor**
Hôtel Oasis,
La Sourderie, 53700 Villaines la Juhel,
Mayenne

| | |
|---|---|
| Tel | +33 (0)2 43 03 28 67 |
| Email | oasis@oasis.fr |
| Web | www.oasis.fr |

## Château de la Villatte

From the village, a drive rises to the top of the butte where a 19th-century château sits in splendour. Isabelle arrived some years ago and her loving restoration knows no bounds. The fine outbuildings are the latest recipients of an immaculate creation – yet still Madame finds time to enjoy her guests; she, or one of her team, is always around. Dimensions are generous throughout and bedrooms are vast, their parquet floors strewn with rugs. Tall windows overlook the steeply sloping park and the valley below, there are marble fireplaces, paintings in gilt frames, an original claw-foot bath. You breakfast on the balcony or in the grand salon, take supper in the dining room, brought to you on fine blue and white china, or, in summer, prepare your own, in the 'rustic' garden kitchen with cooker and barbecue. Visit the medieval fortress of Sainte-Suzanne, borrow the bikes, explore the lovely tree'd grounds. Perfect for couples looking for a quiet, refined retreat.

| | |
|---|---|
| Rooms | 1 double, 1 twin/double: €80–€98 (rooms can interconnect to form suite: €174). Singles €69–€87. Extra bed/sofabed available €26 per person per night. 5% off 2-night stays, 10% off stays of 3 nights or more. |
| Meals | Summer kitchen. Restaurants 10 minute-drive. |
| Closed | Rarely. |

Isabelle Charrier
Château de la Villatte,
53970 Montigné le Brillant, Mayenne

| | |
|---|---|
| Tel | +33 (0)2 43 68 23 76 |
| Mobile | +33 (0)6 85 43 55 99 |
| Email | info@lavillatte.com |
| Web | www.lavillatte.com |

## Château de Craon

Such a close and welcoming family, whose kindness extends to include you. It's a magnificent place, with innumerable expressions of history, taste and personality, and gracious Loïk and Hélène, young grandparents, treat you like friends; Loïk was born here and is happy to share the stories of the house. Everywhere a feast for the eyes: paintings, watercolours, antiques… A sitting room with sofas and a view of the park, an Italianate hall with sweeping stone stair, a beautiful dining room bathed in sunlight, classic French bedrooms in lavender, blue, cream… an original washstand, a canopied bed, a velvet armchair. Outside, there are superb grounds and gardens to explore: 40 acres of river, forests of oak and beech, meadows, lake, ice house, tennis court, pool, a trampoline to bounce and a potager worth leaving home for. The Loire Valley has castles, gardens and sporting activites galore. An enchanting treat for all ages including families with children, history lovers, gardeners or romantics. Guests love it here.

| Rooms | 3 doubles, 1 twin: €100–€160. 1 suite for 2-4: €260. 1 single: €80. |
| --- | --- |
| Meals | Dinner with wine, €30. Restaurants in village. |
| Closed | November – March. |

**Loïk & Hélène de Guébriant**
Château de Craon,
53400 Craon,
Mayenne

| Tel | +33 (0)2 43 06 11 02 |
| --- | --- |
| Email | chateaudecraon@wanadoo.fr |
| Web | www.craoncastle.com |

Entry 155  Map 3

# Loire Valley

Photo: Domaine de la
Tortinière, entry 167

## Château La Touanne

Lush trees and elaborate gates frame the graceful façade. Nicolas and Christine's courteous informality permeates their peaceful 17th-century château. Downstairs, ancestral portraits survey antiques, gilt mirrors and fine porcelain; you have the run of the antler-decked billiard room, panelled green sitting room and chandeliered salon. Breakfast in the stately dining room, where table d'hôtes dinners of locally sourced food and wine are also held. Bedrooms are sumptuous: marble fireplaces, high ceilings, fine oak parquet. One, in imperial purple and white, has a new, regal free-standing bath. Another, gorgeously simple, has been redone in contemporary grey and lime green. A third has ravishing views on three sides and walls papered in a beautiful Jacobean print. The terrace leads into tree-studded parkland, home to the estate farm, chapel, and an orchard concealing the heated pool. Stroll through meadows past the Gothic tower to explore bosky riverside paths, borrow a boat from the boathouse. But come above all for the gracious, relaxing welcome of this authentic family château, just 90 minutes from Paris.

| Rooms | 3 doubles, 1 twin/double: €130–€180. Singles €95–€140. |
|-------|--------------------------------------------------------|
| Meals | Dinner with wine, €35. |
| Closed | Rarely. |

**Nicolas & Christine d'Aboville**
Château La Touanne,
45130 Baccon, Loiret

| Tel | +33 (0)2 38 46 51 39 |
|-----|----------------------|
| Mobile | +33 (0)6 88 76 69 89 |
| Email | nicolas.daboville@orange.fr |
| Web | www.chateau-latouanne.com |

## Château du Boisrenault

Built by a 19th-century aristocrat as a wedding present for his daughter – well overdue, she'd had two sons by the time it was finished – Boisrenault may be turreted, noble and imposing on the outside but it's a family home within. Furniture, objects, pictures, all have a story to tell – and there's no shortage of hunting trophies and stags' heads on the wall. The hostess, Florence, is a gentle soul who leaves sheets of favourite poetry in guests' rooms. Reception rooms are lofty, with huge fireplaces. One sitting room has a baby grand; another, smaller and cosier, is lined with books. As for the bedrooms, each is an adventure in itself. Named after the family's children and grandchildren, they feature a hotchpotch of pieces from different periods, including some excellent antiques; two apartments upstairs have their own fitted kitchens. A delicious pool is discreetly tucked away behind trees in the lovely grounds; table tennis and table football are a godsend on rainy days. Meals, cooked by Florence herself, are served at a vast table in the dining room; be sure to book if you'd like dinner.

| Rooms | 2 doubles, 1 twin: €90–€116. |
| | 1 family room for 4, |
| | 3 family rooms for 3: €134–€150. |
| | 2 apartments for 4–5: €450–€510 per wk. |
| Meals | Dinner €28; book ahead. |
| | Wine from €14. |
| Closed | Rarely. |

**Florence du Manoir**
Château du Boisrenault,
36500 Buzançais, Indre

| Tel | +33 (0)2 54 84 03 01 |
| Mobile | +33 (0)6 89 30 44 16 |
| Email | boisrenault@wanadoo.fr |
| Web | www.boisrenault.fr |

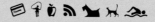

## Château de la Villette

More pretty 19th-century hunting lodge than grand château, la Villette – pale and sedate under its grey roof and with tall shuttered windows – sits in 80 idyllic acres of parkland, close to a huge spring-fed lake. Capable, hospitable, generous Karin – dynamic gardener, fine cook – loves and cares for each inch of the place. A winding staircase leads to a beauty of a bedroom done in Biedermeier style, with a sloping ceiling, honey-yellow walls, white paintwork and serene views; the second room too is seductive. Feather duvets will cosset you, elegant breakfasts (good coffee, homemade jams, fresh croissants and baguettes) and dinners (vegetables from her own organic garden, perhaps a duck fresh from the lake) at the convent table will delight you, and nothing is too much trouble for Karin. You also have a large sitting room with picture windows overlooking the surrounding parkland; curl up with a book here on days when the weather is bad tempered. In summer you can swim or fish in the lake, or boat on it (there's a boat to borrow), have a fine picnic or visit lively markets nearby.

| | |
|---|---|
| Rooms | 1 double; 1 double with separate bathroom: €90. |
| Meals | Dinner with wine, €25. |
| Closed | Rarely. |

Karin Verburgh
Château de la Villette,
St Août,
36120 Ardentes, Indre
Tel       +33 (0)2 54 36 28 46
Email     verburghs@hotmail.com
Web       www.romantik-destinations.com

## Saint Victor La Grand' Maison

The 16th-century château bursts into view from its wooded hilltop, tall turrets and ivy-clad façade towering over the river Anglin. You can saunter down here past the pool and picnic on organic pâté under a 400-year-old oak; just water, trees and birdsong. Inside there are two beautiful sitting rooms, one with old portraits and a roaring fire, the other with a piano, book-lined walls and rugs on polished wooden floors; read by the fire, tinkle on the baby grand, retire to bed. Deeply comfortable rooms in warm reds, blues and pastels have museum-worthy antiques, plush fabrics, gilt portraits, book-lined walls and the deepest peace. Breakfasts of fresh fruit, croissants, charcuterie and confiture maison are served in the delightful dining room with a wood fire in winter; French windows lead to a beautiful grass terrace. Hugely friendly, Madame offers tastings, courses and talks by local savants – and there are gîtes in the grounds. Further afield there is masses to occupy you, from markets to historic sites, churches, wine tastings, walks and fishing. "Simply a delight," says our inspector, "for anybody at all."

| | |
|---|---|
| Rooms | 1 double: €120.<br>2 suites for 2: €150 (can interconnect to form a suite for 4: €200).<br>Dinner, B&B €17 extra per person. |
| Meals | Dinner €15–€20. Wine €8–€20.<br>Restaurant 1.5km. |
| Closed | Christmas & New Year. |

Marie Rouet Grandclément
Saint Victor La Grand' Maison,
36300 Ingrandes,
Indre

| | |
|---|---|
| Tel | +33 (0)6 03 81 51 37 |
| Email | marie@saintvictorlagrandmaison.fr |
| Web | www.saintvictorlagrandmaison.fr |

## Relais de la Mothe

Madame de Rochechouart has put her all into creating a delightful and intimate hotel at this once undistinguished inn. The 18th-century staging post sits at the heart of Yzeures sur Creuse, one of the oldest villages in the Touraine region. It's neat outside – the courtyard clambered by roses and, hidden away, an enchanting private cloister-garden. However, it's the inside that shines: beyond the rustic salon you'll find bedrooms that are individual retreats of unpretentious sophistication, two ideal for disabled guests. Colours are contemporary – parma violet, muted greens – and details appealing; modernity lights original oak floors and dark beams. Bathrooms are state-of-the-art, one marrying bright orange walls with a smart travertine floor. Breakfast (bread from the next-door baker, homemade jams) is good; lunch and dinner even better – the terracotta and chequerboard dining room, open to non-residents, serves great value versions of steak tartare and rabbit pâté. Still peckish? Use the hotel's bikes to reach Michelin-starred restaurant La Promenade in Le Petit Pressigny, just up the road.

| Rooms | 12 doubles, 8 twins: €71–€103. 1 apartment for 4 without kitchen: €114–€150. |
|---|---|
| Meals | Breakfast €10. Dinner €24.80–€36. |
| Closed | January. |

Isabelle de Rochechouart
Relais de la Mothe,
1 place du 11 Novembre,
37290 Yzeures sur Creuse, Indre-et-Loire

| Tel | +33 (0)2 47 91 49 00 |
| Email | relaisdelamothe@gmail.com |
| Web | www.relaisdelamothe.com |

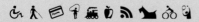

### Château de la Celle Guenand

In the heart of an ancient and unspoilt Touraine village, four hectares of delightful walled park and a fairytale castle with pointy slate turrets that dates from 1442. It's large but not palatial, grand but not ornate, and refreshingly unstuffy. Much is being updated (some bathrooms are still basic), everything is charming, and Stephen is putting all his energies into his new project. You get top mattresses on king-size beds, bedrooms with beautifully proportioned windows (cool conservative shades for the newest), quirky fabrics on the walls and delicious breakfasts served in the breakfast room which has a pretty square piano, or on the terrace in summer. Tuck in to local bread and honey, homemade jams (quince, apricot) and marmalade. After dinner: brocade sofas in faded reds, books to browse and a piano to play. Or take a turn round the garden to find a little wood, a magnificent 500-year-old cedar tree, an orchard, a potager, the remains of a grassy moat and a handsome old metal and glass greenhouse with original ornate shelving for house plants. All this, châteaux by the hatful, and the Brenne National Park. *Children over 5 welcome. Pets by arrangement.*

| Rooms | 4 doubles: €100–€150. |
| | 1 family room for 2-5: €150–€170. |
| | Dinner, B&B €105–€125 per person. |
| Meals | Hosted dinner, €40; |
| | children's menu €20. |
| | Restaurant in village. |
| Closed | 1 November to 24 March. |

| | Stephen Palluel |
| | Château de la Celle Guenand, 14 rue |
| | du Château, 37350 La Celle Guenand |
| Tel | +33 (0)2 47 94 93 61 |
| Mobile | +33 (0)6 76 23 74 77 |
| Email | stephane@chateaucelleguenand.com |
| Web | www.chateaucelleguenand.biz |

## La Chancellerie

On the edge of the hillside village of Huismes is a very charming old manor house of white tufa stone, backed by trees, fronted by parterres. Below ground: a series of extraordinary cellars where Bertrand offers tastings of Chinon wines (delicious, and good value). He and Claire have a real sense of hospitality and love their new home; talented musicians, they host concerts too (note the five pianos). They also love to cook local seasonal food, accompanied by their wines and served in the country dining room or on the terrace. As for the rooms, the family room is in the house itself – vast, lofty, higgledy-piggledy (children will love it), and with a splendid stone fireplace. Three more rooms lie in the more humble wing, each immaculate, each with a table on a strip of terrace outside facing the pretty knot gardens... the newest room is in a loft-like barn with its bed on the mezzanine and a kitchen to die for. Bathrooms are spotless, breakfasts are amazing, and beautiful Chinon is a 15-minute drive. Swim in the river or in your hosts' pool; hire canoes and float down the Vienne.

| Rooms | 3 doubles: €95–€115. |
| | 1 family room for 5: €120–€220. |
| | 1 triple: €110–€250. |
| | Pets €5 per night. |
| Meals | Dinner with wine, €25–€30. |
| | Restaurants 1km. |
| Closed | Rarely. |

Claire & Bertrand Pelourdeau
La Chancellerie,
37420 Huismes, Indre-et-Loire

| Tel | +33 (0)2 47 95 46 76 |
| Mobile | +33 (0)6 60 89 43 23 |
| Email | info@lachancellerie.com |
| Web | www.lachancellerie.com |

## Château de Gizeux

As you approach up the tree-lined drive, the château appears at the top of the rise, guarded by its pepper-pot tower. Through the gateway, then the inner courtyard, and there is Madame, ushering you in for an apéritif with the family (six smiling children) in a vast and magnificent hall, the Francois I Galerie, furnished with 18th-century armchairs and 16th-century murals. So fascinating is the history that the château is open to the public (it feels a privilege to stay here, contributing to the restoration!). One suite, decorated in deep orange and dove grey and on the ground floor, is named after the owner in the days of the French Revolution, 'Julie de la Lorie'; note the gorgeous ceramic stove in its salon-boudoir. The rest are on the first floor, their elegantly dressed windows overlooking the park. All are stylishly furnished, beautifully proportioned and the bathrooms are state of the art, one with tiles hand-painted by Monsieur (who also farms beef cattle). Generous breakfasts are served in your suite, candlelit dinner at separate tables – 'cuisine du terroir' and delicious.

| | |
|---|---|
| Rooms | 5 suites for 2: €135–€185. Extra bed €25. |
| Meals | Dinner with wine, €42; children's menu €15. Restaurants 10km. |
| Closed | Rarely. |

Stephanie de Laffon
Château de Gizeux,
15 rue du Château, 37340 Gizeux,
Indre-et-Loire
Tel    +33 (0)2 47 96 45 18
Email  info@chateaudegizeux.com
Web    www.chambres-hotes-chateau.com

## Château de l'Hérissaudière

Park beside the guardian totems, a glimpse of Madame's spirit, then wander through wild cyclamen beneath giant sequoias, take a dip in the elegant heated pool, enjoy a drink on the flowery terrace, prepare a picnic to eat under the pergola. You could get used to country-house living here, French-style. Madame, charming, cultured, welcomes you as family. Wrapped in 18 acres of parkland, the manor is all light, elegance and fresh flowers. Walls carry old mirrors and bold paintings, tables display intriguing *objets*. Relax in the sunny salon or the splendid library with its books and games table. Bedrooms, over the park, are large, gracious and subtly themed, 'Empire' perhaps, or rich 'Louis XV'. Lovely light 'Chinon' is pretty in pink and white; 'Montlouis', the former hunting room, is wheelchair-friendly. Grand bathrooms have original tiling and marble floors. Tuck into a gourmet breakfast while Madame recommends local restaurants for dinner. The old chapel is now a summer house. Ping-pong, badminton and more are in the grounds, châteaux and golf, riding and cycling trails (bikes to hire) are nearby. *Minimum stay: 2 nights at weekends & high season.*

| Rooms | 2 doubles: €120–€135. |
|---|---|
|  | 3 suites for 2-5: €130–€150. |
| Meals | Summer kitchen. Restaurant 3km. |
| Closed | Rarely. |

Claudine Detilleux
Château de l'Hérissaudière,
37230 Pernay, Indre-et-Loire

| Tel | +33 (0)2 47 55 95 28 |
|---|---|
| Mobile | +33 (0)6 03 22 34 45 |
| Email | lherissaudiere@gmail.com |
| Web | www.herissaudiere.com |

## Hostellerie de la Mère Hamard

Watch the world from your window, the locals clutching their baguettes on their way home. Two pretty townhouses in the centre of a quiet little village, this has been a restaurant-hotel since it was bought in 1903 by a remarkable widow, Madame Hamard, who built up an excellent reputation – Parisian actors loved it and the Duke of Windsor passed by. Here since 1975, Monique and Patrick and their staff still extend a genuinely warm welcome. They have done it up in an attractively modern way with peaceful rooms and bright, crisp bathrooms with pretty friezes. The two big ground-floor rooms have tasteful colour schemes; upstairs there are pale walls and light, bright fabrics; the two smallest rooms under the roof are charming in simple country style; the 'chalet' room over the restaurant is completely different with its wood-slatted walls, and cheerful checked fabrics. Another reason to stay is the seriously good food, traditional with original touches. It's popular with the locals so book your table at weekends. An excellent place to start a family holiday or spend a few days exploring the area.

| | |
|---|---|
| Rooms | 7 twin/doubles: €92–€97. 4 family rooms for 3: €112–€145. Extra bed €15. |
| Meals | Breakfast €12.50. Lunch & dinner €29–€65. Restaurant closed Sunday eve & Mondays. Restaurants 5km. |
| Closed | Early January to mid-February. |

Monique & Patrick Pegué
Hostellerie de la Mère Hamard,
37360 Semblançay,
Indre-et-Loire
Tel        +33 (0)2 47 56 62 04
Email      reservation@lamerehamard.com
Web        www.lamerehamard.com

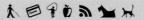

## Château du Vau

Lanky, relaxed philosopher Bruno has turned his family château into a delightful, harmonious refuge for the world-weary traveller. The cosy, book-lined, deep-chaired sitting room is a place where you find yourself irresistibly drawn into long conversations about music, yoga, art... The sunny breakfast room is charming with its stone-coloured tiles and pretty fabrics. Generations of sliding children have polished the banisters on the stairs leading to the large, light bedrooms that are beautifully but unfussily decorated – splendid brass bedsteads, Turkish rugs on parquet floors, old family furniture, pictures and memorabilia – the spirit of zen can be felt in the search for pure authenticity. A flock of sheep graze peacefully in the newly planted orchard, and there's a dreadlocked donkey called Omega. Deer can often be seen bounding across the meadow. With 118 hectares of grounds it is very hard to imagine that you're only 15 minutes from the centre of Tours. On fine summer evenings you can take a supper tray à la Glyndebourne to a favourite corner of the vast grounds.

| | |
|---|---|
| Rooms | 3 doubles: €130. |
| | 2 treehouses for 2: €140. |
| Meals | Dinner with wine €42. |
| | Summer buffets in garden €26. |
| Closed | Rarely. |

Bruno Clément
Château du Vau,
37510 Ballan Miré,
Indre-et-Loire

| | |
|---|---|
| Tel | +33 (0)2 47 67 84 04 |
| Email | info@chateau-du-vau.com |
| Web | www.chateau-du-vau.com |

## Domaine de la Tortinière

It seems unreal, this pepperpot-towered château on a hill above the Indre, the bird-filled woods where wild cyclamen lay a carpet in autumn and daffodils radiate their light in spring. Then there's the view across to the stony keep of Montbazon; this is an exceptional spot with tennis, a heated pool, fishing or rowing on the river, too. Bedrooms are decorated with flair and imagination, be they in the château or in one of the several outbuildings. The smallest is enchanting in its elegant simplicity and fine fabrics; the pavilions, for playing shepherdesses, are charming and beautifully furnished. Bathrooms are luxurious, some smaller than others. For wet nights there's an underground passage to the orangery where you dine – with a dining terrace for summer. Soft lighting, panelled reception rooms, deep comfort and discreet friendliness here in this real family-run hotel: the warm, humorous owners are genuinely attentive, their sole aim to make your stay peaceful and harmonious. Discover the unsung mills and villages of the Indre.

| Rooms | 25 doubles: €119-€320. |
| | 7 suites for 2: €290-€405. |
| Meals | Breakfast €20. Dinner €36-€81. |
| | Restaurant closed Sunday eve |
| | (November-March). |
| Closed | Mid-December to March. |

Xavier & Anne Olivereau
Domaine de la Tortinière,
Les Gués de Veigné, 37250 Veigné,
Indre-et-Loire
Tel     +33 (0)2 47 34 35 00
Email   contact@tortiniere.com
Web     www.tortiniere.com

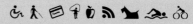

## Château de Reignac

A remarkably balanced restoration is this four-star hotel, full of elegance and charm, where the 'old' is underplayed and the 'new' is discreet. So many personalities stayed or were connected with this château that Erick decided to theme the rooms adding a portrait or special object – and a biography. 'Lafayette', who inherited the château and visited until 1792, is a small suite with two bathrooms all in subtle greens and yellows with an attractive writing desk for your historical novel and a private terrace for balmy evenings. 'Axel de Fersen', a Swedish nobleman who swooned for Marie Antoinette, is in pale blues and yellows with a statue of his beloved and a claw-foot bath. Lime and mauve work wonders in the *grand salon* – enormous sparkling mirrors and flower-dressed chimney – while the smoking room/bar – 'Zanzibar' – is in dark browns with cane furniture. Books can be borrowed from the properly sober library where an Egyptian theme runs through the art on the walls. The guests-only restaurant serves a daily changing menu, full of spicy, original touches. We think you will like it here.

| | |
|---|---|
| Rooms | 6 doubles, 2 twins: €110–€220. 3 suites for 4: €135–€280. 1 apartment for 4 without kitchen: €300–€390 per night. Extra bed/sofabed available €30 per person per night. |
| Meals | Buffet breakfast €16; children's menu €10. Dinner with apéritif €39; children's menu €20. |
| Closed | 5 January to 12 February. |

| | |
|---|---|
| | Erick Charrier Château de Reignac, 19 rue Louis de Barberin, 37310 Reignac sur Indre, Indre-et-Loire |
| Tel | +33 (0)2 47 94 14 10 |
| Email | contact@lechateaudereignac.com |
| Web | www.lechateaudereignac.com |

## Le Cheval Blanc

Bang in the middle of Loire châteaux country, the famous 19th-century staging inn has always been an hotel – but much has changed in the last few years. The main square is now mostly pedestrianised, so the place is brilliantly quiet, and the rooms, all on the first floor, have been beautifully revamped by the new owners. Decorated and furnished with imagination, flair and lots of original timbers, the rooms are all different: from a cleancut 21st-century palette to a more traditional draped look. This is contemporary chic in a highly sophisticated yet unfussy manner. Bathrooms are state-of-the-art stylish, one room has its bathtub and shower proudly centre-stage in the room. Your charming and dynamic hosts are breathing new life into these old bones – fast. The restaurant, long known as one of the best in the region, is furnished and decorated with elegant simplicity so that you can concentrate on the gastronomic delights on your plate. In fine weather, the pretty inner courtyard has peace and shade for breakfast and dinner – and the sheltered pool is a great bonus.

| | |
|---|---|
| Rooms | 7 doubles: €87–€145. 2 suites for 2: €185–€205. Singles €78–€98. Dinner, B&B extra €43–€53 per person. |
| Meals | Breakfast €12. Dinner €32–€58. Wine list €26.50–€47. Restaurant closed Monday & Tuesday. Restaurants 2-minute walk. |
| Closed | January. |

Claire & Alain Guinoiseau
Le Cheval Blanc,
5 place Charles Bidault,
37150 Bléré, Indre-et-Loire

| | |
|---|---|
| Tel | +33 (0)2 47 30 30 14 |
| Email | aguinoiseau@lechevalblancblere.fr |
| Web | www.lechevalblancblere.fr |

## Auberge du Bon Laboureur

This little hotel, a stroll from the glorious château of Chenonceau, was a coaching inn in the 18th century. Now in the hands of the fourth generation, it has expanded higgledy-piggledy into adjoining buildings: the old village school and a house with a 1950s tower, known tongue-in-cheek as 'The Manor'. The pool is in a brilliantly secluded garden over the road. Kept in top condition, bedrooms are light, airy and quietly pretty with plenty of space and storage, classic Jouy fabrics, antiques, books and prints. In the original inn, the heart of the hotel, you find three utterly restful sitting rooms and the elegant dining room with a simpler, more relaxed one next to it. In summer, tables with starched white cloths, candles and flowers are set on the terrace under the trees. A good spot for château-seeing; Amboise, Chaumont, Chambord and more are within easy reach, you can make your visits and be back in time for a swim and glass of fine local wine before dinner. A large potager behind the hotel, overseen by Isabelle, supplies vegetables for Antoine's kitchen. Huge character, charming owners, delightful cuisine.

| | | |
|---|---|---|
| Rooms | 18 twin/doubles: €134–€189.<br>8 suites for 2: €214–€310.<br>Dinner, B&B €62 per person.<br>Extra bed/sofabed available €18 per<br>person per night. |  |
| Meals | Breakfast €18. Picnic €9.<br>Lunch €32–€105.<br>Dinner, set menu, €35–€105.<br>Restaurant closed Tuesday lunchtime. | |
| Closed | Mid-November to mid-December &<br>January. | |

**Isabelle & Antoine Jeudi**
Auberge du Bon Laboureur,
6 rue du Docteur Bretonneau,
37150 Chenonceaux, Indre-et-Loire

| | |
|---|---|
| Tel | +33 (0)2 47 23 90 02 |
| Email | laboureur@wanadoo.fr |
| Web | www.bonlaboureur.com |

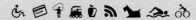

## Château de Pintray

Instant charm and history at the end of the long leafy avenue. This intimate château glows with personality and peculiarity yet this is no museum-piece: youthful, delightful, Anne looks after the B&B while Jean Christophe (who has taken over from his father) produces some of the region's best sweet and dry white wines; enjoy the tastings – they are currently converting to organic status. The house is stuffed full of character and old world charm: find books, games and toys in the communal rooms (including a full sized billiard table in the dining room, and a roaring fire in the sitting room on chilly days). Upstairs to authentic bedrooms, somewhat threadbare carpets, comfortable beds and good antiques totally in keeping with the character of the house. Bathrooms are a good size with big old roll top tubs and walk-in showers. Tuck in to a splendid breakfast at the convivial table before setting off to explore. Start with the parkland surrounding the house, and the vineyards. Then further afield for the great châteaux: Chenonceau, Amboise, Villandry and Azay le Rideau, all within an hour's drive.

| Rooms | 2 doubles: €115. |
| | 1 family room for 4: €115-€165. |
| Meals | Restaurant 2km. |
| Closed | Rarely. |

Anne Ricou & Jean Christophe Rault
Château de Pintray,
Lussault sur Loire,
37400 Amboise, Indre-et-Loire

| Tel | +33 (0)2 47 23 22 84 |
| Email | marius.rault@wanadoo.fr |
| Web | www.chateau-de-pintray.com |

---

## Domaine des Bidaudières

Sylvie and Pascal have made their mark on this classic, pale-stone former winegrower's property. Now helped by their son, they produce a small quantity of wine from their vineyard on the terraced land above the house while cypress trees standing on the hillside behind give it an Italian feel. Sylvie, casually elegant and outgoing, lends sophistication to the whole place not least the bedrooms – fresh, carpeted and contemporary, each decorated in Designers Guild fabric. Some are light, south-facing and have valley views, while the very private suite, once a cave dwelling, is delightfully rustic in character – and has a private terrace for the views. The den-like sitting room, cosy with a wood-burner in the old fireplace (and a billiard table) is also hewn out of the rock. Enjoy breakfast in the stone-flagged conservatory, then while away the afternoon by the splendid south-facing swimming pool on the lower terrace next to the orangerie (you can reach the pool by the lift in the main house). Sun beds are separated by small bushes for privacy and every detail is given attention.

| | |
|---|---|
| Rooms | 4 doubles, 1 twin: €135.<br>1 suite for 3: €150.<br>1 apartment for 5 with kitchenette: €170.<br>1 cottage for 4-5: €1,000-€1,200 per week. |
| Meals | Restaurants 2km. |
| Closed | Rarely. |

**Pascal & Sylvie Suzanne**
Domaine des Bidaudières,
Rue du Peu Morier,
37210 Vouvray, Indre-et-Loire

| | |
|---|---|
| Tel | +33 (0)2 47 23 00 00 |
| Email | contact@chateaudesarpentis.com |
| Web | www.bidaudieres.com |

## Château de Perreux

High on the hillside, with stunning views over water meadows to the Loire – you can see Amboise when the trees are bare – is a romantic château flanked by two little towers, run by a delightful manager. In front is a terraced lawn that drops to the valley; the elegant pool – reached via a rocky tunnel – is on the other side of the road, in a meadow garden bordered by great trees and a winding piece of the river; find a secret corner and lap up the peace. Inside: three salons with panelled walls and coffered ceilings, one in rich red, one with a handsome fireplace and antique wall hangings, the last with bright trumpet-shaped lighting and plain tables for traditional breakfasts. Make the most of the vineyards of Vouvray, then relax in view-filled bedrooms furnished with an uncluttered elegance. Those on the first floor keep their parquet-floored, period feel; on the second comfortable carpet and those at the top, with exposed roof timbers and clean-limbed furniture, have a dramatic yet monastic air. The suites in the towers are delightful. François, a former chef, is always to hand and brilliant at making guests feel at home.

| Rooms | 2 twin/doubles: €135–€165. |
| --- | --- |
| | 6 suites for 2: €155–€260. |
| | 3 family rooms for 4, each with separate shower: €210–€290. |
| | Extra bed/sofabed available €35 per person per night. |
| Meals | Restaurants 1km. |
| Closed | Rarely. |

Olivier Fructus
Château de Perreux,
36 rue Pocé, 37530 Nazelles,
Indre-et-Loire

| Tel | +33 (0)2 47 57 27 47 |
| --- | --- |
| Email | contact@chateaudeperreux.fr |
| Web | www.chateaudeperreux.fr |

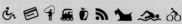

## Château de Nazelles

Up the steep road in the centre of the village to a charming 16th-century manor house with a tiled roof. It faces a shady courtyard cut out of the rock face where a little fountain plays and a winding track leads on into woodland and vineyards. House and garden are an exuberant mix of formal and informal, contemporary and traditional. Winding steps and pathways entice you through a charming series of 'secret' gardens, doorways cut in high hedges offer intriguing glimpses of the rest of the garden, then on over the Loire valley. Rooms are a delight, furnished with simple understated elegance to fully show off the character of the house and most have views over the valley towards Amboise. There's a new room in the oldest part of the main house, with original stone walls and tiled floor, while in the garden there's a little cottage clinging to the rock face, complete with a small kitchen and womb-like sitting room. The breakfast room is serene with a low, beamed ceiling. Great breakfasts, delightful hosts; even the pool is special. The whole place is full of surprises. Nice ones!

| Rooms | 4 doubles: €115–€150. |
|---|---|
| | 2 suites for 4: €260–€300. |
| Meals | Summer kitchen. Restaurants 3km. |
| Closed | Rarely. |

**Véronique & Olivier Fructus**
Château de Nazelles,
16 rue Tue la Soif, 37530 Nazelles,
Indre-et-Loire

| Tel | +33 (0)2 47 30 53 79 |
|---|---|
| Email | info@chateau-nazelles.com |
| Web | www.chateau-nazelles.com |

## Le Fleuray Hôtel & Restaurant

The Newington family hotel is a haven of peace surrounded by fields and grazing cows. The basics at Le Fleuray are ideal: a solid, handsome old manor house with duck pond and barns, mature trees and bushes, swimming pool, hot tub, tennis, kids' park and bikes – all that's needed. Then there's the country-house mood: lightly floral sofas into which you can sink, bookcases, prints and flowers. The rooms in the converted barns are just right for families; slightly cut off from the rest, they have French windows opening onto the garden so each has an individual patio. Those in the main building are a bit smaller but cosy and spotless, with queen-size beds. In summer, you can dine on the terrace. In winter, apéritifs are served in front of a log fire. A young French chef, who comes with quite a pedigree, produces a delicately inventive and well-presented cuisine; the restaurant is one of the most popular in the area. Expect a genuine welcome from family and staff – they know the best châteaux to visit and some lovely walks. Amboise is a short hop away.

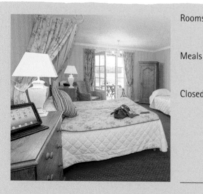

| | |
|---|---|
| Rooms | 9 twin/doubles: €78–€162. 2 suites for 4–6: €158–€248. 12 family rooms for 2–5: €118–€206. |
| Meals | Breakfast €15; children's menu €9. Dinner €29–€39; children's menu from €16. Wine €18–€24. |
| Closed | 22 November to 8 December & 21 December to 26 December. |

**Newington Family**
Le Fleuray Hôtel & Restaurant,
Fleuray, 37530 Cangey-Amboise,
Indre-et-Loire

| | |
|---|---|
| Tel | +33 (0)2 47 56 09 25 |
| Email | contact@lefleurayhotel.com |
| Web | www.lefleurayhotel.com |

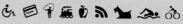

## Château des Arpentis

This superb neo-Gothic château (with 14th-century origins) lies just outside Amboise, yet you are immersed in countryside: the grounds are vast and secluded. Behind, a cliff face is hewn with caves, one of which has become a family suite: sensational, like something out of a fairy tale. To the front: the view! From a sward of lawn and an elegant pool (accessed by a tunnel) the eye is drawn to a lake shrouded by woodland and explored via a riddle of trails. A sense of the regal pervades the interiors; and, as befitting an old hunting lodge, there are hunting trophies in some of the corridors. A cosy guest sitting room feeds into a billiard room (each with a magnificent painted fireplace); the sunny dining room, opening to the terrace, exudes an elegant simplicity and is a beautiful backdrop for breakfast. Each bedroom is marvellous, including a huge raftered suite with its tower annexe and in-room tub. All have gorgeous furnishings, gleaming bathrooms, views over the grounds. Sylvie Suzanne (the owner, and great fun) spends a lot of time here; unsurprisingly, she can't keep away.

| | |
|---|---|
| Rooms | 9 doubles: €140-€210.<br>2 suites for 2-4: €230-€395.<br>1 family room for 2-3: €160-€205. |
| Meals | Restaurants 3km. |
| Closed | Rarely. |

Pascal & Sylvie Suzanne
Château des Arpentis,
37530 St Règle,
Indre-et-Loire
Tel      +33 (0)2 47 23 00 00
Email    contact@chateaudesarpentis.com
Web      www.chateaudesarpentis.com

## Manoir de Contres

Within cycling distance of the finest Loire châteaux, this 19th-century Gothic manor on the edge of Contres sits resplendent in its strolling grounds; repose by the lake with an easel or book. Easy to see why experienced hoteliers Maria and Victor left Paris in search of Sancerre and goat's cheese country. Victor loves cooking for guests, his seasonal menu changes every day so there's no need to go elsewhere for your foie gras or filet de boeuf; Maria is helpful and charming. Up the lift to king-size beds in spacious, pristine bedrooms with spotless blue and white bathrooms: those on the second floor beneath sloping ceilings have a more characterful air, and look prettily to the gardens. Search out the separate pavilion room for extra privacy. Company can be found in the sitting room, beneath very fine beams around the friendly open fireplace with a glass of something from the (neatly concealed) bar. Maestros will welcome the use of the piano, card sharks will enjoy the intimacy of the small blue salon. Come morning, step onto the shaded terrace for a breakfast of homemade jams and croissants.

| Rooms | 6 twin/doubles: €160–€180. |
|---|---|
| | 2 triples: €210. |
| | Cottage – 1 twin/double: €190–€210. |
| | Singles €135–€145. Pets €10. |
| | Extra bed €35. |
| Meals | Picnic available. |
| | Dinner, 4 courses, €33. |
| Closed | 1 January to 12 February. |

**Maria & Victor Orsenne**
Manoir de Contres,
23 rue des Combattants d'Afrique du
Nord, 41700 Contres, Loir-et-Cher

| | |
|---|---|
| Tel | +33 (0)2 54 78 45 39 |
| Email | hotel@manoirdecontres.com |
| Web | www.manoirdecontres.com |

## Château de Nanteuil

Revered grand-mère's house has faded charm – no châteauesque style or opulence but heaps of soul. Find a few crumbly bits outside, rambling greenery and mossy steps, frescoes and trunks in the hall, antlers in the dining room... Bedrooms are light-filled and unashamedly old-fashioned with floral wallpapers, large wardrobes and marble fireplaces; river-water murmurs below your window, and there's an attractive alcove on the landing where you can relax and read the paper; bathrooms are time-warp 70s. Most of all, you'll enjoy Frédéric – he's refreshingly unfussy, occasionally mercurial and serves you excellent organic dinners, perhaps asparagus in season and baked fillet of perch; he was a restaurant owner for many years and really cares about food. He's passionate too about his family home and all its impressive history, and might settle with you by the fire and engage you with his tales and anecdotes; a vintage car rally is sometimes arranged. In summer you can sit on the terrace overlooking the river Beuvron. It's a place you never forget.

| Rooms | 2 doubles: €80-€95. |
| | 2 family rooms for 2-4: €80. |
| | Extra person €20. |
| Meals | Dinner with wine €30. |
| Closed | Rarely. |

**Frédéric Théry**
16 rue Nanteuil Le Chiteau, 41350
Huisseau sur Cosson, Loir-et-Cher

| Tel | +33 (0)2 54 42 61 98 |
| Mobile | +33 (0)6 88 83 79 84 |
| Email | contact@chateau-nanteuil.com |
| Web | www.chateau-nanteuil.com |

## Château de la Rue

This 1810 (but with far more ancient roots) 'Directoire' mansion, approached via a grand avenue of trees, is lived in and loved by adorable Madame, who has been doing B&B for years and knows how to spoil you. You take breakfast in the large, light-filled breakfast room: homemade breads, croissants, jams and cakes; ham, cheeses, eggs for the still hungry. It's definitely worth booking yourselves in for dinner: Véronique rustles up regional specialities like toasted goat's cheese salad followed by guinea fowl with figs or peaches from the garden (in season), game such as wild boar, roe deer or rabbit washed down with a local wine from Vouvray or Cheverny. Sleep peacefully in handsome bedrooms named after famous French female writers, gaily colour-themed ('Mme de Segur'; the smallest, 'Cassandre'; the most luxurious) and the furniture, all antique with the exception of some comfortable sofas, looks as if it has been here forever. Wander the stunning historic walled orchard, visit Château de Chambord, cycle along the river to bustling Blois (restaurants, market, château): the Loire flows at the end of the park.

| Rooms | 3 doubles: €120–€180. |
| | 2 suites for 4: €250. |
| Meals | Dinner with wine, €39, on request. |
| | Restaurants 2km. |
| Closed | January/February. |

**Véronique de Caix**
Château de la Rue,
41500 Cour sur Loire, Loir-et-Cher
Tel     +33 (0)2 54 46 82 47
Email   chateaudelarue@wanadoo.fr
Web     www.chateaudelarue.com

Poitou – Charentes

Photo: Château des Salles, entry 193

## Le Logis d'Antan

Blue shutters against pale walls, faded terracotta roofs – the long façade suggests a simple country elegance. Once a wine merchant's house, then part of a farm, it basks in gardens full of beeches and wild poppies, fruit trees and figs. There's even a little pavilion. Bruno and Annie, ex-journalists with a young family, have created a friendly, unpretentious atmosphere – you'll like their style. Meals (Bruno has been on a cookery course) are eaten at a table seating up to 16 in a typically French dining room – or out on the veranda in good weather. Upstairs, where a mezzanine and maze of passageways make for great hide-and-seek, you can prepare picnics in a communal kitchen. Up here, too, are the double room and the suite, with a bunk-bedded children's annexe. The family rooms are on the ground floor: big, traditional rooms, with their own entrances off the drive. 'Les Pictons', overlooking the front lawn, has exposed stone walls and a grandfather clock; 'La Pibale', its own terrace. Bruno and Annie work closely with a company called Cycling for Softies, so grab the bikes and explore the country.

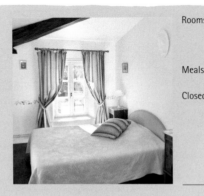

| Rooms | 1 double: €74–€94. |
| --- | --- |
| | 1 suite for 4: €114. |
| | 2 family rooms for 3, |
| | 1 family room for 4-5: €74–€134. |
| Meals | Dinner with wine, €28. Guest kitchen. |
| | Restaurant 12km. |
| Closed | Christmas & New Year. |

Annie & Bruno Ragouilliaux–Di Battista
Le Logis d'Antan, 140 rue Saint-Louis,
79270 Vallans, Deux Sèvres

| Tel | +33 (0)5 49 04 86 75, |
| --- | --- |
| | +33 (0)5 49 32 85 05 |
| Email | info@logisdantan.com |
| Web | www.logisdantan.com |

## Le Logis Saint Martin

Run with efficiency by Edouard Pellegrin, this 17th-century *gentilhommerie* offers that most attractive combination for travellers — solidly comfortable rooms and superb food. It is set conveniently on the outskirts of town, beyond suburbia, in a little wooded valley with a small stream running just outside. The bedrooms are mostly smallish, beamed, traditionally furnished and very comfortable; the bigger rooms, with lovely old rafters, are on the top floor. The tower has been converted into a charming suite with a sitting area downstairs and a smallish stone-walled bedroom up steepish stairs. Food is the thing here — regional, seasonal and served with panache in the colour-washed restaurant or the pleasantly shaded and tranquil garden. New chef Aline Jarriault has worked with the best and there is an innovative yet classic feel, matched by some tempting wines. Choose between the menu terroir and the menu gourmand — or pull out all the stops and work your way through the menu dégustation! As for Saint Maixent l'Ecole, it's a pretty market town not far from Poitiers and La Rochelle.

| | |
|---|---|
| Rooms | 9 doubles, 1 twin: €105–€175. 1 suite for 2: €215–€330. 1 family room for 3: €145–€195. Dinner, B&B €105–€151 per person. Extra bed/sofabed available €15 per person per night. |
| Meals | Breakfast €16. Lunch from €18. Dinner €32–€79. Restaurant closed Sat & Tues lunchtime, all of Mon; open every eve Jul-Aug. |
| Closed | Christmas & 2 January to 7 February. |

| | |
|---|---|
| | Edouard Pellegrin Le Logis Saint Martin, Chemin de Pissot, 79400 St Maixent l'Ecole, Deux Sèvres |
| Tel | +33 (0)5 49 05 58 68 |
| Email | contact@logis-saint-martin.com |
| Web | www.logis-saint-martin.com |

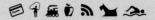

Entry 181  Map 9

## Château de Saint Loup sur Thouet

The Black Prince incarcerated John the Good here in 1356 and it was rebuilt in the 17th century by the Marquis of Carabas, whose magnificence inspired the fairy-tale author Perrault to write *Puss in Boots*. Charles-Henri visited the château on Christmas Eve 1990, fell in love with it – and bought it ten days later. Saint Loup is a listed monument open to the public and its restoration is a gigantic task. Using 18th-century plans, the Comte is also working on the 50 hectares of grounds and kitchen garden. Seven rooms are in the Keep, splendidly medieval, with carved panelling and furniture, four-poster beds, ancient beams and stone fireplaces (not used). All have big bathrooms, some with free-standing baths and one in the guard room, lit by arrow slits overlooking the moat. New doors are made of solid oak with massive locks and keys... a romantic's dream (and a housemaid's nightmare!). Enjoy apéritifs in the walled garden or the orangery across the moat, before finding a restaurant in the village. A jewel of a château, a happy and authentic home.

| Rooms | 18 doubles: €150–€220. |
|---|---|
| Meals | Breakfast €15. |
| | Restaurants 5-minute walk. |
| Closed | Rarely. |

**Comte Charles-Henri de Bartillat**
Château de Saint Loup sur Thouet,
79600 St Loup Lamairé, Deux Sèvres

| Tel | +33 (0)5 49 64 81 73 |
|---|---|
| Mobile | +33 (0)6 80 15 67 36 |
| Email | st-loup@wanadoo.fr |
| Web | www.chateaudesaint-loup.com |

## Château de la Roche Martel

You are perched on a high promontory with a backdrop of woodland and with vast sweeping south-facing views of the surrounding countryside – not all pastoral (a large goat farm is near), but the position is stunning. This is a sensational launch pad for forays to Anjou, Touraine and Poitou. The house has character and history in spades (Henry III is buried here), mullioned windows, a pepperpot tower, a rare covered wooden gallery, the remains of an ancient chapel, a horse in the paddock, century old trees. And now, delightful new owners, she a Polish picture restorer, he an expert on Plantagenet history. Bedrooms glow with gorgeous fabrics and tadelakt walls, the family room with a four-poster and fine stone fireplace, the double in a pretty round tower. All feels generous, the bathrooms are splendid (one with a rare antique wc). Two salons (one facing north, the other south) are yours to slump in, surrounded by interesting objects, books and pictures; one has a large open fire for chilly days. You breakfast in the dining room, attractively laid with fine china, on good local bread and viennoiserie, homemade jam and eggs. *Min. stay: 2 nights in low season.*

| Rooms | 1 double: €120. |
|---|---|
| | 1 family room for 3: €140-€165. |
| | 1 single: €90. |
| | Extra bed €25. |
| Meals | Restaurant 6km. |
| Closed | Rarely. |

**Alicja & Dominique de Cornulier Lucinière**
Château de la Roche Martel, Lieu-dit la
Roche Marteau, 86120 Roiffé, Vienne

| Tel | +33 (0)5 49 22 36 31 |
|---|---|
| Mobile | +33 (0)6 83 43 46 34 |
| Email | larochemartel@orange.fr |
| Web | www.larochemartel.com |

Entry 183   Map 9

## Château de La Plante

The unpretentious stone manor sits high up on the hillside looking down over a vast landscape of arable farmland with the wooded valley of the Vienne in the distance: a large wood protects the house from the north. Wind up a pretty driveway through mature trees, then all opens out and you arrive at the east wing. Very charming. The house has been in Françoise's family for ever (she grew up here) and she and Patrick tend it with loving care, as they do their guests. Period elegance drifts through the bedrooms, named after four great grandmothers: three in the main building with canopied beds, parquet floors and antiques, and a family suite on the top floor of the west wing which has more of a contemporary feel with fresh white painted walls. Serenity reigns supreme; breakfast (continental with homemade jams) is served in the old music room, on good porcelain – fresh flowers sit on the marble mantelpiece. Wander the grassy, natural garden to find a good spot for reading, or join your hosts for an aperitif on the balustraded terrace or under the spreading lime tree. If houses could sing, this one surely would.

| | |
|---|---|
| Rooms | 2 doubles, 1 twin/double: €90–€110. 1 family suite for 4 with separate wc: €140. Children's triple room €60–€80. |
| Meals | Restaurants 10-minute drive. |
| Closed | Rarely. |

Patrick & Françoise Dandurand
Château de La Plante,
86540 Thuré,
Vienne

| | |
|---|---|
| Tel | +33 (0)5 49 93 86 28 |
| Email | patrick.dandurand@orange.fr |
| Web | www.chateaudelaplante.fr |

## Château de Labarom

A delightfully hospitable couple who love having people to stay. Their beautiful, mainly 17th-century, château has a gently fading grandeur and is surrounded by magnificent parkland. Perfect for families, it's a children's paradise with a large swimming pool, plenty of safe space in which to roam and explore and a fascinating pigeonniere. From the dramatic hall the superbly bannistered staircase sweeps you up to the salon gallery that runs majestically through the house and provides a huge space in which to relax – sit, read, dream of benevolent ghosts… The two double bedrooms burst with personality and are roomy and comfortable; children's rooms interconnect. Madame's hand-painted tiles adorn a shower, her laughter accompanies your breakfast (organic garden fruits and four sorts of jam); Monsieur tends his trees, aided by Hermes the dog – he's a fount of local wisdom and is happy to chat about the history of the château too. A warm, wonderful, authentic place, and Michelin stars five miles away.

| Rooms | 2 doubles, 1 twin: €85-€90. Child €20, in connecting room. |
|-------|---------------------------------------------------------------|
| Meals | Restaurants 3km. |
| Closed | Rarely. |

**Éric & Henriette Le Gallais**
Château de Labarom, Route de
Thurageau, 86380 Cheneché, Vienne

| Tel | +33 (0)5 49 51 24 22 |
|--------|----------------------|
| Mobile | +33 (0)6 83 57 68 14 |
| Email | labarom@labarom.com |
| Web | www.labarom.com |

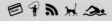

## Hôtel Le Pigeonnier du Perron

René Descartes once owned this little *seigneurie*; its deeds date back to the 15th century. More a country guest house than a hotel, it's been in the family for 150 years. Father and son are fully occupied in their wine laboratory in Cahors; Emilie – hard working, enthusiastic, welcoming – prepares good simple meals (some organic produce, some fish) and runs it all with a small team. Family connections guarantee an excellent selection of wines from Cahors, but also from Poitou and the Loire Valley. Sun-ripened tomatoes, courgettes and peppers are home-grown along with essential herbs for the kitchen, and you can eat on the the stone-flagged terrace in summer. The modest farm buildings are grouped round a sunny courtyard, hollyhocks surge from every nook and cranny and there's a lovely pool. The smallish bedrooms are simply, pleasantly decorated with the odd splash of colour, their floors pale pine, their walls soft-sponged – or of creamy exposed stone. One in the dovecote has a little balcony, many look over the fields and valley. Good value.

| Rooms | 11 doubles, 1 twin: €79–€128. |
| | 2 family rooms for 4: €116–€128. |
| Meals | Dinner €19. Wine €20. |
| Closed | 21 December to 4 January. |

**Emilie Thiollet**
Hôtel Le Pigeonnier du Perron,
Le Perron, 86530 Availles en
Châtellerault, Vienne

| Tel | +33 (0)5 49 19 76 08 |
| Email | reservations@lepigeonnierduperron.com |
| Web | www.lepigeonnierduperron.com |

## Le Relais du Lyon d'Or

The pretty little hotel-restaurant stands in one of Charente's most beautiful medieval villages. American Diana brings her professional experience; Dominique, a fully-fledged French wine expert and dealer, will suggest the perfect bottle be it for dinner or a big event, simple or organic, for connoisseurs or big budgets. The public rooms, rebuilt round old flagstones and beams, are decorated in warm natural colours to enhance the beauty of the original architecture. Bedrooms, some big, some smaller, have intriguing and individual details; rafters for those under the roof, high ceilings and beams or rough terracotta floors for others; none are overdone and all have sparkling bathrooms. The varied menu focuses on traditional dishes and local and seasonal produce, served when possible on the pretty terrace alive with wisteria and roses, hydrangea and geraniums... Masses to see and do: the Valley of the Frescoes including the Abbey at St Savin (UNESCO), the markets of medieval Chauvigny and Loches, the superb Parc de la Brenne for birds, turtles and orchids, Poitiers... or the quiet wonders of nature in the nearby valleys. *Pets by arrangement.*

| | |
|---|---|
| Rooms | 8 doubles: €89-€149. 1 suite for 5, 1 suite for 4: €159-€209. Singles €79-€139. Extra bed/sofabed available €15-€20 per person per night. |
| Meals | Breakfast €13. Dinner €27-€40. Wine €22-€500. Lunch for groups by arrangement. Restaurant closed mid-November to mid-March. |
| Closed | Rarely. |

Dominique Fuscien & Diana Hager
Le Relais du Lyon d'Or,
4 rue d'Enfer,
86260 Angles sur l'Anglin, Vienne

| | |
|---|---|
| Tel | +33 (0)5 49 48 32 53 |
| Email | contact@lyondor.com |
| Web | www.lyondor.com |

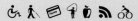

## Hôtel Les Orangeries

The long cool pool beneath the trees will convince you that these people have the finest sense of how to treat an old house and its surroundings. A deep wooden deck, rustic stone walls, giant flower baskets, orange trees, candles at night – all create tranquillity and harmony. The young owners (he an architect) fell in love with the place and have cleverly blended 18th-century elegance with contemporary charm. Oak doors, exposed stone walls, cool stone floors... everything glows with loving care, like valued old friends. Bedrooms are light and uncluttered, those facing the main road are double-glazed but get hot in summer (earplugs can come in handy, too), the split-level apartments are a delight. The Gautiers' passions include the old-fashioned games they have resuscitated for you: croquet and skittles under the trees, two kinds of billiards, backgammon and mahjong. Olivia speaks English and her enthusiasm for house, garden and guests is catching. Award-winning food (Sustainable International Restaurant of the Year) is delicious, local, organic; breakfast, in the garden in summer, is all you'd hope for the price. Exceptional.

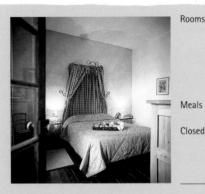

| | |
|---|---|
| Rooms | 11 doubles: €85–€165. |
| | 4 apartments for 4-5 without kitchen: |
| | €145–€215 per night. |
| | Singles €75–€90. |
| | Dinner, B&B €42–€49 extra per person. |
| | Extra bed/sofabed available €10–€18 |
| | per person per night. |
| Meals | Breakfast from €12.50. |
| | Dinner from €28. Wine from €19.50. |
| Closed | Rarely. |

**Olivia & Jean-Philippe Gautier**
Hôtel Les Orangeries,
12 av du Docteur Dupont,
86320 Lussac les Châteaux, Vienne
Tel      +33 (0)5 49 84 07 07
Email    orangeries@wanadoo.fr
Web      www.lesorangeries.fr

## Logis du Château du Bois Doucet

Naturally, graciously, aristocratically French, owners and house are full of long stories and eccentricity. Beautiful treasures abound: a jumble of ten French chairs, bits of ancient furniture, pictures, heirlooms, lamps in a stone-flagged salon, a properly elegant dining room, old dolls and family hunting buttons. There are statues inside and out and the gardens are listed; find a box-hedge maze, topiaries, mature trees and plants, orderly gravel paths and lawns. Bedrooms come with personality; the double and one family suite are in the 20th-century wing – one room can sleep up to four with old family beds and a big oak table where children can draw; the two-storey family suite in the main house is fit for a cardinal – children hop upstairs to their cheerful yellow and blue attic room, and all of you hop downstairs for the bathroom. Monsieur's interests are history and his family, Madame's are art and life; you sometimes have to let yourselves in when you arrive and you will feel part of family life in this delightful people and dog orientated house.

| Rooms | 1 double: €80-€90. |
| | 2 family suites for 4: €150. |
| Meals | Occasional dinner with wine, €30. |
| Closed | Rarely. |

**Hilaire de Villoutreys de Brignac**
Logis du Château du Bois Doucet,
86800 Bignoux, Vienne

| Tel | +33 (0)5 49 44 20 26 |
| Mobile | +33 (0)6 75 42 79 78 |
| Email | mariediane1012@yahoo.fr |

Entry 189  Map 9

## Château de Nieuil

François I built this fairy-tale château as a hunting lodge in the 16th century – and went on to create the Château de Chambord. A gambling count sold Nieuil to the Bodinauds' grandparents; now its hunting days are over and it's become an exciting hotel, paying homage to our feathered friends with a magical bird-spotting walk round the moat. Each room is named after a bird and, if you are not woken by real ones, an alarm will sing 'your' song. A chandelier hung with love letters and a stainless-steel bar bring touches of modern elegance to this country retreat, grand and beautifully decorated. One room has a small children's room up a spiral stair, another a tiny reading room in a turret. Most look onto the ornate gardens at the back, whose newest addition is an eco-cosy star-gazing cabin – book early, it's popular. (There's a gypsy caravan, too.) The breakfast room looks onto the grounds through stained-glass windows, and Madame, a chef in her own right, has trained the young trio who run the restaurant in the old stables: fabulous. Open-hearted, open-armed, these people love what they do, and it shows.

| Rooms | 7 twin/doubles: €130–€250. |
| --- | --- |
| | 3 suites for 2: €275–€420. |
| | 3 cottages for 2: €550 per week. |
| | 1 gypsy caravan for 2: €200 per week. |
| Meals | Breakfast €15. Lunch €25–€55. |
| | Dinner with wine, €55–€80. |
| | Restaurant closed Sunday eve; |
| | Monday & Tuesday lunch Sept–June |
| Closed | Weekdays in October & |
| | 1 November to 5 December. |

Monsieur & Madame Bodinaud
Château de Nieuil,
16270 Nieuil, Charente

| Tel | +33 (0)5 45 71 36 38 |
| --- | --- |
| Email | chateaunieuilhotel@wanadoo.fr |
| Web | www.chateaunieuilhotel.com |

## Le Logis du Paradis

Mellow stones, chunky beams, sensuous fabrics… there's a timeless feel to the beautifully renovated Logis, where Sally greets you as an old friend. The 18th-century buildings (a paradis is where the oldest, finest Cognac was stored) embrace a magnificent oval courtyard. In big, elegant bedrooms you snuggle down in superbly comfortable king-size beds under white linen… and wake in anticipation of a delicious breakfast (on the raised terrace on sunny days, the luxurious dining room in winter). There's a pool in the aromatic garden, books on the landings, a tea and coffee kitchen, a bar in the former distillery shared with the other guests. Pootle down delightfully empty country roads, discover the finest vineyards for a bit of wine tasting, take a picnic to a stunning Atlantic beach. Return to a stroll round the walled parc by the pretty river Né before a four-course table d'hôtes dinner, enjoyed on the terrace in summer. Sally's generous table features market-fresh local produce, fine wines, and a glass of the neighbour's superb XO Cognac to finish with. Highly professional.

| | |
|---|---|
| Rooms | 5 doubles sharing 2 bathrooms: €110–€150. |
| Meals | Lunch €19. Dinner €39, on request. Wine from €12.50. Restaurant 4km. |
| Closed | Mid-January to end February. |

**Sally Brimblecombe**
Le Logis du Paradis,
La Magdeleine, 16300 Criteuil la
Magdeleine, Charente

| | |
|---|---|
| Tel | +33 (0)5 45 35 39 43 |
| Email | info@logisduparadis.com |
| Web | www.logisduparadis.com |

## Domaine du Meunier

A lovely, friendly house built in 1893 as a flour factory and renovated perfectly for you. Find a living room with a library and a piano, a dining room and a games room. Breakfast – at the big friendly table or out on the lawn – is a feast of fruits, breads, cakes, pastries, jams, and coddled eggs from the family's hens; dinner (twice a week in high season) is lively! In summer the sun shines through large windows as dogs and children romp in the gardens, and you wind up the great walnut stair to bedrooms calm and serene. The outbuildings have become gîtes, the 'Pinball Hall' (with 35 machines from the 60s and 70s) hosts events, and the family live in the old mill. Stroll through the walled garden, let the children splash in the pool, doze in an antique deckchair; twice a day high tide means you can swim or sail then return to fresh seafood from local fishermen. Views are gentle, to canal and countryside beyond, while the nearby harbour, pretty with sailing boats, joins the port to the Gironde. Culture abounds with jazz nights and an outdoor film festival. This is a fascinating area… stay a while.

| | |
|---|---|
| Rooms | 3 doubles, 2 twins: €70. |
| Meals | Dinner, €25, twice weekly in high season; book ahead. Restaurants 50m. |
| Closed | Rarely. |

**Ariane & Coen Ter Kuile**
Domaine du Meunier,
36 quai de L'Estuaire, 17120 Mortagne
sur Gironde, Charente-Maritime

| | |
|---|---|
| Tel | +33 (0)5 46 97 75 10 |
| Email | info@domainedumeunier.com |
| Web | www.domainedumeunier.com |

## Château des Salles

A pretty little château set among vineyards and full of character, Salles was built in 1454 and scarcely touched until 1860, when it was 'adapted to the fashion' (profoundly). A century later, the Couillaud family brought the house, vineyard and farm into the 20th century. Behind the fine old exterior you find light, harmony, colour and elegant informality with spiral stone stairs, boldly painted beams and warm, well-furnished bedrooms bathed in soft colours and gentle wallpapers. Salles has a friendly family feel: adorable and elegantly French, Sylvie runs the house with passion and effortless taste, her mother's watercolours hang in the public rooms and decorate bedroom doors. At dinner, refined food made with local and home-grown produce is served with class and estate wines. Sylvie will help you plan your stay, her advice is invaluable. People return again and again to this congenial, welcoming house. One guest said: "She welcomed us like family and sent us home with goodies from her vineyard".

| | |
|---|---|
| Rooms | 1 double, 4 twin/doubles: €88–€160. |
| Meals | Dinner €29–€38. Wine from €15. |
| Closed | November – March. |

**Sylvie Couillaud**
Château des Salles,
61 rue du Gros Chêne, 17240 St Fort
sur Gironde, Charente-Maritime

| | |
|---|---|
| Tel | +33 (0)5 46 49 95 10 |
| Email | chateaudessalles@wanadoo.fr |
| Web | www.chateaudessalles.com |

## Château de la Tillade

You can tell that Michel and Solange like people. They put you at ease in their comfortable home – even when you're secretly terrified of dropping the bone china. The château sits at the top of an avenue of lime trees alongside the family vineyards that have produced grapes for cognac and pineau de Charentes for over two centuries. The original distillery equipment is well worth a visit. Solange holds painting courses in her art studio and her talents as an artist are reflected in her love of fabrics. The bedrooms are marvellously individual, less by design than by natural evolution through the years. Each is like a page out of Michel's memory book: steeped in family history. The claw-foot bath is fit for a princess, the corner room has a wonderful balcony overlooking the drive. Meals are a delight (book ahead), with conversation in English or French around the family table; you are waited on lavishly but without stuffiness. A rare opportunity to get to know a pair of relaxed and charming French aristocrats… breakfast too is round the convivial table.

| | |
|---|---|
| Rooms | 1 twin, 3 family rooms for 3-4 (one room with wc just outside room): €100–€130. Extra bed/sofabed available €25 per person per night. |
| Meals | Dinner €38; book ahead. Restaurant 12km. |
| Closed | Rarely. |

Vicomte & Vicomtesse Michel de Salvert
Château de la Tillade, Gémozac,
17260 St Simon de Pellouaille,
Charente-Maritime

| | |
|---|---|
| Tel | +33 (0)5 46 90 00 20 |
| Email | contact@la-tillade.com |
| Web | www.la-tillade.com |

## Le Moulin de Châlons

The generous, open-hearted Bouquets are a family of perfectionists, and it shows in their beautiful stone mill house sitting gracefully at the water's edge, its sun terrace overlooking the mill race. The restaurant, with its crisp white tables and tankful of lobsters, has earned a huge reputation for finesse; the family hotel is charming. Enter a relaxed salon with a pretty stone fireplace, cosy leather chairs and fresh flowers. Spotless gleaming bedrooms with super sound insulation (against the main road) are traditional; those in the new wing, designed by talented daughter Maud, are ultra-modern and sleek with fluffy tactile touches (faux furs, cushions…). Choose between blue Jouy with bold pebble stencils or elegant antique sofas with rust-and-grey spots and swirls. Bathrooms are immaculate and gorgeous, too; the newest have a serene eastern feel. Neatly tended gardens line the entrance while thoughtful resting places invite you to admire the birds bobbing downstream. Close by are the smart islands of Ré and Oléron; if it's green peace you want, catch a slow boat up the Marais to the *Venise Verte*.

| | | |
|---|---|---|
| Rooms | 5 doubles, 2 twins: €115–€130. 2 suites for 2: €145–€165. 1 family room for 3: €145. |  |
| Meals | Breakfast €13. Lunch & dinner €29–€50. | |
| Closed | Rarely. | |

**Bouquet Family**
Le Moulin de Châlons,
2 rue du Bassin, 17600 Le Gua,
Charente-Maritime

| | |
|---|---|
| Tel | +33 (0)5 46 22 82 72 |
| Email | moulin-de-chalons@wanadoo.fr |
| Web | www.moulin-de-chalons.com |

## Château de Champdolent

On the edge of a village in a pastoral landscape is an 11th-century manor, an 18th-century farmhouse, and a keep, its outline majestic in the setting sun. You sleep under beams in rooms elegant and simple, the largest with its own kitchen and sitting room (designer chairs, huge sofas). Rifle through art books in the library, repair to the guard room with armchairs and immense chimney. Food is taken seriously: Dominique (a sculptor and food producer) and Line (a lover of philosophy whose mother ran a famous restaurant in Paris) are both passionate about food. Breakfast includes homemade cakes and jams, dinner will involve fresh vegetables from their potager, fish from the local market, Line's blanquette de veau or coq au vin followed by her famous tarte tatin – from their own apples of course. They've even won an award for their foie gras (the mysteries of which will be explained to you should you wish to take a cookery course here). Visit markets at Rochefort and La Rochelle, scan the marshes for stork, heron and crane, have a day out sailing or take a picnic to the nearby beach – unknown to the hordes. Super.

| Rooms | 2 doubles: €80. |
| | 1 apartment for 2-3 with kitchen: €120 per night. |
| Meals | Dinner with wine, €27. |
| | Restaurants 15km. |
| Closed | Rarely. |

**Line & Dominique Cozic**
Château de Champdolent,
17430 Champdolent,

| Tel | +33 (0)5 46 82 96 07 |
| Mobile | +33 (0)6 10 34 60 41 |
| Email | d.cozic@gmail.com |
| Web | www.chateaudechampdolent.fr |

## Jardins Alienor

A short stroll from Chateau d'Oléron's tree-lined market square is an elegant hotel that first welcomed guests in the 17th century. Charming owners Laetitia and Marc bought and renovated the original hotel in 2004, extending into adjoining properties to create eight stylish en-suite rooms. Window boxes and pale blue shutters add a flash of colour to the fresh, whitewashed façade, while striking work by local artists is displayed in the salon and the bedrooms. Tranquillity reigns here – sleep deeply in wonderfully comfortable beds and pamper yourself with delicious Keiji products… Oléron is famous for seafood, particularly oysters and mussels; gourmands can indulge in regional specialities in the intimate dining room or eat al fresco in the luscious plant-filled courtyard. If you can bear to leave Jardins Alienor, the island is crisscrossed with footpaths and cycleways, and framed by sandy beaches where you can take to the water on a surfboard, sailing boat or canoe. Back on the mainland, admire Royan's Belle Epoque villas or take a day-trip to La Rochelle.

| Rooms | 7 doubles: €110-€140. |
| | 1 family room for 3: €180. |
| Meals | Dinner €26-€49. |
| Closed | Rarely. |

**Laetitia Le Reun**
Jardins Alienor, 7-11 rue Maréchal Foch,
17480 Le Château d'Oléron,
Charente-Maritime

| Tel | +33 (0)5 46 76 48 30 |
| Email | lesjardinsdalienor@wanadoo.fr |
| Web | www.lesjardinsdalienor.com |

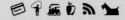

## Eden Ouest

This fabulous building, built in 1745, stands in the old heart of La Rochelle. An immense amount of thought has gone into its renovation, and manager Lise is brimming with ideas as to how they can go the extra mile. Each of the three floors have large windows with pale blue shutters; a balcony runs the length of the first. Sweep up grand stairs to a marble fireplace and muted grey walls, a long polished dining table and a rococo-esque chandelier. Bedrooms are colour coordinated right down to the paintings; most have sofabeds for children, all but one have beautiful bath tubs crafted from wood, and one bathroom's doors open to a patio and salty sea air. Breakfast can be taken in the grand dining room or the courtyard garden when warm: locally sourced treats from markets and artisan shops – traditional breads, croissants, fruit salad, yogurts, three different types of honey... Tread the ancient cobbles, discover an array of interesting shops, restaurants and historic buildings, sample the local apéritifs. The old port is a short stroll – sit and watch the world go by, catch a boat to the marvellous Ile de Ré. *Cot and high chair available.*

| | |
|---|---|
| Rooms | 4 doubles: €125–€255. |
| | 1 suite for 2: €170–€255. |
| | Extra bed €25. |
| Meals | Restaurants 2-minute walk. |
| Closed | Never. |

**Bertrand Patoureau & Lise Humeau**
Eden Ouest,
33 rue Thiers, 17000 La Rochelle,
Charente-Maritime

| | |
|---|---|
| Tel | +33 (0)6 82 62 68 97 |
| Email | contact@edenouest.com |
| Web | www.edenouest.com |

## Maison des Algues

In a residential area, behind private gates on the outskirts of Rivedoux Plage, is a modern single-storey hotel, whitewashed, shuttered and impeccably maintained. The design and the décor have been carefully considered and calm reigns supreme. Nothing is too much trouble for delightful Christian and Jocelyne, who will pick you up from the airport and insist on giving you the best: snowy towels for the bathroom, coloured towels for the pool, delicious pâtisseries for tea. Christian is proud to be a founding member of the Ile de Ré cricket club – hence the cricket pitch in the garden. Guest bedrooms, which open to a smart wicker-chaired terrace, are roomy, restful, flooded with light. After breakfast at 9am – no earlier please, you're here to unwind – slope off to a cushioned sunbed by the pool, spotlessly clean and heated to 28 degrees. Or spin off on a bike (there are ten, in tip-top condition and free of charge) and acquaint yourself with the island: the hollyhocks and whitewashed houses of villages like La Flotte, the fabulous white sand beaches, the chic shops and markets of St Martin. *Minimum stay: 2 nights in high season.*

| | |
|---|---|
| Rooms | 3 doubles ("Saccharine" and "Wakame" interconnect), 2 suites for 2: €125-€215. |
| Meals | Guest kitchen. Restaurants 10-minute walk. |
| Closed | Rarely. |

**Christian & Jocelyne Gatta-Boucard**
147 rue des Algues, 17940 Rivedoux
(Ile de Ré), Charente-Maritime

| | |
|---|---|
| Tel | +33 (0)5 46 68 01 23 |
| Mobile | +33 (0)6 88 48 35 80 |
| Email | information@maison-des-algues.com |
| Web | www.maison-des-algues.com |

Entry 199   Map 8

## Hôtel de l'Océan

A hotel of contrasts: big yet small; hotel and restaurant; perspex by thick curtains; Mediterranean by the Atlantic. The new owners, the delightful Anne and Frédéric, her happy-chef husband, have been running the highly regarded restaurant at L'Océan for ten years. Having left Paris to bring their children up in cleaner air and live a less frenzied life, they now feel completely at home on Ile de Ré and love pointing guests towards its treasures. Set back from the street in a quiet little town, the Océan has 29 bedrooms in sixes and sevens, each cluster with individual flavour, some round a courtyard pungent with rosemary and lavender, some tiny cottages among the hollyhocks. Children love the curtained cabin bed set in a buttercup-yellow alcove. Two new rooms in a wing are large and colonial looking, with super bathrooms (not all with showers) and a calm cool feel. Floors are covered in matting; ships, lighthouses and shells are dotted around against soothing colours. The dining room is another success in cream and palest green-grey. After your apéritif, dinner will involve fresh fish and herbs. *Beach 15-minute walk.*

| | |
|---|---|
| Rooms | 22 doubles, 4 twins: €85–€180. 2 triples: €137–€152. 1 quadruple: €199–€244. |
| Meals | Breakfast €10. Lunch & dinner €24–€50. Wine €14–€40. Restaurant closed Wednesday October–March. |
| Closed | January. |

**Anne & Frédéric Latour**
Hôtel de l'Océan, 172 rue St Martin,
17580 Le Bois Plage en Ré (Ile de Ré),
Charente-Maritime
Tel       +33 (0)5 46 09 23 07
Email   info@re-hotel-ocean.com
Web     www.re-hotel-ocean.com

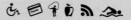

## La Baronnie Hôtel & Spa

A step away from the harbour, a listed monument and a beautiful manor are linked to make one special hotel. La Baronnie, the 'finest house on the island' is over 300 years old. Jasmine scents the air in the delicious cobbled courtyard, and a wooden structure houses a massage room, a jacuzzi, a sauna and small pool. Inside, a stunningly beautiful sideboard is laden with breakfast goodies, from just-squeezed juices to an array of coffees, while an ornate iron staircase sweeps you up to big light bedrooms exuding country chic, finely tuned in gorgeous colours. Imagine pale rugs, thick curtains, elegant cushions, and antiques picked up in brocantes over the years. Some rooms overlook a courtyard and the quietest face the gardens, which are magnificent. Adorable Florence, the ever-attentive owner, knows her island well, its nature and history, its beaches, cycle paths, sand dunes and pines: she helped lead the rise in St Martin's popularity. Perfect for a spoiling weekend – or more: the little town teems with chic shops, restaurants, bars and atmosphere. *Private parking €20 per day.*

| | |
|---|---|
| Rooms | 15 doubles: €149-€399. |
| | 1 suite for 2: €249-€399. |
| | 6 family rooms for 4: €204-€439. |
| | Extra bed/sofabed available €25-€45 |
| | per person per night. |
| Meals | Breakfast €18. |
| | Restaurants 5-minute walk. |
| Closed | 1 November to 24 March. |

**Florence Pallardy**
La Baronnie Hôtel & Spa, 17-21 rue
Baron de Chantal, 17410 St Martin de
Ré (Ile de Ré), Charente-Maritime

| | |
|---|---|
| Tel | +33 (0)5 46 09 21 29 |
| Email | info@hotel-labaronnie.com |
| Web | www.hotel-labaronnie.com |

# Aquitaine

## Château Bellevue-Gazin

This jaunty turn-of-the-century seaside villa ('château' comes with wine making…) set high above the Gironde, is all about light. Sit in the conservatory or on the terrace and drink in the vast westward view down the vineyards and across the estuary. The older *chai* is more in the long low style of nearby farm buildings. Explore the estuary by boat, cross over to the Médoc, or go bird-watching. The house is furnished entirely with antiques and decorated with paintings by Anne-Sophie's talented film-maker and artist relations. The splendid living room/kitchen, all for guests, invites relaxation and informality. Bedrooms have huge views and minimal furniture but you may find a cabin trunk with labels for your collars and studs, or a vast 18th-century armoire from Bergerac, or merely a 1930's hatstand shaped like a bag of golf clubs. Anne-Sophie is an art historian, Alain a civil engineer who made his first wine with grapes bought in the market in Libya; he's come a long way. They keep miniature Falabella horses and both speak excellent English. You will learn a great deal from this engaging couple.

| Rooms | 1 double, 1 twin/double, 1 family room for 3 (all en suite); 1 family room for 4, 1 family room for 3 sharing bathroom: €57–€77. Additional person €15. |
|---|---|
| Meals | Restaurant 3km. |
| Closed | Rarely. |

**Alain & Anne-Sophie Lancereau**
Château Bellevue-Gazin,
5 route de Montuzet,
33390 Plassac, Gironde

| Tel | +33 (0)5 57 42 02 00 |
|---|---|
| Email | bellevuegazin@aol.com |
| Web | www.chateau-bellevue-gazin.fr |

## Château l'Hospital

Vineyards surround the Duhamels' 15th-century Girondine home and Bruno is keen to show you around and share his passion for their Côtes de Bourg reds (if you favour organic wines, take a crate home). He's also in charge of breakfasts – honey, fresh orange juice, homemade brioche, homemade jams – served at one table, indoors or on the covered terrace; drink in the long views. Then take the ferry across the Gironde estuary and in 45 minutes you're in the world of Médoc wines, or drive from the house south: Bordeaux is 30 minutes away. This is an excellent base for the whole of the wine region. Bedrooms are spotless and spacious – no frills, no surprises! – with gleaming new floors and new windows; the suite is a long room divided in two by an archway and steps, and the bathrooms, smart and contemporary, are stocked with handmade soaps. It's peaceful here, with lovely walks through six hectares of vines, there's golf and tennis nearby, cycling routes aplenty, and the nearest restaurants are in Bourg and Blaye, 6km away. But if you don't fancy the drive, dinner can be arranged, with terroir wines, of course, taking pride of place.

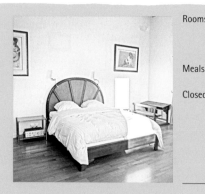

| | |
|---|---|
| Rooms | 1 double with sofa bed: €79-€89. 1 suite for 2 with sofabed in separate room: €79-€89. Singles €69-€72. Extra person €10. |
| Meals | Dinner with wine, €25-€35; children's menu available. |
| Closed | 15 September to 15 October. |

**Christine & Bruno Duhamel**
Château l'Hospital,
33710 St Trojan,
Gironde
Tel     +33 (0)5 57 64 33 60
Email   alvitis@wanadoo.fr
Web     www.alvitis.fr

## L'Hôtel Particulier

In beautiful Bordeaux – a city abuzz with bistro-brasseries and chic boutiques – it's hard to believe such a place could exist: a sanctum of peace behind closed doors. And what doors! Off the busy street, this classic Belle Epoque townhouse is entered via imposing barn-style doors that swing open into a quiet lawned quadrangle, a secret world. There are five guest rooms hidden away here, the quietest at the back: opulent boudoirs that ooze style and indulgence. Ornate fireplaces and polished floors line spacious rooms rendered light and bright by tall, throw-open windows – nature's air con. One has a leafy balcony and delightful mouldings, another comes with its own conservatory. Philippe Starck had a hand in two of the bathrooms, but all have chunky double basins, downy robes and designer fittings. Breakfast is a flexible, communal affair of fresh fruit and local croissants overseen by generous, humorous Alizée and her daughter. The big traditional living room doesn't host dinners – yet. But Bordeaux's mind-boggling array of eateries is on the doorstep.

| Rooms | 2 doubles: €189–€199. |
| | 1 suite for 2, 1 suite for 3: €239–€299. |
| | 1 single: €189–€199. |
| Meals | Breakfast €12. |
| | Restaurants 5-minute walk. |
| Closed | Rarely. |

**Alizée San José**
L'Hôtel Particulier,
44 rue Vital Carles,
33000 Bordeaux, Gironde

| Tel | +33 (0)5 57 88 28 80 |
| Email | info@lhotel-particulier.com |
| Web | www.lhotel-particulier.com |

## Château Lestange

We are full of admiration for Eric and Anne-Marie, who keep this proud old place and its vineyards afloat. They are the loveliest hosts, serving big bountiful breakfasts and welcoming guests as friends. As for the château, built in 1645 and 'modernised' after the Revolution, its charm is undeniable, its paintwork clean and relatively new. Beautiful wooden floors, pale panelled walls, crystal chandeliers and family furniture create a lived-in feel, and the very private family suites (furnished with mirrors and portraits Anne-Marie is still unearthing from the attic) are capacious. One faces a sweet, formal French garden, the other fills with morning sunshine and overlooks the vines. Or stay in the treehouse and hear owls at dusk. Elegant rugs top wooden floors, pretty curtains hang at tall windows, bathrooms are incongruously modern and antiques shine. Wake to breakfast in a vast room before a gilded mirror, then head for Arcachon for boat trips and oysters. Or splendid old Bordeaux, a 15-minute drive – you can see the city skyline from the tranquillity of the château grounds. *Pets by arrangement.*

| | |
|---|---|
| Rooms | 2 family suites for 3: €120–€180. |
| | 1 triple: €120. |
| | 1 family suite can be booked with |
| | triple: €200 per night. |
| Meals | Dinner: set menu €25; |
| | saveur menu €50; book in advance. |
| Closed | Rarely. |

**Anne-Marie Charmet**
Château Lestange,
33360 Quinsac, Gironde

| | |
|---|---|
| Tel | +33 (0)5 56 20 86 14 |
| Mobile | +33 (0)6 73 00 86 19 |
| Email | charmet@chateau-lestange.com |
| Web | www.chateau-lestange.com |

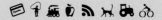

## Domaine de l'Espelette

Madame is happy to serve breakfast until two o'clock; in this haven, she's used to guests oversleeping! The very old house, at the end of a short avenue, sits solidly around two sides of a square below the brow of a hill sheltered by trees; you overlook the sleepy Romanesque village of Haux and its church. Here live three generations: delightful Madame, her two grandchildren, and her sprightly mother – along with horses, a donkey and two cats. Thick walls ensure you won't hear a sound, and you share the living room and the library. Furnishings are traditional, of good quality and character, with touches of marquetry and chintz; books, paintings, magazines abound. There are three spacious bedrooms to choose from, one off the garden, two off the landing (invitingly furnished with books and rattan chairs). Bathrooms are carpeted and generous, with marble basins. As for the garden, it is more of a 'parc joli'. Take a picnic to the stream, swim in the shaded (unheated) pool. For a simple lunch, stroll to the village bar; for shops, restaurants and market, discover Créon. Lovely. *Minimum stay: 2 nights. Over 12s welcome.*

| Rooms | 3 twin/doubles: €100–€150. |
| Meals | Restaurant 1.5km. |
| Closed | 15 August & December/January. |

Silvia Prevost
Domaine de l'Espelette, Route de
Chaumont, 33550 Haux, Gironde

| Tel | +33 (0)5 56 23 37 36 |
| Mobile | +33 (0)6 63 82 01 78 |
| Email | contact@domainedelespelette.com |
| Web | www.domainedelespelette.com |

## Château de Castelneau

A grand distance from the road: a heavenly 14th-century château with Provençal towers. Behind: a shuttered 17th-century façade, a courtyard with outbuildings and an avenue lined with young trees. All around, 100 hectares of vines. The de Roquefeuils are an enthusiastic couple, warm, intelligent and good company, working their socks off to make the estate pay (the claret is delicious!). Guests stay on the upper floor of one of the outbuildings, in bedrooms simple, comfortable and traditional. Floors are carpeted, walls are patterned or plain, bathrooms are functional (showers over baths) and up the tower staircase is a furnished landing with videos for early risers. Downstairs are stone flags, rugs, books, paintings, eclectic aristocratic furnishings. Breakfasts, generous and delicious, are served at an octagonal table before the great chimney breast where winter fires blaze. Outside: a swing slung from the trees, a big grassy area for children to enjoy and a sunny pool behind the chai. Take a tour of the cellars (fascinating), then plunge into the wines of Bordeaux and Saint-Emilion.

| | |
|---|---|
| Rooms | 1 twin/double: €105–€140. 1 suite for 3: €105–€150. |
| Meals | Restaurants 2km. Guests have use of kitchen & barbecue. |
| Closed | Rarely. |

Loïc & Diane de Roquefeuil
Château de Castelneau,
8 route de Breuil, Lieu-dit Châteauneuf,
33670 St Léon, Gironde
Tel      +33 (0)5 56 23 47 01
Email   dianederoquefeuil@gmail.com
Web    www.chateaudecastelneau.com

## Château Lamothe du Prince Noir

A charming quiet spot, convenient for Bordeaux and Saint-Emilion, and a secret castle complete with a moat upon which two white swans and two black swans float. How romantic! It's a family affair: Nicole, husband Ollie (a keen cook) and mother Carla – with help from friendly dog, Lady – greet guests with an apéritif on arrival and delicious dinners on request. Much has already been cleverly restored, some work remains, but the style is light and restrained; stripped and polished floors, Persian rugs, tapestries and Empire side tables. Sleep peacefully in big bedrooms, soak in generous free-standing baths, wake to breakfast served on white linen in the dining room or on the south facing terrace. Wander the garden at will to find hundreds of new trees planted for colour (maple, mimosa, magnolia) but also for fruit (nectarine, peach, plum). Plans are afoot for a kitchen garden, and hens. Visit Bordeaux, picnic on wide beaches, play golf or book a local wine tasting. There's masses to do in gorgeous surroundings, but you may find it hard to tear yourself away from the pages of the fairy tale you've landed in.

| | |
|---|---|
| Rooms | 4 suites for 2 (child's room available across corridor): €190–€235.<br>1 family room for 3-5: €270-€315.<br>Dogs €15 per night. |
| Meals | Light supper with wine, €45.<br>Restaurant 5-minute drive. |
| Closed | Rarely. |

Carla Sobral
Château Lamothe du Prince Noir,
6 route du Stade,
33450 St Sulpice & Cameyrac, Gironde

Tel     +33 (0)5 56 44 91 21
Email   info@lechateaulamothe.com
Web     www.lechateaulamothe.com

## Château de la Vieille Chapelle

A long, leafy lane brings you to a secluded and sumptuous estate, its backdrop sweeping vineyards and raw 12th-century stone – a viticulteur's rambling domain with spacious rooms and an enormous day/living room like a baronial hall, which you are welcome to use. It's an idyllic retreat, a perfect balance of shabby and chic, with every excuse to stay in rather than go out. Each river-view bedroom (one in the house, two adjacent with your own doors onto the front yard) is comfortable and fairly minimalist with cool stone walls (heaven in the heat) and scatter rugs. Bathrooms have walk in wet room showers, with loos hidden behind tiled walls. In the château's galleried dining room, the discreet Madame Mallier serves breakfasts of pastries and cheese and fruit, but bacon and eggs too if you want. Later, book a light meal or full dinner – Madame will join you if kitchen time permits. She can organise an exclusive tour of their renowned cellars. Explore the vineyards, fish, recline, visit colourful local village markets, and let yourself be hypnotised by the fast-running (but unfenced) river and the beauty of glorious Bordeaux.

| | |
|---|---|
| Rooms | 3 doubles (2 in outbuildings): €85. Singles €80. Extra bed/sofabed available €20 per person per night. |
| Meals | Dinner €16-€25. Wine €6.40-€35. |
| Closed | Rarely. |

Fabienne & Frédéric Mallier
4 Chapelle, 33240 Lugon & l'Ile du Carnay
Tel      +33 (0)5 57 84 48 65
Mobile   +33 (0)6 17 98 19 56
Email    best-of-bordeaux-wine@chateau-de-la-vieille-chapelle.com
Web      www.chateau-de-la-vieille-chapelle.com

## Château Claud-Bellevue

On the edge of a sleepy village (no shops, no bars, just blessed silence), a 17th-century priory which was once the house of the Prior of Belvès. Since then it has been a convent, hence the private lych gate to the church. Mellow stone walls are lapped by neatly groomed lawns and gravel paths; a central fountain plays; beyond are 10 hectares of vines. Your hosts, new to chambres d'hôtes and full of plans, give you an effusive welcome and delicious air-conditioned rooms: gilt-edged prints on rustic walls and goosedown as soft as a cloud. A sitting room is kitted out with plenty of comfy sofas and wing chairs, a large fridge is filled with a variety of soft drinks on the house and there's a wide screen TV for those who cannot be torn away. The treats continue at breakfast for Madame is cordon-bleu trained; expect cheeses, fruits, charcuterie and homemade breads, granola and conserves – all served on the terrace or in the breakfast room. Order dinner in (your host eats with you) or hop in the car to Castillon or Libourne for a choice of restaurants. Take a private tour of their own château, discover the wines of Saint Emilion. *Minimum stay: 2 nights.*

| | |
|---|---|
| Rooms | 2 doubles, 1 twin/double: €135–€150. |
| Meals | Light dinner with wine, €40. Afternoon tea included. Restaurants 3km. Private kitchen for guests. |
| Closed | Never. |

**Ana Bockmeulen**
Château Claud-Bellevue,
31 le Bourg,
33350 Belvès de Castillon, Gironde

| | |
|---|---|
| Tel | +33 (0)5 57 49 48 23 |
| Email | abockmeulen@mac.com |
| Web | www.chateauclaudbellevue.com |

Entry 210   Map 9

## Château de Carbonneau

Big château bedrooms bathed in light, a Napoleon III conservatory for quiet contemplation, gentle pastels over classic dados and big bathrooms gleaming with rich tiles – here is a quiet, self-assured family house and readers are full of praise. Good quality comes naturally, history abounds and there's space aplenty for a dozen guests. Outside are delightful grounds with a big fenced pool and 50 hectares of farmland, some of it planted with vines under the appellation Sainte Foy Bordeaux. The rest are used as grazing land for a small herd of Blondes d'Aquitaine cattle. Visit Wilfred's winery and taste the talent handed down by his forebears; you may leave with a case or two. Jacquie, a relaxed but dynamic New Zealander, makes the meals, wields a canny paintbrush and has created a guest sitting room with two smart linen sofas and guidebooks aplenty. Breakfast is served on the main terrace in summer and Jacquie's dinners, enjoyed with the other guests, sound most tempting – she's also recently opened a salon de thé!

| Rooms | 2 doubles, 3 twin/doubles: €90–€145. |
| Meals | Dinner €30. Wine €8–€20. |
| Closed | December – February. |

**Jacquie & Wilfrid Franc de Ferrière**
Château de Carbonneau,
33890 Pessac sur Dordogne, Gironde
Tel     +33 (0)5 57 47 46 46
Mobile  +33 (0)6 83 30 14 35
Email   carbonneau@orange.fr
Web     www.chateau-carbonneau.com

## Château Le Mas de Montet

A nose for fine living brought new owners Paul and Lise to this happy place. At the end of an avenue guarded by plane trees – serenely, gloriously French – is the château, slate-topped and turretted in Renaissance style. Once frequented by Mitterrand and his labradors, it has since been extravagantly restored. Doors open in summer to a big terrace and 50 hectares of parkland with pool, while reception rooms lined with eau-de-nil brocade are sated with auction house finds. Richness and softness bring instant seduction and bedrooms, named after 'Corneille', 'Voltaire', 'Madame de Lafayette', have all you'd hope for the price. The owners do their utmost to make you feel welcome: beds are big and supremely comfortable, four-posters canopied and draped, and bathrooms are Deco-white… the one in the tower has its own chandelier. Paul and Lise adore their garden and house, happily sharing it with you, and also give you a jolly good breakfast. Grand yet easy, uncommercial and full of charm, this is a brilliant place for stressed city souls to unwind.

| Rooms | 4 doubles, 1 twin: €118–€148. |
|---|---|
| | 5 suites for 2: €148–€268. |
| | 2 cottages for 2: €650–€1,200 per week. |
| | Extra bed/sofabed available €25 per person per night. |
| Meals | Breakfast €15. Picnic available. |
| | Restaurant 1km. |
| Closed | 1 November to 1 April. |

**Paul Cavaleiro & Lise Daneels**
Château Le Mas de Montet,
Petit Bersac,
24600 Ribérac, Dordogne

| | |
|---|---|
| Tel | +33 (0)5 53 90 08 71 |
| Email | lemasdemontet@gmail.com |
| Web | www.lemasdemontet.com |

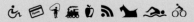

## Château de la Côte

This spectacular 15th-century château has been owned and run by the same charming family since the last century. Travel past golden sunflower fields and the château emerges regally through a forested hilltop. The interior oozes aged grandeur – original stonewalls, wood panelling, a suit of armour in the hall, and huge fireplaces in almost all the rooms. Bedrooms are old-fashioned but impressive with antiques and numerous four-posters to choose from; bathrooms reflect the age of the building (sometimes slightly eccentric but always spotless). Ask for a room in the tower if you don't mind stairs; one has a fabulous private roof terrace – leading up from the bathroom! Views are panoramic. Dinner is a fixed simple menu of local specialities (quite expensive), and a continental breakfast can be taken in the 'tower room' or on the front lawn. Enjoy an aperitif or local wine under an ancient tree and admire the rolling countryside. There's also a pool, children's play area and a secret arbor within the twenty acres of grounds. A wonderful retreat full of character – come for history, romancing, rambling and exploring the Dordogne. *Min. stay: 2 nights, 3 at weekends & high season.*

| | |
|---|---|
| Rooms | 10 doubles: €108–€136. 7 suites for 2: €154–€225. Singles €80–€90. Dinner, B&B €102–€160 per person. Extra bed/sofabed available €15–€25 per person per night. |
| Meals | Breakfast €14–€19. Dinner €29–€59; children's menu €12–€25. Restaurants 3-minute drive. |
| Closed | 15 November to 25 December & 5 January to 15 March. |

**Michel & Olivier Guillaume**
Château de la Côte,
Lieu-dit La Côte,
24310 Brantôme, Dordogne

| | |
|---|---|
| Tel | +33 (0)5 53 03 70 11 |
| Email | contact@chateaudelacote.com |
| Web | www.chateau-hotel-dordogne.com |

## Le Chatenet

Layers of history are here. Brantôme has been home to man since prehistoric times; the grand Benedictine abbey, carved out at the bottom of the cliffs, overlooks the ribbon of the river Dronne that slowly rings the town. Just up the road, a perfect distance from the hustle and bustle, is Le Chatenet, a Périgord-style stone house built at the end of the 17th century. Jane and William are super hosts. Jane will show you the sundial they found under the roof marked 1688, William will point the way to the hidden canopy of trees over a path which leads to the centre of town in a ten-minute stroll. Or you may just want to sit on the stone veranda and follow the sun as it sinks pinkly over the walnut trees and the green valleys. There are big rooms with stunning fabric on the walls, billiards in the games room, rivers to be canoed and grottoes to be explored. There is even a farm down the street with rabbits, chickens and cows, source of your breakfast eggs and milk. Brantôme's bell tower is thought to be one of the oldest in France; they say it must be seen from the inside. Add an extra day, you won't regret it.

| Rooms | 3 twin/doubles: €110–€135. |
|---|---|
| | 2 suites for 2: €150–€195. |
| | Extra bed €25. |
| Meals | Breakfast €12. Dinner from €30. |
| | Wine from €25. Restaurant 1km. |
| Closed | Mid-October to mid-April. |

Jane & William Laxton
Le Chatenet,
Lieu-dit Le Chatenet,
24310 Brantôme, Dordogne

| Tel | +33 (0)5 53 05 81 08 |
|---|---|
| Email | lechatenet@gmail.com |
| Web | www.lechatenet.com |

## Château de Villars

View the château from a teak pool lounger, iced drink in hand: views swoop to forests as far as the eye can see, there's comfort in abundance and old combines with new. Light pours into every room of this neo-classical 'petit château', and the attention to detail is superb. Browse books from the library, relax in the sitting room or on the marvellous terrace with views, enjoy the gym and massage salon too. Bedrooms are immaculate, each with its own style and décor. For self-caterers, tucked between trees, there's a splendid summerhouse on site, and an 18th-century village townhouse too. Breakfast is enjoyed at the long banqueting table or on the terrace, while the owners' love of fine food and wine is expressed in seasonal menus. Only the best fresh produce is used, sourced locally or from the kitchen garden. Dip into the pool, hop on one of the bikes and explore, visit the 13th-century Château de Puyguilhem or the market at watery Brantôme. Or stroll into the picturesque village and capture the feel of a French way of life. *Minimum stay: 2 nights.*

| Rooms | 5 doubles: €125–€165. |
| | 2 houses for 4: €695–€1,495 per week. |
| Meals | Dinner €32–€36. Wine €11–€35. |
| | Restaurants 2-minute walk. |
| Closed | November to mid–April. |

**Bill Davies & Kevin Saunders**
Château de Villars, Près de la Cure,
24530 Villars, Dordogne

| Tel | +33 (0)5 53 03 41 58 |
| Mobile | +33 (0)6 83 26 03 95 |
| Email | chateauvillars@aol.com |
| Web | www.gofranceholiday.com |

## La Commanderie

The setting is special indeed, off a medieval street in a charming hamlet. Go through a stone archway, across generous parkland, beneath majestic trees into the steep-roofed *commanderie*. Here, the Knights of the Order of Malta put up 700 years ago en route to Santiago de Compostela and a low curved toll passage still forms part of the house. It is not so much a hotel as a houseful of guests overseen by diminutive Madame Roux, a considerate, welcoming hostess. An uncontrived collection of antiques warms the friendly bedrooms, each with its own personality on a blue and white theme punctuated by touches of dark blue; ceilings soar, floors of varying ages and diverse patterns are softened by Indian rugs. Downstairs, guests gather at round tables set with antique cane chairs, flowery curtains hang at tall windows, marble busts abound and you get two choices per gastronomic course – just right for this unassuming and atmospheric place. A delightful stone rill snakes through the grass to the pond and the Lascaux Caves are a mile down the road. Great value for what you get, and that includes very good, classic French food.

| | |
|---|---|
| Rooms | 5 doubles, 2 twins: €95. |
| Meals | Breakfast €10. Lunch €22. Dinner €25-€48. Restaurant closed Mondays. |
| Closed | Rarely. |

**Madame Annick Roux**
La Commanderie,
1 place du Verdier, 24570 Condat sur
Vézère, Dordogne
Tel      +33 (0)5 53 51 26 49
Email   hotellacommanderie@wanadoo.fr
Web     www.hotel-lacommanderie.com

## Auberge de Castel-Merle

High above the valley of the Vézère – with peerless views from the terrace – is an atmospheric inn where a Templar castle once stood. It has been in Anita's family for generations, her archaeologist grandfather adding stones from his own digs (Les Eyzies, the capital of prehistory, is nearby). Gentle, helpful and full of good stories, she and Christopher love the place. Years ago they renovated the buildings with great care, keeping the traditional look, and using walnut wood from their own land to restore bed heads and doors. Pastel, pelmets and painted flowers on the walls clothe the dining room; modest, darkish bedrooms in country style have beams, stone walls and wooden floors, there's a bright boutis throw on every bed and shower rooms are curtain'd and compact. Some rooms overlook the courtyard, others the woods. Christopher is an enthusiastic truffle hunter and a wonderful cook, wild boar being one of his specialities; Anita makes beautiful cakes. The hamlet is charming – you can walk to it – and the forest hiking is a joy. Great value.

| Rooms | 7 doubles, 1 twin: €77-€82. |
|---|---|
| Meals | Dinner €19-€30. Wine €9-€28. Picnic available. Restaurant closed lunchtime & Sunday evenings. |
| Closed | 2 October to 4 April. |

**Anita Castanet & Christopher Millinship**
Auberge de Castel-Merle,
24290 Sergeac, Dordogne
Tel     +33 (0)5 53 50 70 08
Email   hotelcastelmerle@yahoo.fr
Web     www.hotelcastelmerle.com

## Manoir d'Hautegente

The ancient manor, first a smithy, later a mill, has been in the family for 300 years but is paradoxically just 50 years old: burned down in the Second World War, it was rebuilt. The millstream has become a fabulous waterfall feeding a pond that shimmers beneath the bedroom windows and the thoroughly kempt garden is a riot of colour. Hautegente is rich inside too with sumptuous dining rooms clothed in silk and hung with well-chosen paintings and prints, though of course you can eat out on the terrace-with-views too — even with your back to the millpond you can see it through ingenious mirrors. There's a cosy drawing room where a large fireplace and a vast array of cognacs summon the sybarite. Lavishly decorated bedrooms have fine thick curtains, antiques and pretty lamps; some are small, some enormous and the soft, expensive feel of padded wall fabrics contrasts with the lovely old staircase leading up from the hall. The rooms in the converted miller's house are more modern; four have mezzanines and the ground-floor room is vast. Bathrooms are all beautifully tiled and properly equipped. A splendid and peaceful place.

| Rooms | 12 doubles: €95–€272. |
|---|---|
| | 5 triples: €224–€272. |
| | Dinner, B&B €111–€288 per person. |
| | Extra bed/sofabed available €25 per person per night. |
| Meals | Breakfast €16; |
| | children's menu €6–€12. |
| | Dinner €49–€110. |
| | Restaurants within walking distance. |
| Closed | Mid-October to 1 May. |

**Patrick & Marie Josée Hamelin**
Manoir d'Hautegente,
Domaine d'Hautegente,
24120 Coly, Dordogne
Tel       +33 (0)5 53 51 68 03
Email    hotel@manoir-hautegente.com
Web      www.manoir-hautegente.com

Entry 218   Map 9

## La Villa Romaine

Smiling, helpful staff will welcome you to the 18th-century farmhouse and its two outbuildings, planted solidly in the ground. Glowing in the sun, these limestone walls enclose a vast courtyard that leads down to an infinity pool – and a wow of a view sweeping the eye over dark forests, green hills, and a village perched on a cliff above the river. Plumb in the middle of the courtyard, a lovely open-sided structure calls you for drinks, a quiet read, or even work; it's the old Halle aux Saumons (salmon market) – we can now only imagine the river below running silver with fish. Fine dining is the attraction here (foie gras, ravioli, veal…) as well as the long, cool, beamed restaurant itself with its bar in one corner and medley of armchairs draped in fashionably greige linen beckoning from the comfortable little sitting area. Crisp white cloths set off sparkling table settings; French windows open to the terrace. Bedrooms, some in the outbuildings, some above the restaurant, are huge; the two-room family suite sleeps six. A choice of eight breakfast teas might give a clue to what is in store. A classy place.

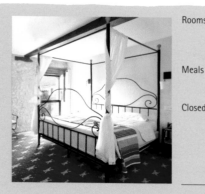

| Rooms | 12 twin/doubles: €125–€175. 1 suite for 2-4, 1 suite for 4-6: €205–€320. 3 triples: €175–€205. |
|---|---|
| Meals | Breakfast €13–€15. Dinner from €32. Restaurant closed mid-November to April. |
| Closed | Never. |

**David Vacelet & Emilie Velut**
La Villa Romaine,
St Rome,
24200 Carsac Aillac, Dordogne

Tel       +33 (0)5 53 28 52 07
Email   contact@lavillaromaine.com
Web     www.lavillaromaine.com

## Manoir de la Malartrie

On the banks of the Dordogne river, a beautifully restored 19th-century manor house with luxurious rooms and a cosy, beamed gîte – an idyllic retreat for sybarites. Inside, charming Ouafaa has blended Moroccan style with Edwardian elegance. Sleep in sumptuous bedrooms, with lovely views and furnished with antiques; treat yourselves in ample bathrooms with dressing gowns and Hermes toiletries. You'll eat well in the magnificent salon or outside on balmier evenings, on Franco-Moroccan meals made with fresh veg from the potager; seldom is there duck, although foie gras with Moroccan spices does appear on the menu. You can also picnic in the grounds or use a small kitchen next to the salon. There's a sleek pool and magnificent gardens with steep slopes to the north bank of the river so you can watch boats sail by, many paths which meander hither and thither among the rosemary, lavender and olive trees, and small terraces, each with their own seating area. Explore grand châteaux or stroll to pretty La Roque-Gageac for shops and restaurants. *Minimum stay: 3 nights. Heated pool available May-October.*

| | | |
|---|---|---|
| Rooms | 4 doubles (1 with terrace): €110–€160. 1 suite for 4: €200–€260. 1 apartment for 2-4: €140–€260. Sofabeds available €30 per night. |  |
| Meals | Dinner with wine & appetizer, €50; available on request for 8 people or more. Restaurants 5-minute walk. | |
| Closed | Mid-December to mid-March (except pre-booked Christmas parties). | |

Ouafaa Diebolt-Balbal
Manoir de la Malartrie,
La Malartrie,
24220 Vézac, Dordogne

| | |
|---|---|
| Tel | +33 (0)5 53 29 03 51 |
| Email | lamalartrie@orange.fr |
| Web | www.manoir-lamalartrie.com |

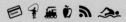

## La Métairie

If you love horses you'll be in your element: you can relax on the terrace and watch them in the next field. You can also ride close by. La Métairie was built as a farm at the beginning of the last century and converted into a 'boutique' hotel some 40 years ago, a U-shaped building smothered in wisteria and Virginia creeper. There's no road in sight and you really do feel away from it all – yet the Dordogne and its clifftop villages are minutes away. Borrow bikes if you're feeling energetic! Bedrooms are charming, cheerful and full of sunshiney yellows and huge beds. They have room for a couple of comfy chairs, too. Bathrooms match – big and bright – and three ground-floor rooms have French windows and a semi-private patio. The pool is big enough for a proper swim and when you come out you can read under the trees that wait for you by the pool. In summer you can eat out here, or on the flowery terrace. The dining room has black and white floors, washed stone walls and well-spaced tables. Go ahead, indulge, order the four-course *menu Périgourdin*. You can swim it off later. Delightful staff, too.

| Rooms | 9 doubles: €135–€195. |
| --- | --- |
| | 1 suite for 2: €195–€330. |
| | Breakfast & dinner €55 per person. |
| | Extra bed/sofabed €35 per person per night. |
| Meals | Breakfast €18. Lunch €18–€50. |
| | Dinner €43–€58; |
| | Menu Périgourdin €55. |
| | Wine €25–€100. |
| Closed | November – March. |

R. & H. Johner & C. Bertschy
La Métairie,
24150 Mauzac & Grand Castang,
Dordogne

| Tel | +33 (0)5 53 22 50 47 |
| --- | --- |
| Email | metairie.la@wanadoo.fr |
| Web | www.la-metairie.com |

## Château Lalinde

Down a little backstreet in Lalinde is a small turreted 1269 château floating above the Dordogne – a fairytale idyll with bags of history. Interesting, calm, charismatic Wilna (born in South Africa, now France-based) is an unforgettable hostess – you could chat for hours! – and a passionate cook: continental yumminess at breakfast (fruit salad, yogurts, local pastries, homemade jams); traditional French dishes with a South African twist at dinner… what a wonderful way to meet her and fellow guests. Classic bedrooms, all with modern bathrooms, come in varying sizes: snug with sloping ceilings (at the top of a steep, spiral stone stair) or larger with balconies and views; one has a wonderful little sitting room in a turret. There's a cute garden and a pool overlooking the river, and a marvellous sitting room clad in 'tufa' stone: historic, cosy, inviting, with a grand fireplace and French windows to a terrace-balcony with magical views. The town is ancient, off the beaten track, delightful, with a weekly market. Bergerac and the Lascaux Caves are close. One of the loveliest places to stay in the Dordogne. *Minimum stay: 2 nights.*

| | |
|---|---|
| Rooms | 5 twin/doubles: €200–€240. Children under 2 stay free. Cot & high chair available at no extra cost. |
| Meals | Lunch, 3 courses, €25. Dinner, 4 courses with wine, €35. Restaurants 5-minute walk. |
| Closed | 1 November to 1 April. |

**Wilna Wilkinson**
Château Lalinde, 1 rue de Verdun,
24150 Lalinde, Dordogne

| | |
|---|---|
| Tel | +33 (0)5 53 22 80 94 |
| Mobile | +33 (0)6 89 38 68 22 |
| Email | twoxscotch@gmail.com |
| Web | www.chateaulalinde.com |

## Chartreuse le Cariol

Arrive on a summer evening at Irene and Marthijn's 12th-century estate house and you will likely hear the buzz of conversation around a laden dinner table. Or perhaps the tinkling of a grand piano from the artist's house. No other sounds, but plenty to see – starting with the bold paintings and sculptures Marthijn de Groot creates in his on-site studio. These artworks brighten the fresh, eclectic décor of the two guest rooms, living and dining rooms and library. A boutique vibe pervades: dark walls, floors and sofas; super-modern lighting; Indian grilles; a glass-topped stone table. Cosy bedrooms (one a generous family size) are on the ground floor, or downstairs by the wine cellar and sauna; both have state-of-the-art slate bathrooms. Step out to a terrace with open views, then wander down to a large swimming pool with a pool house and fire. You can spend all day here – it's that kind of place. Your hosts are a dynamic, creative family who love art, good food (sometimes a spontaneous dinner, maybe a chef) and conversation, and who will gladly point you to cultural events in nearby Beaumont and Bergerac. *Minimum stay: 2 nights, 3 nights in high season. Pets by arrangement.*

| | |
|---|---|
| Rooms | 1 suite for 2: €165. |
| | 1 family room for 5: €290. |
| | Extra bed/sofabed available €39 per person per night. |
| Meals | Dinner, 4 courses with wine, €34.50 (July/August). Restaurants 7km. |
| Closed | Rarely. |

**Irene de Groot**
Chartreuse le Cariol,
Le Cariol,
24440 Naussannes, Dordogne
Tel      +33 (0)5 53 63 97 07
Email    lecariol@icloud.com
Web      www.lecariol.com

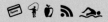

## Château Gauthié

Outside the bastide village of Issigeac is a Périgordian delight run by a young vibrant family. Stéphane has constructed two exotic treehouses, cooks brilliantly and loves wine; Florence is equally capable, equally charming. The dogs wag; the children, thanks to a boated lake in the grounds, live a Swallows and Amazons lifestyle. This is a place that families would adore, country lovers and birdwatchers too, and all those after peace and solitude. Four lofty, light-filled bedrooms, traditionally furnished and freshly white, are comfortable and restful, and bathrooms are spotless. Outside: an infinity pool overlooks the lake below, there's a hot tub to wallow in and the treehouses perch above, their decked balconies gazing over meadows and cows, their mother trees thrusting branches through the floor. Solar-lit paths lead one down through the trees at night, breakfast baskets are winched up in the morning. Visit Issigeac's Sunday market, sail off on the bikes, visit old Bergerac, come back to dinner, a four-course feast matched by a perfect choice of wines. *Minimum stay: 2 nights.*

| | |
|---|---|
| Rooms | 3 doubles, 1 twin: €90–€115. |
| | 1 treehouse for 2: €130–€175 per night. |
| | 1 treehouse for 5 |
| | (1 double, 3 singles; 1 week minimum |
| | in summer): €1,050–€1,540 per week. |
| Meals | Dinner, 4 courses with wine €40. |
| Closed | Mid-November to March. |

Florence & Stéphane Desmette
Château Gauthié,
24560 Issigeac Monmarvès,
Dordogne

| | |
|---|---|
| Tel | +33 (0)5 53 27 30 33 |
| Email | chateau.gauthie@laposte.net |
| Web | www.chateaugauthie.com |

## Hôtel Edward 1er

Some people lounge beside the pool on their honeymoon; Arjan and Marije, your delightful, hands-on hosts, went hotel hunting on theirs. And they found one: a handsome 19th-century turreted townhouse on the edge of a miraculously preserved 13th-century village, voted one of the most beautiful in France. Now they are well established and have seamlessly extended into an adjoining building. Herbs are from the garden, vegetables and fruit are local, fish hails from Bordeaux and Arcachon; everything is made here except bread and ice cream, supplied by artisans. After you have explored the fortified village – four sides set round the huge central square, the surrounding houses corbelled out with arches – further medieval bastides beckon: there are a dozen or so. Arjan has prepared bicycle itineraries and can point out the best place to paddle a canoe. Or you may just want to lounge by the deep-blue pool, honeymoon-style! Lushly comfortable rooms await.

| Rooms | 11 doubles, 6 twins: €67–€210. Singles €65–€118. Extra bed/sofabed available €22–€29 per person per night. |
|---|---|
| Meals | Breakfast €12. Dinner €29.50–€39.50. Wine €19–€50. |
| Closed | 30 November to 14 March. |

Arjan & Marije Capelle
Hôtel Edward 1er,
5 rue Saint Pierre,
24540 Monpazier, Dordogne
Tel       +33 (0)5 53 22 44 00
Email    info@hoteledward1er.com
Web     www.hoteledward1er.com

## Domaine du Moulin de Labique

Ducks on the pond, goats in the greenhouse and food *à la grand-mère* on the plate — the lovely Moulin de Labique glows with warmth and good humour. Shutters are painted with *bleu de pastel* and the 13th-century interiors have lost none of their charm. The Belgian owners, Christine and Patrick, share dinners (seasonal, local, delicious) in wonderfully relaxed fashion. Bedrooms are a match for the rest of the place and are divided between those in the main building above a vaulted *salle d'armes*, those in the barn, reached via a grand stone stair, and a suite in the old bread and prune-drying ovens. There are chunky roof beams, seagrass mats on ancient tiles, lovely old iron bedsteads, antique mirrors and papers sprigged in raspberry and jade green. One room has a balcony, the suite in the barn has a terrace, and some bathrooms have Portuguese tiles: there's much to captivate and delight. Outside, old French roses, young alleys of trees, a bamboo-fringed stream and an exquisite, child-safe pool. Book a long stay, and make time for tastings at the Monbazillac domaines.

| | |
|---|---|
| Rooms | 3 doubles, 2 twins: €110–€140. |
| | 1 suite for 4: €199. |
| | Dinner, B&B €83–€99 per person. |
| Meals | Dinner €31. Wine €16–€30. |
| Closed | Rarely. |

**Patrick & Christine Hendricx**
Domaine du Moulin de Labique,
St Vivien,
47210 Villeréal, Lot-et-Garonne
Tel    +33 (0)5 53 01 63 90
Email  moulin-de-labique@wanadoo.fr
Web    www.moulin-de-labique.net

## Domaine de Pine

Hidden among 52 acres of sunflower fields lies a beautifully proportioned stylish, intimate hotel – and a self-catering cottage, too. Built for a baron 200 years ago, it's been transformed by an English couple with impeccable taste into a haven of luxurious modern comfort including a heated pool, WiFi in every corner – and period style. Delicious breakfasts, light lunches and scrumptious dinners are served on fine white linen with freshly-cut garden flowers; enjoy elevated views from the terrace. Four elegant bedrooms (some air-conditioned) are large and light (the higher the lighter) with beams and great views; soft creams and whites dominate. In the bathrooms you'll find fluffy towels and dressing gowns. Summer calls for lazing on sumptuous loungers, happy hour is between five and six, and all this can be enjoyed by self-caterers, too. In winter visit the new fitness room then cosy up by a roaring fire and enjoy a candlelit supper in the blue and white dining room. Step out for medieval town markets or music festivals, or explore the estate – tons of choice. *Pets by arrangement.*

| | |
|---|---|
| Rooms | 3 doubles (2 rooms can interconnect): €99-€235. 1 suite for 4: €145-€190. Singles €79-€149. Dinner, B&B from €115 (for 1) & €180 (for 2). Extra bed/sofabed available €15 per person per night. |
| Meals | Lunch & dinner from €35. Restaurants 2-minute drive. |
| Closed | Rarely. |

Marcus & Cathy Becker
Domaine de Pine,
47470 Blaymont, Lot-et-Garonne
Tel     +33 (0)5 53 66 44 93
Mobile  +44 (0)7831 115599
Email   email@ddpine.com
Web     www.domainedepine.com

## Moulin de Larroque

In a beautiful corner of the Lot-et-Garonne, 90 minutes from Bordeaux, is a small special place housed in a watermill once used in the production of armagnac. Millstream and mill pond lie prettily behind; in front is a sweep of mown parkland and willows. Owned and run by a charming young couple, centred on a corridor off which five bedrooms lie, this small hotel is furnished in functional French style. It is aimed primarily at couples, with its classic bedrooms (all doubles, no twins), characterful colourful bathrooms and – very popular this! – indoor sauna, steam room and pool; spa towels and slippers are supplied. You are super-near the road to Barbaste (yet double-glazed against it) so can whisk into town for dinner. And you are wonderfully close to old Nérac. Glide under the historic Pont Vieux, treat yourself to armagnac-dipped cherries, and glistening produce at the market. The moulin has no communal space (bar a vast loft space for weddings and a breakfast room with smart tables) but the bedrooms, with their wooden floors and delicately patterned walls, are cosy and charming.

| | |
|---|---|
| Rooms | 5 doubles: €88–€119. Extra bed/sofabed available €20–€25 per person per night. |
| Meals | Breakfast €9. Restaurants 1.5km. |
| Closed | Rarely. |

**Béatrice & Jean-Philippe Guitton**
Moulin de Larroque,
47230 Barbaste, Lot-et-Garonne

| | |
|---|---|
| Tel | +33 (0)5 53 97 23 34 |
| Mobile | +33 (0)6 80 70 60 49 |
| Email | guitton.jean-philippe@wanadoo.fr |
| Web | www.moulin-larroque.com |

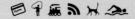

## Château de Baylac

The charming Darrigrands discovered their enchanting B&B in fairy tale style... Wandering through remote woodland, they stumbled upon an ancient château abandoned for decades. Restoring the neglected building became a labour of love for the whole family. It is still blissfully off the beaten track, only the bucolic sounds of deer and cows chewing the cud breaks the silence, but interiors are now fabulously stylish. Each bedroom has its own charm and character – from playful 'Vivaldi' to the minimalist chic of 'Perce-Neige', but all have big comfortable beds with good linen, plenty of space and bathrooms with dressing gowns and walk-in wet rooms. Breakfast is in the dining room at one large table or outside on sunny days, and can include bacon and eggs if you want – otherwise locally made jam and honey, freshly baked bread, ham and cheeses. Dinner will be fresh and regional – Madame comes from a farming family so ingredients will only be the best – and served beneath sparkling chandeliers. Explore Béarn on horseback or from a hot air balloon, wander colourful markets, fish, hike, sail and even ski

| | |
|---|---|
| Rooms | 2 doubles: €138. |
| | 3 suites for 2: €138. |
| Meals | Dinner with apéritif, wine & coffee, €37; book in advance. |
| | Restaurants 6km. |
| Closed | Never. |

Jacqueline & Patrick Darrigrand
Château de Baylac,
64190 Bugnein,
Pyrénées-Atlantiques

| | |
|---|---|
| Tel | +33 (0)6 07 80 72 54 |
| Email | patrickdarrigrand@yahoo.fr |
| Web | www.chateaudebaylac.com |

## Château d'Orion

The arrival is stunning: fields of sunflowers and maize, grazing sheep and views to the distant Pyrénées before a swoop through a handsome gate and a three-storey château with 16th-century roots. Elke and Tobias, genuine and kind, ask only that you make yourselves at home; they love to share their deep knowledge of the history and the region, having turned the château into a place of vibrant cultural exchange – seminars, exhibitions, concerts. The ground floor has two sitting rooms (one doubles up as a dining space) with antique furniture, comfortable chairs and sofas, old paintings, prints, and very precious old wallpaper with a heron and palm tree theme. Breakfast (outdoors on sunny days) on fresh fruit, homemade yogurt, homebaked spelt bread with hazelnuts and walnuts. You can ask for supper too – from tapas and salad to three courses with local trout and patty pan velvet soup. Upstairs to bedrooms you could happily do a polka in, with super mattresses and fine linen; carpets are woollen and cream; bathrooms are traditional with towel warmers. Take a turn around the pretty, productive potager, bask in peace and quiet.

| | |
|---|---|
| Rooms | 5 doubles: €104–€184. Extra bed €20. |
| Meals | Dinner, 3 courses, €30. Cold meat platter €20–€30. Restaurants 10km. |
| Closed | Never. |

Merle Staege
Château d'Orion,
1 L'Église, 64390 Orion,
Pyrénées-Atlantiques

| | |
|---|---|
| Tel | +33 (0)5 59 65 07 74 |
| Email | info@chateau-orion.com |
| Web | www.chateau-orion.com |

## Hôtel Laminak

You are well looked after here. Cheerful new owners Pascale and Martial have devoted their careers to hospitality and are well-travelled. They've kept the enchanting feel of a simple little hotel (intimate, friendly) and redecorated the bedrooms (not vast but very attractive). Find pale beige and blue fabrics with flashes of red-striped Basque, maritime or bull-fighting themed artwork, lovely views over to green hills and crisp bathrooms with shining tiles. Unbend on a comfy sofa in the sitting room – it's cosy in here and there's lots of work by local artists; on balmy days discover plenty of boltholes in the garden, on the terrace or by the super swimming pool. All is relaxed and you can make yourself at home. Breakfasts are generous affairs with homemade jams and cakes, delicious local farm produce (cheese, ham, saucisson). You are on a quiet road outside the village of Arbonne with a few discreetly screened neighbours, it's a ten-minute hop to the best surfing coast in Europe and the heady charm of Biarritz, or the antiques fair at Ahetze, or a championship golf course – and the mountains are worth a week's effort in themselves. *Children under 2 free.*

| Rooms | 12 twin/doubles: €79–€139. Extra bed/sofabed available €17 per person per night. |
|-------|--------------------------------------------|
| Meals | Breakfast €11.50. |
| Closed | Rarely. |

Pascale & Martial Mazabraud
Hôtel Laminak,
Route de St Pée, 64210 Arbonne,
Pyrénées-Atlantiques

| Tel | +33 (0)5 59 41 95 40 |
|-----|---------------------|
| Email | info@hotel-laminak.com |
| Web | www.hotel-laminak.com |

## Château d'Urtubie

Urtubie is old, very old: built in 1341 with permission from Edward III. The keep is still intact, though the roof was changed in 1654 to resemble Versailles. Your host Laurent, generous, charming, passionate about the place, is a direct descendant of Martin de Tartas who built it. Inside, all is elegant and inviting, and that includes the bedrooms, reached by a stair (or discreet lift). The first-floor 'prestige' rooms are light, airy, classical, imposing, and the 'charm' bedrooms on the second-floor are smaller. All are air-conditioned and are beautifully maintained, while bathrooms stock the family's new range of soaps and creams made from shea butter and verbena. On the outskirts of this pretty little Basque town, a hop from the motorway (you barely hear it) and five minutes from the beach, Urtubie is a sweet retreat in fine gardens with an elegantly decked pool. Don't imagine it's stuffy: Laurent couldn't be easier or more welcoming. His wife is the mayor, his brother and sister-in-law have a Michelin-approved restaurant 500m away.

| Rooms | 1 double, 8 twin/doubles: €90–€175. |
| | 1 single: €85–€175. |
| Meals | Breakfast €12. Restaurant 500m. |
| Closed | Christmas. |

Laurent de Coral
Château d'Urtubie,
Urrugne, 64122 St Jean de Luz,
Pyrénées-Atlantiques

Tel      +33 (0)5 59 54 31 15
Email    info@chateaudurtubie.fr
Web      www.chateaudurtubie.fr

## Arguibel

Guéthary is one of the best-kept Basque secrets. The beaches are charming, the coastal walks breathtaking, there are friendly bars and an artistic history; Debussy, Ravel and Chaplin spent heady summers here. A mile outside the village (with restaurants; you'll need a car), behind a deceptively conventional façade, discover a gloriously daring and theatrical hotel, its boutiquey flourishes the right side of kitsch and its bathrooms pure works of art. Art Deco furniture, 18th-century Jouy, 21st-century sculpture and rock 'n' roll memorabilia inhabit the same space and form an astonishingly harmonious whole. Humorous touches and references to local literati abound. Each big bedroom (four reached via the sweeping stair) has its own cocooning high-tech luxury (iPods etc) and a balcony with an unbroken view of rolling hills and the Pyrénées. In spite of the vast salon, the chic library/bar, the separate tables at breakfast, there's a warmly personal mood. Fifteen minutes up the coast is grand old Biarritz, paradise for surfers and chic shoppers; south, the atmospheric 'vieille ville' of the port of St Jean de Luz.

| | |
|---|---|
| Rooms | 3 doubles: €120–€210. |
| | 2 suites for 2: €200–€285. |
| Meals | Breakfast €16. Restaurants 1400m. |
| Closed | 5 January to 13 February. |

**François Blasselle**
Arguibel, 1146 chemin de Laharraga,
64210 Guéthary, Pyrénées-Atlantiques

| | |
|---|---|
| Tel | +33 (0)5 59 41 90 46 |
| Mobile | +33 (0)6 75 68 68 06 |
| Email | contact@arguibel.fr |
| Web | www.arguibel.fr |

## Villa Le Goëland

Every room has an ocean view, the wonderful family bedroom has "the finest view in Biarritz". Villa Le Goëland is lush, lavish and inviting. Dominating the ocean, yards from the beaches of glamorous Biarritz, the only privately owned villa of its kind to have resisted commercial redevelopment has opened its arms to guests. Turrets were added in 1903; Paul's family took possession in 1934; now he and his wife, young, charming, professional, are its inspired guardians and restorers. They live in an apartment upstairs and know all there is to know about the pleasures of Biarritz: casino, museums, boutiques, golf, surf, spa. Oak floors, magnificent stairs and sunshine-filled balconies that go on for ever; the salon and dining room each have one so fling open the tall French windows. Bedrooms, not cosy but lofty, are panelled and parquet'd, beds are king-size, the two suites have terraces, bathrooms date from the 1900s to the 1960s, and every window watches the waves. Breakfasts bring *viennoiseries*, served by Paul with a smile. The final touch: a private parking space for every guest, a godsend in this town.

| | |
|---|---|
| Rooms | 2 doubles: €150–€270. |
| | 2 suites for 3: €150–€270. |
| Meals | Breakfast €10 – free on presentation of a Sawday's guide. Restaurant 20m. |
| Closed | November – February. |

**Paul & Élisabeth Daraignez**
12 plateau de l'Atalaye,
64200 Biarritz, Pyrénées-Atlantiques

| | |
|---|---|
| Tel | +33 (0)5 59 24 25 76 |
| Mobile | +33 (0)6 87 66 22 19 |
| Email | info@villagoeland.com |
| Web | www.villagoeland.com |

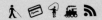

Entry 234   Map 13

## Hôtel Arraya

The drive to the village of Sare is breathtaking: winding road, red and white farmhouses, rolling hills. The hotel, which dominates Sare's square, has been in the family for three generations; it was a salon de thé after the war (and the 'gâteau Basque' is still delectable). Lawned terraces are the new gardens, a lap pool is planned, and the views of La Rhune tempt you to catch the mountain train. Pass the dappled dining terrace and the little shop (Basque linen, Basque pottery, homemade jam) to enter a double-glazed haven, overseen by smiling Madame. Two salons greet you – charming furniture, overstuffed sofas, a bar full of armagnacs, flowers from the garden. Upstairs, across two floors, with fire doors encased in handsome oak, are 16 bedrooms, sumptuous and serene, the quietest facing the garden. We loved the chests of drawers topped with old jugs and basins, the impeccable beds, the hand-sewn soft furnishings. Splash out on a 'prestige' suite if you can: the bathrooms are magnificent. Lovely Saint-Jean-de-Luz and its harbour are 12km, the hiking is marvellous, the beaches are close. *Parking on-site.*

| | |
|---|---|
| Rooms | 14 twin/doubles: €94–€195. |
| | 2 family suites for 2-4: €190–€245. |
| | Dinner, B&B €36 extra per person. |
| Meals | Breakfast €11. Dinner €27–€50. |
| Closed | 1 November to 31 March. |

Laurence & Jean Baptiste Fagoaga
Hôtel Arraya,
Place Centrale, 64310 Sare, France,
Pyrénées-Atlantiques

| | |
|---|---|
| Tel | +33 (0)5 59 54 20 46 |
| Email | hotel@arraya.com |
| Web | www.arraya.com |

## Hôtel 202

No Room 101, this! Hôtel 202 is spanking new and full of personality. In a secluded spot among the pines and mimosas of Hossegor – mecca for surfers and golfers – this Art Nouveau/contemporary Basque-style building is 50 metres from the golf course and a short hop to the beach. Inside, all is effortlessly chic – edges curve, white surfaces gleam, light floods through arched windows. Owner Jérôme runs the place with a passion for detail, a charming 'hands-on' attitude, a love for this region. Bedrooms have crisp white linen, furry throws and good-sized balconies that overlook the pool or the pines. Funky canvas message-paintings hang above the bed: 'Surf's up', 'Hello world!'. A breakfast buffet and fresh smoothies are served on the wooden decking or in the bright spacious bar area and there are plenty of restaurants for dinner nearby – just ask. Surf competitions run during the summer and a shuttle bus ferries you from the hotel in peak season (July/August) to the lake. Run by friendly and efficient staff, this is a cool and quirky place from which to explore Les Landes. Fabulous.

| | |
|---|---|
| Rooms | 21 doubles: €120–€250.<br>2 suites for 2: €210–€460. |
| Meals | Breakfast €14. Restaurants 2km. |
| Closed | Early January to early February. |

Jérôme Lacroix
Hôtel 202,
202 av du Golf,
40150 Hossegor, Landes

| | |
|---|---|
| Tel | +33 (0)5 58 43 22 02 |
| Email | contact@hotel202.fr |
| Web | www.hotel202.fr |

## Domaine de Sengresse

A spectacular tree-lined drive delivers you to a 17th-century domaine, and the entrance hall sets the tone: raw silk framing windows, a Steinway on a sparkling floor, oil paintings from Michèle's mother. What you have here is a rare combination of elegance and rustic charm and, in the manner of the best country hotels, the owners' personality. Michèle and Rob, welcoming and charming, are there to look after you but never intrude. You'll love the bedrooms of luxury and light, the calm colours, the exposed beams, the elegant breakfasts on the terrace, the candlelit dinners beneath an ecclesiastical chandelier. No room downstairs is out of bounds. The food is organic, home-grown, bountiful and delicious (you may eat romantically à deux if you prefer). Breathtaking parkland surrounds you and the grounds are never-ending, peaceful with hammocks and hidden corners, and a pool by the old stone barn. Board games in the dresser, a children's library under the stairs… and Les Landes, with its markets for foodies and brocanteurs, its surfing for beach bums, its 'petits châteaux' at Gaujacq and Amou. *Minimum stay in house: 2 nights.*

| | |
|---|---|
| Rooms | 3 doubles, 2 twins: €115–€135. 1 house for 2-6: €100–€165. Singles €95–€125. Extra bed/sofabed available €25 per person per night. |
| Meals | Dinner with wine, from €35. |
| Closed | Rarely. |

Michèle & Rob McLusky
& Sasha Ibbotson
Domaine de Sengresse, Route de Gouts,
40250 Souprosse, Landes

| | |
|---|---|
| Tel | +33 (0)5 58 97 78 34 |
| Email | sengresse@hotmail.fr |
| Web | www.sengresse.com |

Limousin & Auvergne

Photo: Château du Bois
Noir, entry 239

## La Maison des Chanoines

Built for the canons (*chanoines*) of Turenne, this ancient hotel-restaurant has been in Claude's family for 300 years. No wonder the family held on to it: the 16th-century, mellow-stoned house with its steep slate roof is one of the loveliest in a very lovely village. Chantal, charming and gracious, takes care of guests from dawn to dusk, always with a smile. The pretty bedrooms, freshly decorated, are scattered among outbuildings, two of them approached via a little bridge from the garden. Well lit, they have parquet floors and white walls; bathrooms ooze fluffy towels. The stone-flagged breakfast room feels ancient and airy. Dining takes place in the cosy old cellar whose ceiling vaults over just six white-clothed tables – nicely intimate – or under a fairy-lit pergola in the garden amid honeysuckle and roses where you are asked to "pour your ice-bucket water onto the tomatoes." The food is a delight; Claude is the chef and will use only the freshest, most local produce for his much-praised regional dishes. Ask about their three-day gourmet stay. Great value. *Private parking available.*

| | |
|---|---|
| Rooms | 2 doubles , 1 twin/double, 2 suites for 2-3, 1 family room for 4, all with private entrance: €85-€155. |
| Meals | Breakfast €10. Dinner €35-€50. |
| Closed | Wednesdays (except during school holidays). |

Chantal & Claude Cheyroux
La Maison des Chanoines,
Route de l'Église,
19500 Turenne, Corrèze

| | |
|---|---|
| Tel | +33 (0)5 55 85 93 43 |
| Email | maisondeschanoines@wanadoo.fr |
| Web | www.maison-des-chanoines.com |

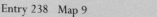
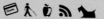

## Château du Bois Noir

Tree-lined drive, parkland setting, terraced garden, blush-pink stucco façade – this is the real deal: a Renaissance-style, 19th-century French château. Dutch couple Henk and Henriette spent three years restoring the rooms to a low-key opulence; no bling, no ostentation, just quietly luxurious. Huge bedrooms, with floor-to-ceiling windows (except the under-eaves triple room), soft carpets and velvet drapes, are graciously traditional. Beds are made-to-measure – two four-poster – colours and furnishings solid and rich. Most have tiled fireplaces, one a romantic tower salon, another bursts with sunny yellow colours. Vast bathrooms are cool with marble. There's an elegant, light-filled salon, billiards room and handsome, chandeliered dining room with vast stone-carved fireplace. Dine here or on the terrace on generous breakfasts, with typical local dishes for three course dinners. Explore Sarlat, gardens of Périgord Noir, walking in the Vézère Ardoise or relax in the château's terraced garden with its shady gazebos and views over parkland; perfect for evening aperitifs. With attentive hosts, this is a hotel of huge charm.

| Rooms | 2 doubles: €99–€135. |
|---|---|
| | 1 suite for 2: €165. |
| | 1 triple: €150. |
| | Cot €10. Extra bed €22. |
| Meals | Breakfast €13. Dinner €29. |
| Closed | November – March. |

Hendrikus Van Ampting
Château du Bois Noir,
Le Bois Noir,
19310 Perpezac-le-Blanc, Corrèze

| Tel | +33 (0)5 55 84 48 29 |
|---|---|
| Email | info@chateau-du-bois-noir.com |
| Web | chateau-du-bois-noir.com |

## Le Jardin des Lys

A handsome house in the heart of a pretty medieval town where mysterious little streets bustle and church bells gently peal. Leave the car in the square and step inside. From an impressive hall, a twisting staircase leads to big balconied bedrooms where all is über-spotless and new. Luxuriously dressed windows overlook the church; rich colours and baroque wallpapers are the backdrop for fireplaces and leather chairs; TV, tea trays and pillow bonbons complete the elegant scene. Choose a room with a 180cm bed – two have them; come with the family and take the suite. Bathrooms are immaculate with corner baths and showers created out of marble that twinkles like the starlit sky. Look forward to a buffet breakfast of compotes and fresh bread in an airy dining room immaculately furnished with Louis XIV tables and chairs. Your discreet hosts leave you to your own devices so come and go as you please (note the handy entry code). Stroll to restaurants, public garden, museum – return to a pretty garden plump with hydrangea. And don't forget to bring back Limousin chocolates from the Chartier family's tiny shop.

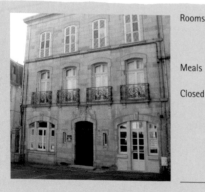

| Rooms | 2 doubles, 2 twin/doubles: €89–€99. 1 suite for 4: €119. Singles €89. Extra bed/sofabed available €15 per person per night. |
| Meals | Cold meats & cheese platter €20. Wine €15. Restaurants 50m. |
| Closed | Rarely. |

Joël Chartier
Le Jardin des Lys, 3 place de la
Collégiale, 87400 St Léonard de Noblat,
Haute-Vienne

Tel     +33 (0)5 55 56 63 39
Email   le-jardin-des-lys@orange.fr
Web    www.le-jardin-des-lys.com

Entry 240   Map 9

## Château du Fraisse

A grand frontage, charming outbuildings, immaculate grounds: the setting is beautiful and your sleep will be sound: you feel you are in the middle of nowhere. After 800 years of family and estate symbiosis, Le Fraisse is a living history book, mainly a rustic-grand Renaissance gem by the great Serlio – pale limestone, discreetly elegant portico, Henry II staircase, an astonishing fireplace in the drawing room. Your lovely hosts – two generations live here – greet you with warmth and happily tell you about their house and its fascinating history; they do afternoon tours for the public and you can get married here, too; many do. The guest quarters are in one wing, with a stunning breakfast room to relish (Madame's homemade jams, too) and four large and lofty bedrooms; if you return late at night, the main door will be locked and you must climb the steep old spiral stair. There are draped curtains at tall windows, elegant antiques and paintings and prints, small beds, pretty wallpapers, a few bold colours; one bathroom has a fragment of a 16th-century fresco and baths have hand-held showers. There's an excellent restaurant nearby.

| Rooms | 1 double, 1 twin: €90-€100. |
| | 1 suite for 4, 1 suite for 3: €135-€150. |
| Meals | Restaurants 6km. |
| Closed | Mid-December to mid-January. |

|  | Marquis & Marquise des Monstiers |
| | Mérinville |
| | Château du Fraisse, |
| | Le Fraisse, 87330 Nouic, Haute-Vienne |
| Tel | +33 (0)5 55 68 32 68 |
| Email | infos@chateau-du-fraisse.com |
| Web | www.chateau-du-fraisse.com |

## Château du Ludaix

Pure château with a touch of humour, Ludaix is glamorous, dramatic, hospitable, fun. David and Stephanie are natural hosts and lavish care on house and guests; they do training workshops and film shoots too. David is exploring the archives of this Belle Epoque château – "a living history book" – and rebuilding the ancient waterworks and the woodland walks. Stephanie, with an abounding energy, collects objets d'art and brocante pieces. To a background of warm bold colours, English and French antiques – from old to Art Deco – are enhanced by myriad hats, costumes, clocks, chandeliers and the odd tented ceiling, all pulled together with a designer's panache. Some bathrooms do not have doors, some loos are behind screens, there's no lift, heaps of stairs… the charm of this place is all-pervading. Now the gatehouse, La Maison de Gardien, has opened its doors too, with a bedroom suite up and another down – a luxurious self-catered retreat. As for the four-course dinners, if Stephanie's cakes are anything to go by, they will be imaginative and delicious. *Whole house available.*

| | |
|---|---|
| Rooms | 2 suites for 2, 1 suite for 3, 1 suite for 4: €120–€180. |
| Meals | Dinner, 4 courses with wine, €40. |
| Closed | Rarely. |

**David Morton & Stephanie Holland**
Rue du Ludaix,
03420 Marcillat en Combraille, Allier
Tel     +33 (0)4 70 51 62 32
Mobile  +44 (0)7739 431918
Email   stephanie@rapport-online.com
Web     www.chateauduludaix.com

## Château de Clusors

Atop a hill, and up an avenue of lime trees, this small château has gazed on untouched countryside since the 14th century. Steeped in history (Henri is full of stories; Madame de Montespan once stayed here), the place is still a working farm: friendly and down-to-earth, Madame manages a herd of Charolais cows. Up the spiral stone stair are big bedrooms with fine furniture and excellent modern bathrooms; breakfast is set before family portraits and a bookcase stocked with leather-bound tomes. The large sitting room has a grand fireplace with carved fleur de lys and family arms, a billiard table and collection of lovely old armchairs. Outside: a big garden with an orchard, formal box and rose areas and a pool in a sunny, secluded corner; rest in the shade of a big tree and admire the magnificent view. You'll find a good choice of restaurants within 10km, and guests can use a smart kitchen to prepared picnics; the Thieulins have masses of knowledge on the history of the area and interesting places to visit. Wonderfully, authentically French.

| Rooms | 2 triples: €105. |
| | Extra bed €20. |
| Meals | Cold meats and vegetable platter, €10. |
| | Restaurants 1km. |
| Closed | Rarely. |

Christine & Henri Thieulin
Château de Clusors,
03210 St Menoux, Allier

| Tel | +33 (0)4 70 43 94 69 |
| Mobile | +33 (0)6 70 79 27 75 |
| Email | henri.thieulin@orange.fr |
| Web | www.chateaudeclusors.com |

## Château de Vaulx

Creak along the parquet, waltz around the salon, sleep in one tower, wash in another (Chambre Athénaïs is irresistible!). Is it real or a fairy tale? Embraced by coniferous forest, the castle has been in the family for 800 years. Expect turrets, a moat, and an interior that holds endless treasures: paintings and sketches of ancestors, dark antiques adding to the mystery, furnishings worthy of the troubadours who sang here. It's an adorable château owned by an adorable pair who welcome you like long lost friends. Philippe and Martine are nurturing Château de Vaulx as their parents did, with joy – and updating a bit; new bathrooms are on their way but won't lose any of the character. With luck you'll be treated to a glass of pear schnapps in the huge kitchen, in among the copper pots and pans. Make friends with the dogs and the donkey, stroll from peaceful lawn to sweeping view, settle into one of their sociable dinners at the delicious, candlelit table. Breakfast is a feast of brioche, yogurt, eggs, cheese, and honey from their hives. A haven of hospitality and peace. *Arrival from 5pm.*

| Rooms | 2 doubles: €80-€100. |
|---|---|
| | 1 family room for 3: €100-€130. |
| | Extra bed/sofabed available €30 per person per night. |
| Meals | Dinner with wine, €30. |
| Closed | November – April. |

**Guy & Régine Dumas de Vaulx,**
**Philippe & Martine Vast**
63120 Ste Agathe, Puy-de-Dôme

| | |
|---|---|
| Tel | +33 (0)4 73 51 50 55 |
| Mobile | +33 (0)6 42 01 11 94 |
| Email | ph.vast@orange.fr |
| Web | www.chateaudevaulx.fr |

## Domaine de Gaudon – Le Château

The contrast could scarcely be greater. In the wilds of deepest Auvergne with nature bounding free all round, you find new Medici urns lining the edges of a great park. Inside the 19th-century splendour of glossy oak panelling, mouldings and original wall coverings, this totally natural, endearing couple have created a glamorous backdrop, all brass and satin, gilt and quilting, for their superb French antiques show. Gleaming luxuriously, big bathrooms are in keeping. Alain is a dab hand at wall panels and mouldings, Monique knows exactly what she likes in fabrics and colour combinations (Prussian blue and gold, canary yellow and gold, green and orange), they simply love having guests and breakfast is designed to dazzle you as your bedroom did. Gaudon is a Gîte Panda in a wildlife conservation area with some superb specimen trees, a young arboretum, a wetland observation spot and innumerable frogs, bats, birds and insects (there are samples in frames indoors). Herons fish in the pond, woods invite explorers, children love the place, and there's a fabulous new well-being centre. Astonishing.

| | |
|---|---|
| Rooms | 3 doubles, 1 twin: €120. 1 suite for 2: €140. Extra bed €25. |
| Meals | Supper trays available. Restaurant 4km. |
| Closed | Rarely. |

**Alain & Monique Bozzo**
Domaine de Gaudon – Le Château,
63520 Ceilloux,
Puy-de-Dôme

| | |
|---|---|
| Tel | +33 (0)4 73 70 76 25 |
| Email | domainedegaudon@wanadoo.fr |
| Web | www.domainedegaudon.fr |

## Château Royal de Saint-Saturnin

Oodles of atmosphere, rooks aplenty and views over one of Auvergne's wonderful romanesque churches. A volcanic region is the perfect cradle for this magnificently turreted and castellated fortress, high on the forested fringes of one of France's most beautiful villages, Saint Saturnin. A stone spiral, worn with age and history, leads to five sumptuous bedrooms – regal four-posters and an inspired blend of antique and modern furniture – in the oldest wing of the 13th-century 'monument historique'. The Louis XIII suite, its bathroom tucked into a tower, spans the castle's width; views are to tumbling rooftops and that perfect church, and the gardens and parkland behind (heaven for weddings). The vaulted dining room, decked with gleaming copper pans, is the backdrop for relaxed breakfast spreads. Redolent with royal history, the château has been lovingly, painstakingly returned to its original glory, yet, thanks to your friendly, well-travelled hosts, is in no way intimidating. Catherine de Médicis and La Reine Margot were once owners and a Renaissance garden is now being made. Château Royal is open to the public.

| Rooms | 2 doubles: €200-€240. 2 suites for 2-3, 1 suite for 2-5: €240-€270. Extra bed/sofabed available €20-€40 per person per night. |
| Meals | Breakfast €15. Restaurant 0.5km. |
| Closed | 11 November to 31 December & 1 January to 20 March. |

Emmanuel & Christine Pénicaud
Château Royal de Saint-Saturnin,
Place de l'Ormeau,
63450 St Saturnin, Puy-de-Dôme
Tel      +33 (0)4 73 39 39 64
Email  contact@chateaudesaintsaturnin.com
Web    www.chateaudesaintsaturnin.com

## Auberge de Chassignolles

The 1930s inn sits opposite the medieval church and next to the ruins of a 13th-century castle, its bar happily occupied by friendly locals. At 950 metres, the village has lovely views over fields and forests, stretching to the peaks of the Auvergne and Mont Dore. You'll find pure mountain air, a slow pace, and a place to stay with a slice of pizzazz thanks to new owner Peter, fresh from his restaurant success in Bristol. It hums with unpretentious good looks, young staff and seriously delicious, locally-sourced food. Upstairs, tall windows light old parquet, white walls and warm old furniture in plain simple rooms – a 1930s inlaid bedroom suite dressed in pure white linen, a deep and friendly armchair. One room above the restaurant is a library/sitting room and there's a meadow with farmyard animals, veg plot and fruit trees over the road. The pretty, old-style restaurant – country furniture, check cloths, crinkly lamps, a fascinating mixture of old crockery – is the place for *cuisine du terroir*, all freshness and taste. It's a perfect focus for revived community life and a boon for travellers.

| | |
|---|---|
| Rooms | 6 doubles, 1 twin sharing bathroom: €45-€65. 1 family room for 4: €50-€65. Extra bed €15. |
| Meals | Breakfast €7.50. Picnic €10. Sunday lunch €25; other days on request. Dinner €25 (except Monday). Wine €10-€80. |
| Closed | Early November to early May. |

Peter Taylor
Auberge de Chassignolles,
Le Bourg,
43440 Chassignolles, Haute-Loire

| | |
|---|---|
| Tel | +33 (0)4 71 76 32 36 |
| Email | aubergedechassignolles@gmail.com |
| Web | www.aubergedechassignolles.com |

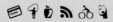

### Instants d'Absolu – Écolodge du lac du Pêcher

Sledge with dogs through the forest, ride horses at night and hear stags 'bark', cook with wild plants, fish for trout, snow-shoe in winter – tempting! Peace and serenity reign supreme, at this remote eco-lodge by the Lac du Pêcher, a 17th-century farmhouse originally built of lava and wood, now extensively and invitingly remodelled. The owners, generous and thoughtful, are committed to the happiness of their guests. It's a place for those who love wild nature, wholesome pampering and food in tune with the seasons. It's bliss to retire to harmonious bedrooms, each evoking the spirit of nature: they have sheep and goat skins for carpets; stylish basins of wood, marble, granite or lava; and huge views of forest, volcano or lake. In the sitting room, sofas wear fur cushions, a chandelier drips with glass, a fire crackles, an 'indoor garden' brings the outside in. In the restaurant, curtains are changed according to the seasons: linen for summer, virgin wool for winter. There's a spa for reiki, shiatsu, reflexology, massage with lava stones... and a garden with outdoor 'pillows' by the lake. *Free spa access when you buy dinner.*

| | |
|---|---|
| Rooms | 7 doubles: €189-€220. |
| | 4 suites for 2: €229-€290. |
| | 1 single: €154-€165. |
| | Spa €15 per person; |
| | private spa for 2 €45. |
| Meals | Dinner €33. |
| Closed | Mid-November to mid-December & |
| | mid-March to Easter. |

Laurence Costa
Instants d'Absolu – Écolodge du lac du Pêcher, Lac du Pêcher,
15300 Chavagnac, Cantal

Tel      +33 (0)4 71 20 83 09
Email    info@ecolodge-france.com
Web      www.ecolodge-france.com

## Château de Sédaiges

An amazing opportunity to see, experience, and sleep in a château – 11th century with mock gothic additions and in the family for 800 years. Here you can feel the history, and are encouraged to do so by your delightfully energetic and sophisticated hostess (joined by a tribe of grandchildren who occupy the attics in summer); you get a great welcome. Open to the public and endlessly fascinating for young and old, the château houses a famous collection of old-fashioned toys dating back to 1860, tapestries given by Louis XVI, fabulous parquet floors, murals, antiques, woodwork… in the UK all this would be roped off! There's no lift, the plumbing can be erratic and some of the beds are creaky and small, but mostly the bedrooms are charming, even lavish, and it feels like a privilege to stay (it is). Breakfast is dispatched from a kitchen festooned with copper pans to a grand and distinctive dining room, and the park is well kept with a large swimming pool discreetly tucked away. Don't expect pomposity, just cultured open-mindedness and a love of fine things. A paradise for children. *Overflow room for children.*

| | |
|---|---|
| Rooms | 2 doubles: €130.<br>3 suites for 2-4: €130-€160.<br>Extra bed €20. |
| Meals | Restaurant in village. |
| Closed | October – April. |

**Bab & Patrice de Varax**
Château de Sédaiges,
15250 Marmanhac, Cantal

| | |
|---|---|
| Tel | +33 (0)4 71 47 30 01 |
| Email | chateau15@free.fr |
| Web | www.chateausedaiges.com |

## Château de Lescure

On the southern slope of Europe's largest extinct volcano, where nine valleys radiate, stands an atmospheric 18th-century château guarded by a medieval tower where two rustic vaulted bedrooms soar. The twin has the right furbelowed drapery and, in the big inglenook kitchen, Sophie, a committed environmentalist who inherited this house and is passionate about it, serves home-smoked ham, veg from her organic garden, fruit from her orchard. She also knits and grows plants for materials including hemp and linen. Michel's passions are heritage conservation and blazing trails across the hills straight from the door – old pilgrim paths and trade paths – fascinating. They are bilingual hosts who may invite you to join in bread-making and cooking. The garden is big and fun with terraces down and across to the kitchen garden with its medieval layout of square beds: find a plethora of flowers, ancient trees, and a hedge-protected lawned seating area for games or lazing about. There are monuments of great age to explore and absolutely brilliant walks for historians and anybody interested in the countryside. *Minimum stay: 2 nights in high season.*

| Rooms | 1 twin; 1 double with separate shower room, 1 double with separate shower room downstairs: €90. Extra bed €30. |
|---|---|
| Meals | Dinner with wine, €20–€30; children's menu €10. |
| Closed | December/January. |

Michel Couillaud
& Phoebe Sophie Verhulst
Château de Lescure, 15230 St Martin
Sous Vigouroux, Cantal
Tel    +33 (0)4 71 73 40 91
Email  michel.couillaud@orange.fr
Web    www.chateaudelescure.com

## Auberge de Concasty

Half a mile high lies the river-ploughed plateau: strong air, wild country, vast space. Built 300 years ago, the family mansion stands prouder than ever, and clever, delightful Martine has brought everything up to date: jacuzzi, hammam, massage, yoga (and more!) and organic food and veg from her brother's farm to keep you blooming. The dining room, with its vast inglenook, and the covered patio overlooking the pool and the view, are the stage for lovingly prepared shows of foie gras and asparagus, scallops and confits (you can watch: Martine chats happily while cooking), the supporting cast an impressive choice of wines; great breakfasts, too. Bedrooms – in the main house, the barn or the renovated chestnut dryer – are stylishly rustic with space, good floral fabrics and an evocative name each – nothing standard here, especially that view. The magnificent new family room in ivory and soft blue is the height of sophistication. You will love the smiling, attentive staff, the warm family atmosphere, the freedom in the air. *Some rooms with balcony or terrace.*

| | |
|---|---|
| Rooms | 11 doubles: €88–€158. |
| | 1 suite for 2: €156–€192. |
| | Extra person €18–€28. |
| | Dinner, B&B extra €41–€51 per |
| | person; children under 2 free. |
| Meals | Brunch €17. Dinner €36–€44. |
| Closed | December – March. |

Martine Causse
Auberge de Concasty,
15600 Boisset,
Cantal

| | |
|---|---|
| Tel | +33 (0)4 71 62 21 16 |
| Email | info@auberge-concasty.com |
| Web | www.auberge-concasty.com |

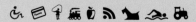

Midi-Pyrénées

Photo: Hôtel Restaurant
Le Vert, entry 252

## Hôtel Restaurant Le Vert

The alchemy of family tradition – three generations and 30 years for this Belgo-German couple – has rubbed off onto the very stones of their beautiful, authentic country inn where Bernard's skills shine from the kitchen. It feels like a private house: fresh flowers, glowing silverware and old flagstones leading you from the small lobby to the dining room. Glance at the blackboard for the day's special to get your appetite going and, if the weather is right, head for a table on the flowered terrace. The local foodies are greeted as friends here, always an auspicious sign. Ingredients are vital to Bernard – organic and local whenever possible – and he works wonders with them. This is Cahors wine territory: delightful, chatty Eva will advise. The rooms in the garden annexe are big, cool and elegant with beamed ceilings, stone walls and antique furniture lightened by simple white curtains and delicate bedspreads. The pool is hidden on the far side of the green and shady garden. In a country where politicians are authors and cooks are philosophers, Bernard's ivory tower is in the kitchen.

| Rooms | 6 twin/doubles: €85–€130. Dinner, B&B €85–€107 per person. Extra bed/sofabed available €15 per person per night. |
|---|---|
| Meals | Breakfast €10. Dinner €28–€32. |
| Closed | 1 November to 31 March. |

**Bernard & Eva Philippe**
Hôtel Restaurant Le Vert,
Le Vert, 46700 Mauroux, Lot

| Tel | +33 (0)5 65 36 51 36 |
| Email | info@hotellevert.com |
| Web | www.hotellevert.com |

## Hôtel Relais Sainte Anne

In the centre of beautifully preserved Martel, step in from the quiet street, take a deep breath, feel the still magic of the place. The fabulous garden has endless secret corners and pathways running through high box-edged lanes. The several buildings that house the bedrooms were once a girls' school, the delightful covered terrace was their playground, the old school house is now an oriental suite exuding opulence and space. Warm old stones and terracotta, fine fabrics and heavy rugs abound. We loved the lighter rooms, too, and the three simpler yet pretty rooms for smaller budgets: such a friendly touch. Bathrooms are original and fun: black and terracotta, a bit of gilt or candy stripe, a flowery frieze. All this, a perfectly lovely family (Madame still says "I'm so happy here," and gets a kick out of each new decorative idea) and innovative cuisine, served on the terrace or in the intimate dining room by a big open fire. A 'lovers' table' dressed with roses and candles can be set under the porch of the little chapel. Sophistication without self-consciousness – a rare treat.

| Rooms | 7 doubles, 4 twins: €85–€185. |
|---|---|
| | 4 suites for 2: €155–€275. |
| | 1 single: €49–€190. |
| Meals | Breakfast €13–15. |
| | Dinner, market menu, €28–€40. |
| | Wine €19–€90. |
| Closed | 12 November to 1 April. |

Ghislaine Rimet-Mignon
Hôtel Relais Sainte Anne,
Rue du Pourtanel, 46600 Martel, Lot

| Tel | +33 (0)5 65 37 40 56 |
|---|---|
| Email | relais.sainteanne@wanadoo.fr |
| Web | www.relais-sainte-anne.com |

## Le Mûrier de Viels

You won't meet a soul on the drive to get here, except possibly a wild deer. This intimate hotel, made up of a sprinkling of 18th-century buildings on several lush levels, hides among the oak woods and gazes down on the river with beautiful views of the valley. Come for a smiling welcome and an atmosphere of relaxed comfort: Joséphine and Oz left stressful lives in Britain to realise their dream of owning a small hotel and bringing up a family in France. The layout is charming, with reception, restaurant and guest rooms scattered among terraces and secret corners. The pool area has a great view, as do most of the rooms; there's space and blissful tranquillity. In the bedrooms where rustic stone walls rub shoulders with white plaster you'll find stylish modern French furniture and soothing colours, big walk-in showers, good reading lamps and fat pillows. The suite has a fitted wardrobe with antique doors, a comfy raffia sofa and a stunning view through a huge window. Every room is pristine. Treat yourself to Oz's beautiful cooking on the terrace or in a dining room bright with yellow leather chairs.

| | |
|---|---|
| Rooms | 3 doubles, 1 twin: €65-€140. 1 suite for 3: €90-€105. 2 family rooms for 3: €100-€150. 1 cottage for 2-4: €450-€750 per week. |
| Meals | Breakfast €10. Picnic available. Dinner €25-€30. Wine €10-€27. |
| Closed | 13 November to 28 February. |

**Joséphine Porter & Oz Shariss**
Le Mûrier de Viels,
12700 Causse & Diège, Aveyron
Tel        +33 (0)5 65 80 89 82
Email     mail@le-murier.com
Web       www.le-murier.com

## Château de Labro

In a large park with vast pastures, woods and every imaginable tree, this fine 16th-century château has all the ingredients for a magical stay. A tree-lined drive leads to an old gated entrance beyond which a walled vineyard hides a huge pool and a lawn. Nearly all the bedrooms are large, with fine parquet floors and views to slate roofs, the garden or the foothills of the Massif Central. Those in the main house are dedicated to local artists, others, off a stone-flagged courtyard, have four-posters and a delectable treehouse, complete with chandelier, sits in the branches of an ancient oak tree. A generous breakfast is laid on elegantly dressed tables in the old pigsty and there's a large salon with chesterfield sofas behind the fine wooden bar. Check out the magnificent wine rack (sample their 'Marcillac'); indulge in special food in a gorgeous setting. Local folk Giselle and Sylvain look after it all with ease and charm, owner Monsieur Rouquet pops in from time to time. Take a trip to the Gorges du Tarn or the Roquefort cheese caves, hike or bike in the wonderful L'Aubrac. Enchanting.

| | |
|---|---|
| Rooms | 12 doubles, 1 twin: €90–€170. 3 triples: €145–€185. 1 treehouse for 2: €250 per night. 1 apartment for 4 with kitchen & living room: €250 per night. |
| Meals | Breakfast €14. Dinner €29–€41. Wine €14–€79. |
| Closed | Rarely. |

**Jean & Nizou Rouquet**
Château de Labro,
Labro, 12850 Onet Le Château,
Aveyron

| Tel | +33 (0)5 65 67 90 62 |
|---|---|
| Email | jmrouquet@wanadoo.fr |
| Web | www.chateaulabro.fr |

## Le Domaine de Perches

Sheltered below the country lane, the 17th-century pale-stone, elegant building faces south, revelling in the lush fruitful valley that flows away beyond the garden. Inside are superb high beamed rooms; you'll find privacy even in the public rooms: club-like morning room, library with a vast classical fireplace, immense white-furnished salon in the former winery — you choose. Or plunge into the pool discreetly sited below the terrace, then sit under a willow by the frog-sung lily pond (maybe your prince will come?). Bedroom moods vary: in the big mushroom-masculine double, glowing antiques and two armchairs; in the suite, a smallish bedroom and a smart sitting room; in the romantic ivory and grey double, a draped bedhead and a clawfoot tub. All are superbly comfortable and have excellent lighting. It is a beautifully kept home where you will find artistic flair, a love of cooking (fresh vegetables in season, local wines) and stimulating company. Monsieur is passionate about architecture and design and his lovingly collected antiques and works of art add sparkle to the sobriety. A place of genuine class. *Minimum stay: 2 nights in high season.*

| | |
|---|---|
| Rooms | 1 double, 1 twin/double: €150–€165. 1 suite for 2 with sitting room: €185–€205. Pets by arrangement €15 per night. |
| Meals | Dinner with wine, €50, on request. Restaurants 10-minute drive. |
| Closed | Never. |

M. Guyomarch
Le Domaine de Perches,
Perches, 81600 Gaillac, Tarn

| | |
|---|---|
| Tel | +33 (0)5 63 56 58 24 |
| Mobile | +33 (0)6 08 88 19 29 |
| Email | domainedeperches@orange.fr |
| Web | www.domainedeperches.com |

## Château Touny les Roses

If you're on the trail of local hero Toulouse-Lautrec, then this pretty country estate will be right up your street. Set in seven hectares of garden and vineyard, the château's pleasing traditional exterior gives no hint of what awaits. Inside art is everywhere: in the flagged entrance hall and the striking red room where breakfast is served is an ever-changing backdrop of modern paintings. The big bedrooms meld old fashioned comfort with contemporary touches that evoke Mondrian or the heyday of the Moulin Rouge. In huge bathrooms two basins and separate baths and showers are the rule, not the exception. The château's verdant grounds are no less impressive – 300 roses bloom in the formal garden, there's woodland to explore and behind the house a pathway leads to a private jetty on the Tarn. You're just 15 minutes from the beautiful medieval city of Albi, a World Heritage Site: if you want to roam, bikes and kayaks are available – but with fishing, badminton, pétanque, a pool and BBQ on hand, you could happily stay put. In summer friendly hosts Thierry and Sophie serve breakfast in the garden, and can also organise dinner.

| Rooms | 2 doubles: €99–€138. |
| | 2 suites for 4: €99–€169. |
| | Extra bed available. |
| Meals | Dinner, 4 courses with wine, €29. |
| | Cold plate with wine, €23. |
| | Restaurants 1km. |
| Closed | Rarely. |

Sophie & Thierry Bosschaert
Château Touny les Roses,
32 chemin de Touny,
81150 Lagrave, Tarn
Tel        +33 (0)5 63 57 90 90
Email      thierry@touny.fr
Web        www.tounylesroses.com

## Hôtel Cuq en Terrasses

Come to the Pays de Cocagne, the brochure says. Where is that, you ask? It is an imaginary land of pleasure in the once prosperous pastel-producing Tarn. Philippe and Andonis gave up good jobs in Paris to buy this 18th-century presbytery after falling in love with the region. Perched in mouthwatering gardens on the side of a hill, the multi-level mellow stone edifice looks – and is – utterly inviting. All the rooms, including the two-floor suite by the saltwater pool, exude character and finesse. All are different, with original terracotta floors, hand-finished plaster, exposed beams, a Chinese vase here, an antique bed there. It is worth staying just for the bathrooms, lovely with hand-painted tiles. Evening meals, on the terrace in summer, are a delight for eye and palate: something different each day, fresh from the market, beautifully balanced by wines from the region. Guests are full of praise, for the food and the gardens, the pool and waterfall, the blissful views, the wonderful hosts. We cannot fault it. *Children over 10 welcome.*

| | |
|---|---|
| Rooms | 3 doubles, 3 twin/doubles: €85-€165. 2 suites for 2: €160-€205. Dinner, B&B €92-€128 per person. Extra bed/sofabed available €20 per person per night. |
| Meals | Hosted dinner €38; book ahead. Wine €16-€25. |
| Closed | 21 October to 21 April. |

**Philippe Gallice & Andonis Vassalos**
Hôtel Cuq en Terrasses,
Cuq le Château,
81470 Cuq Toulza, Tarn

| | |
|---|---|
| Tel | +33 (0)5 63 82 54 00 |
| Email | cuq-en-terrasses@wanadoo.fr |
| Web | www.cuqenterrasses.com |

Entry 258   Map 15

## L'Abbaye Château de Camon

Camon… the name carries images of pious folk, wrapped in sackcloth and arriving by donkey. Art history buffs will swoon trying to find which bits were built when, but it was first recorded as a Benedictine Abbey in 928. Now Peter, who managed luxurious Samling Hotel in Cumbria, and his wife Katie, an interior designer and young mother, run the place hands-on like a B&B (though breakfast is extra). They give you monks' bedrooms with vaulted ceilings, tiny glistening floor tiles and tall 28-pane windows looking south to the hills; rooms on the second floor are squarer; all have soft colours, lovely fabrics, spoiling bathrooms. Relax in the huge salon with its exquisite 18th-century plasterwork and floral ceiling, or take tea in the sheltered cloister garden. Breakfast is served, most elegantly, on a long high terrace running the length of the château and overlooking formal gardens with lawns, mature trees and swimming pool. The refined *menu dégustation* is a memorable dining experience, the wine list is superb and you are in the heart of Cathar country, near the medieval delights of Mirepoix. *Minimum stay: 2 nights. Pets by arrangement.*

| | |
|---|---|
| Rooms | 5 doubles: €140–€200. 1 suite for 4: €255–€275. Singles €135–€165. Extra bed/sofabed available €30 per person per night. |
| Meals | Breakfast €18. Wine €18–€44. Menu dégustation €46, every evening except Wednesday. |
| Closed | 1 November to 31 March. |

**Katie & Peter Lawton**
L'Abbaye Château de Camon,
09500 Camon,
Ariège

| | |
|---|---|
| Tel | +33 (0)5 61 60 31 23 |
| Email | katie@chateaudecamon.com |
| Web | www.chateaudecamon.com |

## Au Château

A beguiling mix of grandeur and informality. The house is filled with light and life, thanks to this young Anglo-French family who obviously adore their "Maison de Maître" – a fine example of Napoleonic architecture and which feels very rural thanks to its enclosed grounds, but is only a short walk from the village centre. Original features abound – wood panelling, marble fireplaces and a grand staircase. Softly contemporary bedrooms, two in a separate building, are airy spaces that mix the best of modern with the loveliest of traditional: pale beams and white plaster walls, bold colours, luxurious silks, elegant antiques. There's a country-style breakfast room and a fully equipped kitchen so you can make your own suppers – then eat al fresco on the terrace. Visit historic towns, explore the Canal du Midi, let the kids roam free in the garden, splash in the pool, stroll to the charming village – an ancient 'Bastide' town with a newly-restored 'voie verte'. Walk or cycle for miles without worrying about cars – bliss! Further afield you can golf, ride, canoe and explore a colourful, very French, market every day of the week.

| | |
|---|---|
| Rooms | 1 double: €65-€70. |
| | 2 suites for 2-3: €85-€90. |
| | 1 family room for 4: €115-€130. |
| | 1 triple: €80-€105. |
| Meals | Restaurants 5-minute walk. |
| Closed | Rarely. |

**Kathrin Barker**
Au Château, 1 bd des Fossés de Raoul,
82210 St Nicolas de la Grave,
Tarn-et-Garonne

| | |
|---|---|
| Tel | +33 (0)5 63 95 96 82 |
| Email | kathrin.barker@sfr.fr |
| Web | www.au-chateau-stn.com |

## Château de Projan

The interiors are remarkable and the proportions grandiose, a pleasure to stride. And the history of the 18th-century château is fascinating: ask Richard and Christine to tell you the stories. Eclectic, quirky and entertaining is the mix of antiques with paintings, tapestries and sculpture from the Art Nouveau, Cubist and Art Deco periods; equally special, the inlaid marble floor at the foot of the staircase. First-floor bedrooms have wide oak boards, tomette tiles, antique writing desks; one great room has a 15m ceiling with original mouldings, others still have their timber frames. Most astonishing are the recent panelled bathrooms, gleaming with massive mirrors and huge showers. There are two dining terraces with views across to the Pyrénées, a hall-cum-piano room, fireplaces for chilly evenings… make yourselves at home in grand fashion, book in for cookery courses, Armagnac tastings, fabulous sejours. The kitchen opens to the ground-floor hall so you can watch chef/patron Richard prepare his Gascon specialities, which you can then savour accompanied by local wines. Welcoming, and perfect for the jazz festival in Marciac.

| | |
|---|---|
| Rooms | 6 doubles, |
| | 1 family room for 4: €130–€200. |
| | Singles €100–€130. |
| | Dinner, B&B €115–€140 per person. |
| | Extra bed/sofabed available €15 per |
| | person per night. |
| Meals | Breakfast €14. Dinner €38–€60. |
| Closed | February, last week in October & 21 to |
| | 28 December. |

Christine & Richard Poullain
Château de Projan,
32400 Projan,
Gers
Tel       +33 (0)5 62 09 46 21
Email   chateaudeprojan@gmail.com
Web     www.chateau-de-projan.com

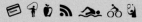

## Le Relais de Saux

Three to five hundred years old, high on a hill facing Lourdes and some dazzling Pyrenean peaks, the house still has a few unregenerate arrow slits, left over from sterner days. You come in through the multi-coloured garden that spreads across lawns and terraces with corners for reading or painting. Bernard Hères inherited Saux from his parents and, with the help of his late wife's flair and energy, opened it to guests. He knows the area thoroughly and can guide you to fine walks, climbs or visits. Return to deep armchairs in the dark old-beamed salon with its peaceful garden view (some traffic hum outside). Bedrooms with carpeted bathrooms are in the same traditional, elegant mood with draped bedheads and darkish plush or flock-papered walls. One has no fewer than four tall windows, another has an old fireplace, the two second-floor rooms are big yet cosy beneath their lower ceilings. Lourdes' torchlit Marian Procession – praying the rosary in all the languages – is a moving experience. But a word of warning: be careful on leaving the dual carriageway on your return.

| | |
|---|---|
| Rooms | 3 doubles, 2 twin/doubles: €96–€103. |
| Meals | Restaurant 2km. |
| Closed | Occasionally. |

Bernard Hères
Le Relais de Saux,
Route de Tarbes, Le Hameau de Saux,
65100 Lourdes, Hautes-Pyrénées
Tel      +33 (0)5 62 94 29 61
Email    contacts@lourdes-relais.com
Web      www.lourdes-relais.com

# Languedoc – Roussillon

Photo: Le Mas Trilles,
entry 268

## Château La Villatade

A vast 19th-century wine vat is the novel tasting room for the aromatic wines still made at this lovely old farmhouse, where sweet gîtes cluster around a big square courtyard and the views are incredible on a fine day. Sophie and Denis invite you to share their home and their passion for wine making… their welcome is irresistible. The B&B suite looks out onto the courtyard, with its own sitting room and kitchen corner, while the Forge is a little house surrounded by vines, close by but very private and with a great view. A large fireplace, a tiny kitchen, its own piece of garden under the willow tree in the shade… heaven! The décor throughout La Villatade is contemporary and charming, walls are limewashed, terracotta tiles are cool, and all you hear are the cicadas. As for the grounds, they're idyllic: teeming trout, flourishing potager, horse and donkey in the paddock, and a long, long, 18th-century stone pool, chlorine-free and fed by two wells, absolute bliss on a hot day. Mingle in the courtyard for the weekly wine-tasting and nibbles, explore the Languedocian villages and the marvellous Minervois. *Minimum stay: 2 nights in high season.*

| Rooms | 1 suite for 2, 1 house for 2: €98–€115. Extra bed/sofabed available €20 per person per night. |
| --- | --- |
| Meals | Dinner with wine, €20. |
| Closed | January. |

**Sophie & Denis Morin**
Château La Villatade,
La Villatade,
11600 Sallèles Cabardès, Aude

| Tel | +33 (0)4 68 77 57 51 |
| --- | --- |
| Email | villatade@wanadoo.fr |
| Web | www.villatade.com |

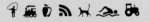

## Hôtel d'Alibert

Expect Renaissance-style arches and alcoves, a twisting spiral stone stair, and a gallery overlooking a courtyard with columns dating to 1561: the place is unlike any other. History-soaked Hôtel d'Alibert is masterminded by Frederick – "call me Fredo". He is hugely entertaining, a lover of food and wine, and his great-grandparents began the original auberge and café. Best of all, this is in the heart of a peaceful medieval village, ten miles from the cacophony and splendour of Carcassonne. Find exhibitions, marble sculptures, art books and magazines in the sitting room, and white tablecloths, a large fireplace and high ceilings in the restaurant: a rustic-elegant backdrop for dinner. The cuisine is rich, traditional and 'du terroir': wild mushrooms, tête de veau, cassoulet à la Carcassonnaise, pâtisseries maison. Bedrooms are up that spiral stair, each with its own décor, the highest with the views. All have warm colours, large windows, super bathrooms, heaps of space. Pretty tables are laid in the courtyard for summer breakfasts. Markets, castles and wineries abound.

| | |
|---|---|
| Rooms | 4 doubles; 1 double sharing bathroom with single: €90. 1 single sharing bathroom with 1 double: €80. |
| Meals | Breakfast included. Dinner €29. Wine €28–€50. Restaurants 5-minute walk. |
| Closed | Never. |

**Frédéric Guiraud**
Hôtel d'Alibert,
Place de la mairie,
11160 Caunes Minervois, Aude
Tel     +33 (0)4 68 78 00 54
Email   Frederic.dalibert@wanadoo.fr
Web     www.hoteldalibert.com

## Château Haute Fontaine

Vineyards crossed with wild walks circle this unpretentious, sea-breezy château, home to sociable British hosts beyond a mighty pine-flanked drive... it's a stunning approach. Paul and Penny bravely plunged head first into the French world of wine and are now sailing smoothly with a small local team. Explore the garrigue-rich estate, tour the cellars: it is quite something to be shown around, and fascinating to pick up the stories and the info. There's an embracing inner courtyard for breakfast; jasmine clambers, herbs tumble and tables cluster, and you mingle with guests from the three gîtes – and cats, of which there are many. Slumber in the former grape-pickers' dwelling in 'Syrah', 'Marsanne', 'Vermentino' or 'Merlot', simple and homely with a family feel, and up steepish stairs. Beds are wicker or wrought-iron, shower rooms large and shared, there are terracotta tiles, ochre walls and a kitchen for twilight feasts. It's a sociable place too, good for families with children who want to make friends. You are just outside a small village so can walk to a restaurant for dinner... and coasts and culture await.

| | |
|---|---|
| Rooms | 2 doubles, 1 triple sharing 2 bathrooms and wcs: €60–€75. 1 single sharing 2 bathrooms and wcs with all: €50. |
| Meals | Breakfast €6. Guest kitchen. Restaurant 1km. |
| Closed | 1 September to Easter. |

**Paul & Penelope Dudson**
Château Haute Fontaine,
Domaine de Java, Prat de Cest,
11100 Bages, Aude

| | |
|---|---|
| Tel | +33 (0)4 68 41 03 73 |
| Email | haute-fontaine@wanadoo.fr |
| Web | www.chateauhautefontaine.com |

Entry 265   Map 15

## La Fargo

Water runs everywhere in this ancient converted forge, an oasis in unspoilt Corbières countryside. Christophe gives you a large house with a very relaxed vibe and the option to make light meals in a kitchen, order in a chef, be catered for if you are a group of 10, or drive to the lovely village where there are plenty of good restaurants. Bedrooms are all large, light and unfussy with polished concrete floors, big beds, vast windows and sliding doors to private patios and little gardens festooned with bamboo and papyrus; bathrooms are super, some with beautiful black marble baths, and all with separate loos. You breakfast in the dining room on homemade fig and kiwi jam, yogurt, honey, fresh bread and viennoiseries from the local bakery. Hang around here floating in the infinity pool – a natural de-stresser – or head for Carcassone for a good day out. You can birdwatch, walk, fish, explore vineyards, castles, medieval abbeys – or potter in La Fargo's potager and orchard, play the piano, gather some fruit and laze on a wooden lounger. A river swim is heaven.

| | |
|---|---|
| Rooms | 8 doubles, 2 twins: €120–€150. 2 family rooms for 4: €140–€170. Extra bed €20. |
| Meals | Breakfast €15. Dinner €30 available for groups of 10+. Restaurants 5km. |
| Closed | October – April. |

**Christophe & Dominique Morellet**
La Fargo,
11220 St Pierre des Champs, Aude
Tel     +33 (0)4 68 43 12 78
Email   contact@lafargo.fr
Web     www.lafargo.fr

## Château des Ducs de Joyeuse

The drive up is impressive, the castle even more so: 1500s and fortified, part Gothic, part Renaissance, standing in its own patch of land on the banks of the Aude. A large rectangular courtyard is jolly with summer tables and parasols, the stately dining room has snowy linen cloths and flowers, the staff are truly charming and helpful, and the menu changes daily depending on what is fresh. Vaulted ceilings and well-trodden stone spiral stairs lead to formal bedrooms with heavy wooden furniture, some beamed and with stone fireplaces; there's a heraldic feel with narrow high windows, studded doors and smart bedspreads in navy blue and bright red. Ask for a room with a watery view. Bathrooms glow with tiled floors, bright lights and stone walls – some up to two metres thick: perfect sound insulation. Historical information about the building is on display everywhere, owners Isabelle and Vincent are full of ideas and can help you plan your trips out. Hearty souls can knock a ball around the tennis court then cool off in the outdoor pool – or brave that lovely river. Good value.

| Rooms | 10 doubles, 11 twins: €118–€152. |
| | 2 family rooms for 4: €178–€233. |
| | 12 triples: €193–€275. |
| | Dinner, B&B extra €48 p.p per night. |
| Meals | Breakfast €16. Dinner €29–€79. |
| | Wine €21–€125. |
| Closed | Early November to early April. |

Isabelle & Vincent Nourrisson
Château des Ducs de Joyeuse,
Allée du Château, 11190 Couiza, Aude
Tel      +33 (0)4 68 74 23 50
Email   reception@chateau-des-ducs.com
Web     www.chateau-des-ducs.com

## Le Mas Trilles

Stéphane and Amparo have taken over the family's rambling, honey-coloured 17th-century farmhouse; some old-fashioned touches, and their personal welcome makes it feel more like home than hotel. First to greet you are the sounds of birdsong and rushing water, then, perhaps the head-spinning scent of orange or cherry blossom from the lovely redolent garden. There are two comfortable sitting rooms, one with its original beams, both with paintings, cool terracotta tiles and places to read and relax. Many bedrooms, larger in the main house, are reached by unexpected ups and downs; all have shower-in-bath systems. There are some fine antiques, a few little terraces, and woods and mountains beyond. The largest room has magnificent views of the Canigou mountain, the spiritual home of the Catalan nation; cheaper rooms are quite small. Breakfast on the sweet terrace with homemade fig or apricot jam or in front of a crackling fire on chilly days. Down by the river there are fine views of the mountains and an intoxicating feeling of space.

| Rooms | 11 doubles: €85–€229. |
| | Pets €13 per night. |
| | Cots €12 per night. |
| | Extra beds €15–€29. |
| Meals | Breakfast €13.50; children under 12, €10. |
| | Restaurant 200m. |
| Closed | Early October to late April. |

Stéphane & Amparo Bukk
Le Mas Trilles,
Le Pont de Reynès, 66400 Céret,
Pyrénées-Orientales
Tel      +33 (0)4 68 87 38 37
Email    info@le-mas-trilles.com
Web      www.le-mas-trilles.com

## Domaine de la Fauvelle

A tree-lined avenue leads to La Fauvelle – an impressive building, built as a ceramic factory in 1850 and bought by the present Norwegian owners in 2001. They've restored everything stylishly and created a comfortable, relaxed and welcoming place to stay. A vast entrance hall leads to a dining and lounge area with high ceilings, modern art and grand arched windows. Enjoy breakfast here or under the grape vines on the terrace overlooking lawn, palm trees and a large saltwater pool – lots of choices including bacon, omelettes, cheese, croissants, fruit, jams and juices; an enormous antique cupboard serves as a bar. The big ground floor bedrooms all have French windows and views on to the bird-filled garden or patio; find fresh, clean lines with splashes of Catalan colours, polished terracotta floors and mosaic-walled en suites. Walk into lively Thuir for supper (10 minutes); visit local vineyards; take a peek at Spain from Canigou – one of the highest mountains in the Pyrénées. Pretty village Castelnou with its château on the hilltop is festooned with small shops and restaurants and sandy beaches are a 30-minute drive. *Parking on-site.*

| | |
|---|---|
| Rooms | 14 twin/doubles: €115–€125. Extra bed available €15. |
| Meals | Restaurants 10-minute walk. |
| Closed | 1 December to 1 March. |

Morten Norli
Domaine de la Fauvelle,
60 av Fauvelle, 66300 Thuir,
Pyrénées-Orientales

| | |
|---|---|
| Tel | +33 (0)4 68 50 50 50 |
| Email | morten.norli@lafauvelle.com |
| Web | lafauvelle.com |

Entry 269   Map 15

## Relais des Chartreuses

Up in the wooded hills above Le Boulou is a French farmhouse hotel with a young modern interior and astonishingly good food. Every evening is a culinary adventure so prepare yourself for a seasonal chalked-up set menu and a beautiful list of local wines. You enter via a pretty terraced garden, one of several: you can chase the sun (or the shade) all day. Friendly staff usher you up and down steps to calm, restful and chic bedrooms – each one creatively inspired, each different from the last. Prices reflect – fairly – the differences in size, so the priciest is 'Le Pigeonnier', a secluded suite with the luxuries of air con and a private terrace. Splashes of colour lift greys, taupes and whites, reclaimed materials and quirky artefacts abound, and some bathrooms have his and her showers. It's a brilliant place for forays to Spain and the south coast; dreamy Collioure, beloved of Matisse, is 20 minutes away, Céret, Picasso's favourite, is even closer – seek out the Musée d'Art Moderne and the Saturday market. Return to a stylish lounger, slip into a cool pool.

| | |
|---|---|
| Rooms | 9 doubles, 3 twin/doubles: €80-€170. 1 family room for 4-5: €210-€270. Outer building – 1 suite for 4: €210-€270. Singles €70-€80. Dinner, B&B extra €45 per person. Extra bed/sofabed available €25 per person per night. |
| Meals | Buffet breakfast €15; children's menu €10. Dinner, 4 courses, €38; children's menu €25. Wine €16-€76. Restaurant 5km. |
| Closed | Christmas & 2 January to 5 March. |

Anne Besset Lissorgue
Relais des Chartreuses,
106 avenue d'en Carbouner,
66160 Le Boulou, Pyrénées-Orientales

Tel     +33 (0)4 68 83 15 88
Email    relaisdeschartreuses@gmail.com
Web     www.relais-des-chartreuses.fr

## Château d'Ortaffa

Medieval Ortaffa sits in a pocket of sunshine between the Pyrénées and the lively port of Collioure, and this big old winemaker's château – once the Episcopal palace of the bishops, adjoined to historic residential buildings – perches on its ancient fortified walls. Large French windows open to the terrace, where breakfast comes with a stunning tableau of mountains and sea with village rooftops tumbling below. Slip into a beautifully restored house, luxurious and with a relaxed holiday feel, whose elegant, pastel-shaded library and guest rooms display your hosts' love of antiques and fine art. Your room may have Picasso prints, bookshelves, an antique child's bed, or quirky graffiti in the loo; one beauty, in pale greys and blues, reveals remnants of the former chapel. Alain (once in advertising) and Michelle (in antiques) are friendly, articulate and know their patch well. Roll down to the port for seafood, slide south along the coast to Spain… for Cadaques, Figueras, Girona. A special spot, away from the bustle of Collioure. *Minimum stay: 2 nights on weekdays. Pets by arrangement.*

| Rooms | 2 doubles; 1 suite for 2-3, 1 suite for 2-5: €110-€130. Extra bed/sofabed available €30 per person per night. |
|---|---|
| Meals | Restaurant in village. |
| Closed | Rarely. |

**Michelle & Alain Batard**
Château d'Ortaffa,
8 rue du Château, 66560 Ortaffa,
Pyrénées-Orientales

| Tel | +33 (0)6 64 14 53 42 |
| Email | chateau.ortaffa@gmail.com |
| Web | www.chateau-ortaffa.com |

## Le Clos de Maussanne

Just off the road and surrounded by vineyards, the unusual 18th-century house, formerly a convent, is smaller inside than it looks. Just one room deep, it is elegantly tall and furnished with sober panache. The lovely salon/dining room, the heart of the place, looks onto noble old plane trees; there's a covered terrace full of tables and a super restaurant kitchen downstairs: Bruno's reputation for good food has spread far and wide, with a surprise a day on the menu and two chefs in the kitchen for big events. Corinne, the other pillar of the house, is both efficient and delightful. The bedrooms, which overlook the garden, are gorgeous with their quiet cream walls, chunky modern furniture, big beds, piqué covers. The largest room has lime-washed timbers to the roof and a pale floor leading out to a private terrace. The final flourish? Elisabeth Baysset's atmospheric paintings. Visit the lovely pedestrianised old quarter of Pézenas and return to a beautiful pool in its walled garden. There's a clutch of cats, a dogs' playground with jumps – and the motorway right there for immediate access.

| Rooms | 4 doubles: €125–€155. |
| | Singles €90. Extra bed/sofabed |
| | available €25 per person per night. |
| Meals | Dinner from €28. Wine €17–€115. |
| Closed | Rarely. |

**Bruno Saurel & Irwin Scott-Davidson**
Le Clos de Maussanne,
Route de Pézenas,
34500 Béziers, Hérault

| Tel | +33 (0)4 67 39 31 81 |
| Email | contact@leclosdemaussanne.com |
| Web | www.leclosdemaussanne.com |

## L'Auberge du Cèdre

No wonder guests return to this big, bustling, ethically-run house. Lively, charming Françoise and her multi-lingual husband Lutz welcome walkers, climbers, cyclists and families. There's a special space for workshop groups, too, separate from the big comfy sitting room. Bedrooms are plain, beamy, white, with the odd splash of ethnic colour and terracotta floors that gleam. Beds, beautifully designed by Lutz and made by local craftsmen, are all twins/doubles. Only a few bathrooms are now shared but the wonderful atmosphere of good humour and laughter has not been affected by the improvements and this is still not a place for luxury-seekers. Art exhibitions are constant, everywhere something beautiful catches the eye. Meals of local and organic produce are chosen from a blackboard menu. It's perfect for families: a swimming pool, space to run around in, boules under the chestnut trees before you turn in for the night. The auberge sits in the middle of the Pic Saint Loup vineyard, one of the best in the Languedoc and Lutz's excellent wine cellar is another reason to prolong your stay.

| | |
|---|---|
| Rooms | 11 twin/doubles; 4 twin/doubles with separate shower & shared wc: €72–€108. 4 suites for 2-4: €114–€208. 1 triple with separate shower & shared wc: €72–€107. 1 apartment for 6 (self-catered or with meals at the auberge): €120–€205 per night. Dinner, B&B €50–€93 extra p.p. |
| Meals | Light lunch €15. À la carte €29–€45 (weekends). Wine €9–€98. |
| Closed | Mid-November to mid-March. |

Françoise Antonin & Lutz Engelmann
L'Auberge du Cèdre,
Domaine de Cazeneuve,
34270 Lauret, Hérault

| | |
|---|---|
| Tel | +33 (0)4 67 59 02 02 |
| Email | welcome@auberge-du-cedre.com |
| Web | www.auberge-du-cedre.com |

## La Lozerette

In September 1878, Robert Louis Stevenson set off from Le Monastier, with Modestine the donkey, to walk the 220 kilometres to St Jean du Gard. Towards the end of his journey he stopped off at the Cévennes village of Cocurès, on the river Tarn, just above the National Park. Here, Pierrette runs the country inn started by her grandmother and passed on to her by her parents. Laid-back staff, warm and friendly, handle all comers to this busy hotel. Pierrette herself is hands-on, running the reception, taking orders in the (excellent) restaurant, managing the wine cellar: a trained sommelier, she will pick you out just the right bottle; her cheeseboard is to die for. Bedrooms, mostly a good size, colour coordinated but not twee, have wooden floors, oh-so-comfortable beds and stripey, checked or flowery décor. The small bar with its cheerful bucket chairs is charming, the gardens pretty, the balconies bright with flowers. The whole hotel shines. Take a drink into the garden or play boules, walk in the National Park, follow Stevenson's trail – on foot, donkey or horseback. Good value, one of the best.

| Rooms | 12 twin/doubles: €65–€100. |
| | 8 family rooms for 4: €96–€109. |
| | Singles €82–€105. |
| | Dinner, B&B €61–€80 per person. |
| Meals | Breakfast €9–€15. |
| | Lunch & dinner €18–€50; |
| | children's menu €11.50. |
| Closed | November – March. |

Pierrette Agulhon
La Lozerette,
Cocurès,
48400 Florac, Lozère
Tel        +33 (0)4 66 45 06 04
Email    lalozerette@wanadoo.fr
Web     www.lalozerette.com

## Château Massal

On the edge of the red-roofed town – one side facing woodland, the other the road, and a many-terraced garden rambling behind – is one of our favourite 'petits châteaux.' Step back in time as you climb a spiral stone stair and cross creaking boards to big beautiful bedrooms with a château feel. Warm deep colours, mosaic floors and walnut parquet set off family furniture to perfection. Light floods in through tall windows, there's a small TV salon especially for guests, and quirky touches abound; one room has a bathroom in the tower, another houses an ancient grand piano. As for Madame, she welcomes you as she would a friend. One of an old French silk family who have been here for generations, she is as elegant and delightful as her home, and full of interest and energy. After a sociable breakfast around the big dining room table, she will tell you all the places to see in this magnificent area, and if there are four of you, she will cook dinner; at weekends you may meet her charming daughter. Take a picnic to the lovely garden, drink in the peace.

| | |
|---|---|
| Rooms | 4 doubles: €68-€98. |
| | Child's bed available. |
| Meals | Restaurant 5km. |
| Closed | Mid-November to March. |

Françoise & Marie-Emmanuelle du Luc
Château Massal,
Bez & Esparon,
30120 Le Vigan, Gard
Tel       +33 (0)4 67 81 07 60
Email     francoiseduluc@gmail.com
Web       www.cevennes-massal.com

## Château de Potelières

Down the grand avenue, through the majestic gates, to a perfect château surrounded by olive groves. It was renovated in the 1780s but the history goes back centuries. Enter to find a hallway flooded with light and a wide stone stair to galleries above, off which terracotta and parquet-floored salons lie. Florence and Eric arrived in 1999, spent a year restoring – brilliantly – then opened to guests. The golden yellow dining room opens up to a balustraded front terrace, glassed-in for autumn and spring and open in summer (ideal for weddings), where buffet breakfast feasts are taken. Find a library and a music room, a fabulous billiard room and a scarlet salon with a fire that can be lit on cooler nights. Outside: secluded benches under vast trees, a sleek gallery by the pool with loungers and parasols, and orchards for homemade jams. All you hear is the flowing of the fountain and the distant church bell. Enjoy stunning Uzès (35km) with its cafés, galleries and market, and the gorges and grottos of the Parc National. Return to fine bedrooms with great tall windows and bathrooms with fabulous showers. *Babes in arms stay free. Cot available.*

| | |
|---|---|
| Rooms | 6 doubles: €100–€180. |
| | 1 suite for 3, |
| | 2 suites for 4: €150–€255. |
| | Child's bed available (for children aged 2-10), €15 p.p. per night. |
| Meals | Restaurant 5-minute walk.. |
| Closed | 5 October to 18 December & 5 January to 31 March. |

Florence & Eric Odin
Château de Potelières,
Le Village,
30500 Potelières, Gard

Tel     +33 (0)4 66 24 80 92
Email   infos@chateau-potelieres.com
Web    www.chateau-potelieres.com

## L'Enclos des Lauriers Roses

The tiny reception gives no clue as to what lies beyond; a hamlet within a village. Step across a sunny dining room, through French windows – and blink. Scattered around three swimming pools is a cluster of cottage rooms. Newly built of pantile and stone recovered from old village houses, most have a private terrace or garden. Large, airy and prettily furnished with painted Provençal pieces and fabulous mattresses, each has a different charm – 'Mimosa' has a finely upholstered yellow bed, 'Amarilys' has big chunky terracotta tiles. Walls are white, ceilings neatly beamed, there might be a bed tucked under a stone arch or extra beds for children on the mezzanine. Bathrooms are modern and marbled and a fridge keeps drinks chilled. Madame supervises the excellent restaurant, Monsieur does the wine – 500 bottles in the cellar – and their sons take care of the buildings and garden. Eat on the terrace or in the dining room; the locals love the cooking, too. Nîmes, Avignon and beaches are less than an hour, swim in the Gorges du Gardon, walk among the pines. As for the village, it's charming.

| Rooms | 11 twin/doubles: €80–€190. |
|---|---|
| | 10 family rooms for 4: €120–€290. |
| | 2 triples: €95–€130. |
| | Dinner, B&B €80–€130 extra p.p. |
| | Extra bed/sofabed available €15 per person per night. |
| Meals | Breakfast €15. |
| | Lunch & dinner €24–€45. |
| Closed | Christmas & New Year. |

**Bargeton Family**
L'Enclos des Lauriers Roses,
71 rue du 14 Juillet,
30210 Cabrières, Gard

| Tel | +33 (0)4 66 75 25 42 |
|---|---|
| Email | reception@hotel-lauriersroses.com |
| Web | www.hotel-lauriersroses.co.uk |

Rhône Valley – Alps

## Le Clair de la Plume

Set in a sea of lavender, laden with literature, history and flowers, Grignan is a treat of a little town. So is this welcoming hotel within its sheltering walls (some rooms are in another charming house 100m away). Push the heavy gates of the pink *maison de maître* onto a special place. Jean-Luc Valadeau has created a warm hospitable "home with all the comforts of a hotel". He and his staff are a community, ushering you through deliciously elegant rooms where antique pieces catch your eye, and the small terraced garden has a natural pool and a lovely view over the town. Peaceful bedrooms are divided between the main and the second house. A combination of great taste and authenticity mixes Louis Philippe wardrobes, country-style wicker, luxurious bathrooms, washed or ragged walls, original tiles and shining oak planks. After a generous breakfast, walk into town or borrow bikes and explore the picture-perfect villages. Then return to the organic garden restaurant for exotic selections of teas and mouthwatering pâtisseries among the roses or a delectable dinner in the main restaurant – or both.

| | |
|---|---|
| Rooms | 2 doubles, 10 twin/doubles: €99–€395. 3 family suites for 4: €395–€495. Extra bed/sofabed available €45 per person per night. |
| Meals | Breakfast €19. Lunch €24.50. Dinner €45. Garden restaurant (lunch & tea July/August), €24.50. |
| Closed | Never. |

Jean-Luc Valadeau
Le Clair de la Plume,
2 Place de Mail,
26230 Grignan, Drôme

| | |
|---|---|
| Tel | +33 (0)4 75 91 81 30 |
| Email | info@clairplume.com |
| Web | www.clairplume.com |

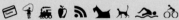

## Château les Oliviers de Salettes

After three years of renovations and meticulous attention to detail from gentle owners Robin and Dominique, the hotel runs like clockwork. The building that exists today, a three-storey house of impressive proportions with a turret at each end, was part of a much larger château, the centre of a vast vineyard. Now it lords it over five hectares of finely landscaped parkland, with dining terraces, boules pitch and infinity pool, and panoramas that reach to the Alps. Honeymooners, families, the lazy and the lively: all will love it here. Apart from cookery lessons, wine tastings and electric-bike rentals, there's tree climbing and paragliding, canoeing and windsurfing, riding and golf. And a sweet spa to recover in: how about a bamboo massage? Uncluttered bedrooms are full of lofty splendour and furnished in classic French style, their stone walls and great beams intact; bathrooms (one in the dovecote) are state of the art. But dinner is the highlight of the stay: beautiful food from beautiful produce accompanied by heavenly views. The 'menu du midi' is great value. *Sofabed available in some rooms.*

| Rooms | 13 doubles (6 in outbuilding): €99–€169. 8 suites for 2 (1 in outbuilding), 1 suite for 4 with private terrace: €169–€415. Singles €99–€159. Dinner, B&B €154–€214 per person. Extra bed/sofabed available €39 per person per night. |
|---|---|
| Meals | Breakfast €16. Lunch €15-29. Dinner, 4 courses, €43; 5 courses, €65. Wine €26–€60. Restaurants 1km. |
| Closed | Rarely. |

**Robin Leyssens & Dominique Berger**
Château les Oliviers de Salettes,
1205 route du Château,
26450 Charols, Drôme

| Tel | +33 (0)4 75 00 19 30 |
| Email | contact@chateau-lesoliviers.com |
| Web | www.chateau-lesoliviers.com |

## La Treille Muscate

It's love at first sight with this jewel of a 17th-century Provençal mas set in a medieval village of pottery and antiques sellers. Inside are stone walls, old beams, vaulted ceilings and a superb ancient fireplace. From two of the salons, some of the bedrooms and the popular dining terrace, the views over the Rhône valley and the forests are breathtaking, the distant power station just an outline; there's also an exquisite enclosed garden for quiet moments. Rooms – four with private terraces – are an inviting and elegant blend of traditional and comfy modern, with choice antiques much in evidence and lots of colour variations, offset by bursts of dazzlingly pure white. The traditional indoor public areas, dressed in stonework and earth tones, are equally welcoming, and the cooking gets rave reviews from France's top sources, with the décor sharing the billing. Owner Katy, a former language teacher in France and England, clearly loves her work and greets her guests like old friends. Hiking, horse riding, golf, great markets and summer festivals round out the menu. The Rhône Valley at its most romantic.

| Rooms | 8 doubles, 3 twins: €70-€160. 1 suite for 2: €120-€150. Extra bed/sofabed available €18 per person per night. |
|---|---|
| Meals | Breakfast €12. Dinner €20-€40. Wine €18-€82. |
| Closed | 7 December to 12 February. |

**Katy Delaitre**
La Treille Muscate,
26270 Cliousclat, Drôme
Tel      +33 (0)4 75 63 13 10
Email    latreillemuscate@wanadoo.fr
Web      www.latreillemuscate.com

## Château de Fontblachère

Framed by a forested valley and mountainous horizons, this 17th-century château marries Provençal peace with deep comfort and style. Bernard greets you in a courtyard whose manicured hedges and white roses dissolve into parkland: a panoramic pool, Japanese fish pond, tennis court, jacuzzi… Under vaulted ceilings are more treats: a large, sunny sitting room with log fire, piano, candles, art and polished boards; an orangery dining room with Turkish cushions and walls decorated with vintage rugs, opening onto a pretty covered courtyard. Dine on iced melon soup, asparagus, roast quail, local goat's cheese; breakfasts are good too with local jams and strawberries, and sprightly Bernard cooks, serves, pours and chats all the while. Immaculate bedrooms are all on the first floor and have original terracotta flooring with quantities of beautiful kilims, marble fireplaces topped with old mirrors, flowers and excellent beds with fine white linen. Plenty of space for families too. The valley cries out for walking, riding and fishing in the Rhône; summer operas and great markets will keep you happily busy too.

| Rooms | 2 family rooms for 2-3, 1 family room for 2-4, 1 family room for 2-5: €115-€255. |
| Meals | Dinner with wine, €35. Restaurants 3km. |
| Closed | 16 September to 14 June. |

Bernard Liaudois & Eric Dussiot
Château de Fontblachère,
07210 St Lager Bressac, Ardèche

| Tel | +33 (0)4 75 65 15 02 |
| Mobile | +33 (0)6 11 18 23 83 |
| Email | eric.dussiot@yahoo.fr |
| Web | www.chateau-fontblachere.com |

## Château de Balazuc

A remarkable place. This 11th-century château, above the Ardèche river and the tiny village of Balazuc, is imposing from the outside and relaxed within. Find an inspired 'ancient meets modern' style; the main living room has an enormous fireplace and wide stone floor; the dining room has a big wooden table with a multi-coloured mat running the length of it and seven red lamps hanging above. The warmly friendly Lemaires – multilingual former journalists – invite you to mingle in the evening for drinks and nibbles. Breakfasts are convivial affairs too, served either in the vaulted dining room or out on the view-filled terrace: a whopping great board with local cheeses and ham, jams, honey, chestnut spread, pancakes, fruits, perhaps a pear and cinnamon gâteau… Choose from hugely comfortable, radically different rooms – soft linen, Moroccan touches, balconies, a huge chain armour curtain… sleep to the sound of owls, the river – and chirping frogs in summer. Explore the village, visit the Grotte Chauvet cave – the oldest art gallery on earth – go canoeing, walking, cycling. Fabulous.

| | |
|---|---|
| Rooms | 4 doubles: €140–€180. |
| Meals | Restaurants within walking distance. |
| Closed | 1 December to 31 January. |

Luc & Florence Lemaire
Château de Balazuc,
07120 Balazuc, Ardèche

| | |
|---|---|
| Tel | +33 (0)9 51 39 92 11 |
| Mobile | +33 (0)6 07 16 66 58 |
| Email | contact@chateaudebalazuc.com |
| Web | www.chateaudebalazuc.com |

## Château Clément

On a wooded hill filled with birds and views, overlooking the spa town of Vals les Bains and the valley beyond, this ornate 19th-century château has seen service as both a wartime prison and a holiday centre. Constantly renovated by Éric and Marie-Antoinette, it is now both luxurious eco-hotel and family home. An extraordinary wooden staircase sweeps you up to airy bedrooms of understated elegance and contemporary details that complement original glowing parquet, antiques, tall views to gardens and the undulating Ardèche. The apartment is a must for families. Magnificent new garden-level rooms in exciting contemporary style have designer furniture, subtle led lighting, jacuzzi baths, private terraces. House and setting may be grand but the young Chabots are as welcoming as can be, grow their own fruit and veg and dine with their guests. Éric, an experienced cook and pâtissier-chocolatier, works his magic at dinner. Breakfasts are fabulous too. Let yourself be enticed from the rose-rich garden and the elegant salons to the summer pool on the sunny south terrace. A cocoon for the senses, a magical place. *Min. stay: 2 nights in high season. Pets by arrangement.*

| Rooms | 2 doubles: €180–€200. |
|---|---|
| | 2 suites for 2, 1 suite for 2-6: €230–€600. |
| | 1 apartment for 4, 1 apartment for 10 (loft for 8-10): €2,000–€4,000 per week. |
| | Singles €135–€250. Extra bed/sofabed available €50 per person per night. |
| Meals | Dinner with wine, €75–€100, on request. |
| Closed | Mid-November to mid-March. |

Marie-Antoinette & Éric Chabot
Château Clément, La Châtaigneraie,
07600 Vals les Bains, Ardèche

Tel       +33 (0)4 75 87 40 13
Mobile    +33 (0)6 72 75 03 36
Email     contact@chateauclement.com
Web       www.chateauclement.com

## Château de la Motte

The fairy-tale good looks of this Roannais château in peaceful parkland charm from the outset. Henrik and Liliane lavish it with care and sound judgement, bringing back its traditional 18th-century allure with fine furniture and art collected over decades in the business. Sophisticated Swedish francophiles, they can chat and advise in an impressive range of languages and see that you get the most out of your stay, whether you simply want to unwind by the pool or in the sauna, or take off in a hot-air balloon. Your rooms are supremely comfortable as well as stylish and you'll want to linger over brioche and homemade jams at breakfast. At dinner there's a choice of menus – local meat and game are outstanding – and wines are from the modest to the more rarified. It's a special treat to dine out on the island in the little house made for the Paris World Exhibition in 1889. Or you might want to push the boat out and dine at Le Prieuré in nearby Ambierle under a former Troisgros chef. You're well-placed too for visits to vineyards, breweries and chocolatiers; to historic Charlieu and St Haon le Châtel.

| | |
|---|---|
| Rooms | 4 doubles, 1 twin/double, 1 four-poster: €110–€150. 1 suite for 4: €180. Singles €90–€100. Extra bed/sofabed available €25 per person per night. |
| Meals | Dinner €28–€35. Wine from €15. Restaurant 5km. |
| Closed | Mid-December to February. |

Henrik & Liliane Lantz
Château de la Motte,
42640 Noailly, Loire

| | |
|---|---|
| Tel | +33 (0)4 77 66 64 60 |
| Email | chateaudelamotte@wanadoo.fr |
| Web | www.chateaudelamotte.info |

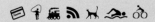

## Château de Chambost

Take a step back in time... it takes little to imagine the owners' aristocratic ancestors residing in this impressive, 16th-century hillside château. Traditional going on lavish, it's still fit for Lyonnais elite. In the first floor reading/sitting room find imposing boar-heads mounted on the walls, armchairs upholstered in oriental fabric and quantities of books and glossy magazines. Bedrooms are decked out in toile de Jouy and period furniture, exquisite marquetry parquet floors, floral linen and trays with pretty china cups; one's still adorned with original 1850s parrot-flocked wallpaper and some have views across the valley to the village. In the basement lies another gem: a striking umbrella-vaulted dining room, where guests eat together round a convivial table, and vivacious, friendly hostess Véronique serves beef reared on the château's estate and homemade cheeses; you're welcome to have aperitifs and nibbles with the family beforehand. The cows have bagged most of the garden, but guests can retire to the elegant sitting room to plan countryside forays beyond.

| Rooms | 2 doubles, 1 twin: €90–€100. |
| | 1 family room for 3: €115. |
| Meals | Dinner with wine, €30. |
| | Restaurant 15km. |
| Closed | Rarely. |

Vivien & Véronique de Lescure
Château de Chambost,
69770 Chambost Longessaigne, Rhône
Tel      +33 (0)4 74 26 37 49
Mobile   +33 (0)6 30 52 04 84
Email    infos@chateaudechambost.com
Web      www.chateaudechambost.com

## Château de Briante

A gorgeous stop-over in the vineyards if you are keen to see how a winery really works. You stay in this exotic-looking château – all glowing-pink stone and striking towers, surrounded by baize-green parkland. It's grand but with a lovely laid-back unpretentious touch thanks to young and enthusiastic owners Lauren and her husband, who are passionate about what they do. Rooms in the Tuscan-style wing mix original features – polished floors and wood panelling – with cool furnishings – vintage chairs and modern art. Sleek in silvers and coffees, all have flat screen TVs, well-dressed beds and heavenly green views; two have sun-drenched balconies. Breakfast on local cheese and hams in the ground floor dining room, then slip through French windows to stroll the parkland – with its rose-decked orangerie – explore the vineyards or cool off in the good-sized pool. When you're feeling peckish you can nip into Saint Lager or Belleville, where there are plenty of restaurants to choose from. Do organise a wine tasting here – the family have been producing excellent Beaujolais wines since 1787. You will taste, learn and be charmed. *Cot available. Pets welcome, ask in advance.*

| Rooms | 3 doubles: €130-€150. Extra bed/sofabed available €20 per person per night. |
| Meals | Restaurant 1.5km. |
| Closed | Never. |

Lauren Schneider
Château de Briante,
810 route de Briante,
69220 St Lager, Rhône

| Tel | +33 (0)6 83 31 28 50 |
| Email | lfaupin@gmail.com |
| Web | www.domainedebriante.fr |

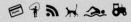

Entry 286   Map 11

## Château de Marmont

An amazing avenue of plane trees delivers you to an authentic 'time warp' château experience – and private access directly onto the second hole: bring the golf clubs! Madame, a classical historian, is a joy, and her house as colourful as she. Find family heirlooms polished to a honeyed finish, period details and interesting collections, original wallpapers, a billiard room you can use and many good books in English and in French – tempting to find a comfortable, quiet spot and just curl up to read. Up the grand stairs is a bedroom with books and fresh flowers, and a bathroom with a claw foot bath and trompe-l'œil walls. Elegant breakfasts are taken in the orangery, windows flung open to the garden in summer, or by the fire on chillier mornings: classical music plays, the candle is lit, the coffee is hot, the oranges and the squeezer are to hand, bread is fresh from the village and the homemade jam is delicious. The peace is deep (no babbling TV, no internet connection for interruptions) so it won't suit those looking for a wild time, but people who love houses and history will be very happy indeed here.

| Rooms | 1 double: €95. |
| | 1 family suite for 3-5: €140. |
| Meals | Restaurant 3km. |
| Closed | Rarely. |

Geneviève & Henri Guido–Alhéritière
Château de Marmont,
2043 route de Condeissiat,
01960 St André sur Vieux Jonc, Ain
Tel       +33 (0)4 74 52 79 74
Web      www.chateau-marmont.info

## Château de Tanay

Surrounded by flat lands, a magnificent château in acres of parkland with pool. Inside is equally splendid. A sleek modern décor illuminates fine stonework and medieval beams, there's a games room for children, a grand piano for musicians and, beneath the great carved fireplace, a convivial breakfast table. In summer you can tuck into croissants, hams and jams by the moat beneath the willow. Spend the day in charming old Lyon or treat the family to the Parc des Oiseaux... return for a château tour with your hosts (Monsieur has a passion for history), trot off for dinner at the local pizzeria. Tasteful bedrooms, two large, two smaller but still a good size, with compact bathrooms spotless and chic, lie in the courtyard stables but the family room is in the château itself – with an amazing massage bath. Your hosts have heaps of information about the area: the Hameau Dubœuf wine museum is not far and the region is brilliant for Beaujolais. No food here but some good restaurants in town; pick one right on the river. *Extra bed available.*

| Rooms | 4 twins/doubles: €95–€130. |
|-------|----------------------------|
|       | 1 family room: €160–€200. |
| Meals | Restaurant 1km. |
| Closed | 1 October to 31 March. |

**Benoît Haym**
Château de Tanay,
Chemin de Tanay,
01600 Saint-Dider-de-Formans, Ain

| Tel | +33 (0)6 63 94 70 27 |
|-----|----------------------|
| Email | info@chateau-tanay.com |
| Web | www.chateau-tanay.com |

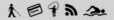

## Château de Pâquier

Old, mighty, atmospheric – yet so homely. On the edge of a picturesque village is an alpine château with huge rooms, lofty beams and windows with breathtaking views. Beyond: horses, hens (whence breakfast's eggs) and terraced gardens beautiful to wander. Bedrooms are up an ancient spiral staircase that sets the imagination reeling; with their handsome wardrobes, polished beds and toasty terracotta floors, they are sober, comfortable, elegant and uncluttered. Twice a week, kind generous Hélène prepares dinner in her modernised 17th-century tower kitchen (wood-fired range, stone sink, cobbled floor). She makes her own bread, honey, jams and walnut aperitif, and the wines come from their Montpellier vineyard. If you like get-up-and-go there's masses to do: watersports at Lac de Monteynard, skiing at Gresse and Vercors (downhill and cross country), hiking and biking... and there's an 'accrobranche' in the forest! The château is ten minutes from the main road to Grenoble and yet is utterly tranquil. Stay one night and you'll wish you'd stayed more.

| Rooms | 3 twin/doubles: €90–€110. |
| | 2 family rooms for 5: €86–€146. |
| Meals | Dinner with wine, €16–€27. |
| Closed | Rarely. |

Jacques & Hélène Rossi
Château de Pâquier,
Chemin du Château,
38650 St Martin de la Cluze, Isère

| Tel | +33 (0)4 76 72 77 33 |
| Email | chateau.de.paquier@free.fr |
| Web | chateau.de.paquier.free.fr |

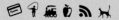

## Château de la Commanderie

Grand it appears, and some of the makers of that grandeur – Knights Templar, princes and prime ministers – gaze down on you in the dining room, a favourite restaurant for the discerning palates of Grenoble. Yet the atmosphere is of an intimate family hotel. The whole place is awash with antiques and heirlooms, breakfast is delicious, good taste prevails and flowers add that touch of life and genuine attention. And there are massages galore in the sumptuous spa. Bedrooms are in four buildings, old and new, adding to the sense of intimacy. Rooms in château and chalet are traditional with carved wooden beds and gilt-framed mirrors, though some of them give onto a small road. The Orangerie's rooms (as you'll discover once you have negotiated the rather plain corridors) look out over fine parkland, and are deliciously peaceful. The least expensive rooms are in the Petit Pavillon, on the roadside. But whichever you choose, you will be beautifully looked after by the Beaumont brothers – they grew up here – in this smart suburb of Grenoble. *Signs for 'La Commanderie' indicate an area of town, not the château.*

| | |
|---|---|
| Rooms | 42 twin/doubles: €102–€190.<br>Singles €102–€180.<br>Dinner, B&B €107–€123 per person. |
| Meals | Buffet breakfast €16.50.<br>Lunch & dinner €30–€84.<br>Wine €30–€50. Restaurant closed<br>Mondays, Saturday lunch & Sundays. |
| Closed | 20 December to 3 January. |

**Monsieur de Beaumont**
Château de la Commanderie,
17 av d'Echirolles, Eybens,
38230 Grenoble, Isère

| | |
|---|---|
| Tel | +33 (0)4 76 25 34 58 |
| Email | resa@commanderie.fr |
| Web | www.commanderie.fr |

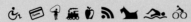

## Château des Allues

A breathtaking setting for an atmospheric château, 13th century and facing the mountains. There's an incredible feeling of openness and space here, and a house party feel if you stay. Stéphane's warm personality gives the place soul, and he loves to connect with guests; Didier too is charming. Gourmet meals are served in a characterfully splendid dining room and the food is innovative and delicious, with vegetables from the potager – a glory. Inside: flowers, paintings, sculptures, quirky-chic antiques, music classical and modern, and comforting old-style suites with huge walk-in wardrobes and tip-top bathrooms. The rooms vary in style, some lofty and handsome with four-poster beds, others floral with an English country theme. What's so lovely here is that the house looks over a wide valley giving you an incredible feeling of tranquillity, and in spite of the mountains, there's no sense of being hemmed in. Breakfasts, a fine spread of savoury and sweet, include homemade brioche and jams and set you up for the day. Climb snow-topped peaks, collapse by the pool, visit the Château de Miolans. *Cot available.*

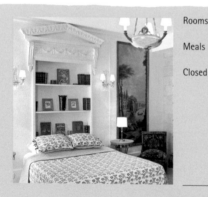

| Rooms | 2 doubles: €140-€165. |
| | 2 suites for 4, 1 suite for 2: €150-€240. |
| Meals | Dinner with wine, €48, book in advance. Restaurants 5-minute drive. |
| Closed | 3 weeks in December. |

Stéphane Vandeville
Château des Allues,
73250 St Pierre d'Albigny, Savoie
Tel        +33 (0)6 75 38 61 56
Email      info@chateaudesallues.com
Web        www.chateaudesallues.com

## La Ferme du Chozal

Meals with family and friends taste best in the mountain air. From the suntrap terrace of this small hotel you can try fish from the lakes, meat from the pastures, and edible flowers from the garden. Ferme du Chozal has some of the best views in the village; on a clear day you can see Mont Blanc. Frédéric and Anne-Christine offer you home-baked bread for breakfast, homemade yogurts and jams, Beaufort butter and cheeses, eggs, ham and fruit salads, and their staff, young and multi-lingual, are charming. Wake to green fields, birdsong and cowbells, hike to the Cormet de Roseland's glorious lake, and return to new pine, old beams, soft beds and deep baths. Cosy up in a little library filled with magazines, board games and books (and DVDs for the mini cinema), laze by the heated pool, soak in the jacuzzi with an aperitif. In the second chalet (connected by a tunnel) is that wonderful restaurant and its excellent cellar. Some bedrooms have low beams, others have balconies.

| Rooms | 6 doubles, 1 double (in outbuilding): €120-€375.<br>1 suite for 4 (1 double & bunkbed room): €215-€320.<br>4 family rooms for 2-4: €120-€240.<br>Breakfast & dinner €52 per person; children €35. |
| --- | --- |
| Meals | Dinner from €32. |
| Closed | Rarely. |

Anne-Christine & Frédéric Boulanger
La Ferme du Chozal,
73620 Hauteluce, Savoie

| Tel | +33 (0)4 79 38 18 18 |
| --- | --- |
| Email | informations@lafermeduchozal.com |
| Web | www.lafermeduchozal.com |

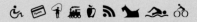

Entry 292   Map 12

## Hôtel Le Cottage Bise

Not many hotels are blessed with such an eye-capturing lakeside position; gazing from the terrace at the sun setting over the Roc de Chère, you could be in a Wagner opera. The three buildings that make up this supremely well-run hotel resemble – quelle surprise! – Alpine chalets; what's more, they are set in well-planted gardens with a classy pool and perfectly gravelled pathways. Jean-Claude and Christine run their relaxed and not-so-small hotel with quiet Savoyard efficiency and a proper concern for your comfort. Rooms, each one different, come in two styles: traditional, with floral papers and antique paintings, and contemporary, with paler walls and modern art; all are big with swish bathrooms and the balconied suites have splendid views to the lake and mountains. The food – served in the restaurant or on the lake-view terrace – is first class (note, half-boarders have less choice). You are away from the bustle of Annecy but close enough to dabble if you wish... the old quarter is a delight. Sail, windsurf, waterski, pedalo – the lake laps at your feet.

| | |
|---|---|
| Rooms | 25 twin/doubles: €140–€270. 6 suites for 4: €300–€450. |
| Meals | Breakfast €21. Lunch €30–€75. Dinner €47–€75. Wine €25–€70. Restaurants 5-minute walk. |
| Closed | October – April. |

Jean-Claude & Christine Bise
Hôtel Le Cottage Bise,
Au Bord du Lac,
74290 Talloires, Haute-Savoie
Tel     +33 (0)4 50 60 71 10
Email   cottagebise@wanadoo.fr
Web     www.cottagebise.com

## Les Chalets de la Serraz

You can gaze out to the Aravis mountains and the magnificent Etale Massif from your bedroom window (or dinner table) at this traditional Savoyard once-upon-a-time farmhouse: it's easy to imagine following in the trails of Vincent Vittoz, just one of the famous sons of snowy La Clusaz. For this is essential Haute-Savoie make no mistake. In winter the snowfields drift right up to the timbers and after a local breakfast, served to your bedroom if you wish, you can ski straight to the lifts. This place has been in energetic Raphaël's family since 1874, but the welcome is friendly and the homely feel is apparent throughout: find animal skins and an open fire in the communal sitting area – great for relaxing with a hot chocolate after a challenging day on the slopes. Families love it here. Stay in the hotel or in one of the chalets with their authentic and cosy mix of pine, oak and stone. South facing views soar across the pool towards peaks and running streams. In summer, everyone dines outside in a convivial way and there's plenty to do round and about including visiting cheese farms in the high pastures.

| | |
|---|---|
| Rooms | 3 twin/doubles: €260–€300. 1 suite for 2: €280–€445. 1 family room for 4: €405–€430. 1 triple: €330–€555. 1 chalet for 2-4, 2 chalets for 2-5: €385–€465 per night. |
| Meals | Prices include breakfast & dinner. Wine list €30–€40. |
| Closed | Rarely. |

**Raphaël Gallay**
Les Chalets de la Serraz,
3862 route du Col des Aravis,
74220 La Clusaz, Haute-Savoie

| | |
|---|---|
| Tel | +33 (0)4 50 02 48 29 |
| Email | contact@laserraz.com |
| Web | www.laserraz.com |

## Villa Rose

Don't be fooled by the perfectly typical exterior of this 1900s Alpine villa set back from the busy road and looking innocent behind wooden shutters and box hedges. Step inside to four floors of precisely designed rooms with unusual ornaments, feathery lampshades, bright modern colours – silver, black, lime green, bright pink. A large sitting room in cool greys and creams has plenty of comfy seating, a warming log fire, roses by a local artist on the floor, silvery reindeer on the walls; the sun room is off here with long views facing east. Upstairs is the dining room where you eat under the steely eye of a cow's head sculpture, or out on the terrace in summer months. Bedrooms differ in style, but all have stunning beds, fine Italian linen and towels, robes, slippers, TVs and bathroom treats. Staff are laid-back and friendly, breakfast is flexible and includes Welsh rarebit or sausage and bacon hash, coffee and tea are available all day and there's an honesty bar. A spoiling place from which to ski (car to main lift included of course), or enjoy summer. *Children over 6 welcome. Parking on-site.*

| | |
|---|---|
| Rooms | 4 doubles: €275-€350. |
| | 1 suite for 4: €325-€395.. |
| | Dinner, B&B: €325-€495 per room per night. |
| Meals | Breakfast included. |
| | Restaurants 2-minute walk. |
| Closed | Rarely. |

Selina
Villa Rose,
74 Place des Sept Monts,
74340 Samoens, Haute-Savoie

| | |
|---|---|
| Tel | +33 (0)7 84 27 51 72 |
| Email | info@villarosesamoens.com |
| Web | www.villarosesamoens.com |

Hotel Rhône Valley – Alps

## Au Coin du Feu-Chilly Powder

The homeward piste takes you to the door; the cable car, opposite, sweeps you to the peaks. The chalet is named after its magnificent central fireplace… on one side gleaming leather sofas, on the other, red dining chairs at a long table. Everything feels generous here: great beams span the chalet's length, windows look up to the cliffs of the Hauts Forts, high ceilings give a sense of space. There's a reading room on the mezzanine above the living area with books, internet, antique globe and worn leather armchairs, and a small bar made of English oak by a carpenter friend. Bedrooms are Alpine-swish and themed: there's the 'Toy Room' for families, the 'English Room' that sports a bowler hat. The carpets are sisal, one room's four-poster is veiled in muslin and the bathrooms have luxury bathrobes and shower heads as big as plates. The chef produces the best of country cooking, and Paul and Francesca can organise everything, including torchlight descents. There's massage, a sauna, a hot tub outside, DVDs to cheer wet days – even an in-house crèche. A great spot for families.

| | |
|---|---|
| Rooms | 9 twin/doubles: €100.<br>8 family rooms for 4: €120-€150.<br>Winter dinner, B&B €895-€1,425 p.p. per week. |
| Meals | Picnic €10. Dinner with wine, €45. |
| Closed | Rarely. |

**Paul & Francesca Eyre**
Au Coin du Feu-Chilly Powder,
2740 rue des Ardoisières,
74110 Morzine, Haute-Savoie

Tel +33 (0)4 50 74 75 21
Email paul@chillypowder.com
Web www.chillypowder.com

Entry 296   Map 12

## The Farmhouse

The day starts with a breakfast spread in the cattle shed – now a deeply atmospheric dining room – and ends with a slap-up dinner hosted by Dorrien. Many years ago he gave up England for the oldest farmhouse in Morzine – the lovely, steeply pitched Mas de la Coutettaz at the peaceful end of town. Push open the mellow carved door to find a 1771 interior of dark chunky beams, huge Morzine slate flags and patina'd pine doors with original mouldings. Big, characterful, comfortable bedrooms, whose bathrooms promise white robes and lavish lotions, are reached via a central stone stair; some have mountain views. At the end of the garden is an exquisite little mazot, its bedroom up a steep outside stair. Morzine is the perfect staging post for the Avoriaz and Portes du Soleil, so come for hiking, biking, swimming in the lakes; in winter, a 'ski host' at the farmhouse introduces you to the runs, and dinners are lively. Return to a hot toddy in the bar and a crackling log fire, lit at the merest hint of chill, even in summer. Final proof (as if you needed it) that you will adore The Farmhouse and long to return.

| | |
|---|---|
| Rooms | 3 doubles, 2 suites for 2: €90-€260. 2 family rooms for 4, 1 family room for 3: €90-€312. 3 cottages for 2: €90-€260 per night. Winter dinner, B&B €250-€442 for 2. Ask about singles prices. |
| Meals | Dinner, 4 courses with wine, €30-€40. Dinner, B&B mandatory December to April, on weekly basis. |
| Closed | May & October/November. |

Dorrien Ricardo
Le Mas de la Coutettaz, 429 Chemin de
la Coutettaz, 74110 Morzine

| | |
|---|---|
| Tel | +33 (0)4 50 79 08 26 |
| Mobile | +33 (0)6 80 91 63 21 |
| Email | info@thefarmhouse.co.uk |
| Web | www.thefarmhouse.co.uk |

Provence – Alps – Riviera

## La Bastide de Boulbon

It will fire your imagination. Leave the main road for a secret, dead-end village. There, on the hill, are windmills and a huge castle, old houses line the quaint narrow streets that climb to the summit. In the middle, is this impressive 200-year-old mansion. Jan and Marie-Claire came from Belgium three years ago and have already made their mark by combining proper professional skills with genuine pleasure in receiving guests. They have put their heart and soul into the renovation and decoration and have done a fabulous landscaping job on the garden. Four huge taupe parasols marry the dining patio to the elegant façade with its same-coloured shutters; the giant centuries-old plane trees and trickling stone fountain teach a gentler sense of time. Inside, elegant proportions, clean lines, modern simplicity and the subtlest palette of neutral and dusky tones, with the occasional bold piece of art, make for restful spaces. Be prepared to eat well: Marie-Claire grew up in one of Brussels' best restaurants and has taken on a new French chef. The scene is set for a luxurious, relaxing stay.

| | |
|---|---|
| Rooms | 2 doubles, 4 twin/doubles: €145–€175. 2 suites for 4: €205–€240. |
| Meals | Breakfast €17. Dinner €15–€20. Wine €22–€80. |
| Closed | November – March. |

**Jan De Mulder & Marie-Claire Callens**
La Bastide de Boulbon,
Rue de l'Hôtel de Ville,
13150 Boulbon, Bouches-du-Rhône

| | |
|---|---|
| Tel | +33 (0)4 90 93 11 11 |
| Email | contact@labastidedeboulbon.com |
| Web | www.labastidedeboulbon.com |

## Mas de l'Oulivié

The olive groves, lavender fields and chalky hillsides of Les Baux are a dream of a setting for this Provence-style hotel, roofed with reclaimed terracotta, sheltered by cypress and oleander. The hotel reflects owner Isabelle's passion for sustainable tourism, she is a respected contributor to the local economy and every detail has been carefully considered: food from local producers, local artisan furniture, painted and waxed walls, homemade tiles round the fabulous pool (it has a gentle slope for little ones and a hot tub). Furnishings are fresh, local, designed for deep comfort. Bedrooms are gorgeously coloured, country-style with an elegant twist, some have their own grassy sitting area, the suite has a private patio, the road is discreet. Filled with flowers in the summer, the bright and cosy living-room has a rustic fireplace. The Achards love to provide guests and their children with the best and that includes a superb well-being and massage room, delicious lunches by the pool, electric bikes for the hills. One of the crème de la crème of Provence's 'hotels au naturel' – near oh-so-pretty Les Baux.

| Rooms | 25 doubles: €111–€420.<br>2 suites for 2: €384–€660.<br>Extra bed/sofabed available €40 per person per night. |
| --- | --- |
| Meals | Breakfast €18; children's menu €9.<br>Poolside lunch €9–€35.<br>Wine €17–€39. Restaurants 2km. |
| Closed | 11 November to 24 March. |

**Emmanuel & Isabelle Achard**
Mas de l'Oulivié, Les Arcoules,
13520 Les Baux de Provence,
Bouches-du-Rhône

| | |
| --- | --- |
| Tel | +33 (0)4 90 54 35 78 |
| Email | contact@masdeloulivie.com |
| Web | www.masdeloulivie.com |

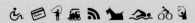

## Mas du Vigueirat

A small pool cascading into a larger pool, a walled garden with quiet corners, wisteria, honeysuckle, trees of all sorts… and nothing to disturb the view but meadows, woods and horses. You'll find it impossible to leave this tranquil, scented spot – although St Rémy (galleries, Van Gogh museum) is just up the road, and Arles, Avignon, the lavender fields and olive groves of Les Baux de Provence are not much further. High plane trees flank the drive to the dusky pink, grey-shuttered Provençal farmhouse and inside all is light, simplicity and gentle elegance. Bedrooms are uncluttered spaces of bleached colours, limed walls and terracotta floors. Views are over the beautiful garden or meadows; ground-floor 'Maillane' has a private terrace. The high-beamed dining room/salon is a calm white space with a corner for sofas and books. and if the weather's warm you'll take breakfast under the plane tree. After a dip in the pool or a jaunt on the bike, pop into St Rémy for cafés, galleries, boutiques and one of the best weekly markets (Wednesdays) in Provence.

| | |
|---|---|
| Rooms | 3 doubles: €145–€165. |
| Meals | Picnic available. |
| | Poolside meals in summer €15–€20. |
| | Restaurants 3km. |
| Closed | Christmas. |

Catherine Jeanniard
Mas du Vigueirat, 1977 chemin du
grand Bourbourel, 13210 St Rémy de
Provence, Bouches-du-Rhône

| | |
|---|---|
| Tel | +33 (0)4 90 92 56 07 |
| Email | contact@mas-du-vigueirat.com |
| Web | www.mas-du-vigueirat.com |

## Le Mas des Carassins

Walking distance from lovely St Rémy, the charming mas settles gently into its leafy cocoon, a massive garden bursting with oleanders, lavender, lemons and fine pieces by local designers and Balinese artists. After a swim – in one of two pools – you have boules, badminton and bikes to hire. This is Van Gogh country and the hotel lies within the conservation area of Roman Glanum. In the pretty dining room, oil paintings by a friend add a splash to white walls and meals are a special feast of market produce accompanied by excellent local wines. Air-conditioned bedrooms in the old mas are dreamy, washed in smoky-blue or ochre shades; dark wrought-iron beds are dressed in oatmeal linens and white quilts; ground-floor rooms open to small gardens or wooden decks. In contrast, the newest rooms are done with contemporary furniture, Parisian and Balinese art, pebble showers. All is spotless and every room is air-conditioned. The young owners have thought of everything: pick-up from the airport or train, car hire, tickets for local events – and there's parking, a bonus so close to town. *Over 12s welcome.*

| | |
|---|---|
| Rooms | 19 twin/doubles: €110-€255. 3 suites for 2: €208-€255. Extra bed/sofabed available €27-€36 per person per night. |
| Meals | Breakfast €16. Dinner €36. Wine €18-€85. Restaurants 5-minute walk. |
| Closed | January to early March & 2 weeks in December. |

**Michel Dimeux & Pierre Ticot**
Le Mas des Carassins, 1 chemin Gaulois, 13210 St Rémy de Provence, Bouches-du-Rhône

| | |
|---|---|
| Tel | +33 (0)4 90 92 15 48 |
| Email | info@masdescarassins.com |
| Web | www.masdescarassins.com |

## Le Mas Saint Florent

Legend has it the Minister of Communications installed France's first telephone in this grandiose mansion, an ensemble of stone balustrades and shuttered windows set among olives, plane trees, chestnuts, a rose garden and bamboo. And there are art exhibitions, a small lake and a pool, with pool house and barbecue. Bedrooms are sumptuous; sink back on a mountain of cushions amid period furniture, oriental rugs, sculptures, mirrors, lamps. Most are big and 'Les Lauriers' is immense, with billowing red curtains and velvet sofa; some have fireplaces; one has a terrace and claw foot bath. It's a wow of a place – a fantasy fulfilled for Gilbert and his partner – but it's Mother who sews the soft furnishings and who greets you on arrival. Theatre sweeps through the common rooms: antique chairs, Chinese rugs, photographs, flowers, fireplaces, a black baby grand, chess board, fossil sculptures, cubic art… even the flooring is remarkable! You can dine in if you wish, pop into Roman Arles or perhaps Avignon, 35 minutes away; in Camargue there are village festivals, markets, walking and wildlife galore.

| Rooms | 3 doubles: €179-€214. |
| | 1 suite for 4: €363-€418. |
| | 2 family rooms for 3: €214-€274. |
| | Singles €145-€240. Extra bed/sofabed |
| | available €10 per person per night. |
| Meals | Breakfast €16.50. |
| | Dinner €36. Wine €18-€38. |
| Closed | Never. |

**Gilbert Poirier**
Le Mas Saint Florent, Route de la Crau,
13280 Raphèle lès Arles,
Bouches-du-Rhône

| Tel | +33 (0)4 90 97 02 79 |
| Email | massaintflorent@orange.fr |
| Web | www.le-mas-saint-florent.com |

## Le Mas de Peint

In the heart of the Camargue, book in for an energetic, gastronomic short break and live as a 'cowboy'! Lucille and son Frédéric are warm, kind and proud of their beautiful farm – 250 bulls, 15 horses and swathes of arable land. Lucille creates a sober, elegant French country-farmhouse feel – no flounces or flummery, just impeccable style. They both miss Jacques, husband and father: a legend in the area, he died in 2010. Bedrooms are deep green or old rose; generous curtains are checked dove-grey; floors come tiled or wool-carpeted. There's eye-catching quirkery everywhere – a collection of fine pencil sketches, an antique commode – and some rooms with mezzanine bathrooms under old rafters. Breakfast royally in the big family kitchen or on the wisteria-draped terrace, then drift over the serene canal to the secluded pool, encircled by teak loungers, scented with jasmine. We recommend dinner: the fabulous, innovative chef delivers light, elegant regional food under a muslin canopy at tables aglow with Moroccan lamps; follow with coffee and cognac in the clubby cigar room or the seductive salon. *Min. stay: 2 nights at weekends, 2 high season. Pets by arrangement.*

| | |
|---|---|
| Rooms | 2 doubles, 6 twin/doubles: €245-€330. 4 suites for 2, 1 family suite for 4 (2 adults & 2 children): €395-€465. Extra bed/sofabed available €35 per person per night. |
| Meals | Breakfast €12-€22. Lunch, à la carte €41-€66. Dinner €59-€97. Restaurant closed Thursday. |
| Closed | Early January to mid-March & mid-November to mid-December. |

**Lucille & Frédéric Bon**
Le Mas de Peint,
Le Sambuc, 13200 Arles,
Bouches-du-Rhône

| | |
|---|---|
| Tel | +33 (0)4 90 97 20 62 |
| Email | contact@masdepeint.com |
| Web | www.masdepeint.com |

## Mas de la Rabassière

Fanfares of lilies at the door, Haydn inside and Michael smiling in his chef's apron. Rabassière means 'where truffles are found' and epicurean dinners here are a must; wines from the neighbouring vineyard and a sculpted dancer grace the terrace table. Cookery classes using home-produced olive oil and advice on what to see and where to go, jogging companionship and airport pick-ups are all part of Michael's unflagging hospitality; nobly aided by Thévi, his Singaporean assistant. Michael was posted to France by a multi-national and on his retirement slipped into this lush corner of Provence. The proximity of the canal keeps everything green: revel in the well-tree'd park with its grassy olive grove, roses galore, lilies, jasmine, and white and blue wisteria. There's a large library in English and French, and bedrooms and drawing room are comfortable in English country-house style: generous beds, erudite books, a tuned piano, fine etchings and oils, Provençal antiques. Come savour this charmingly generous house – and Michael's homemade croissants and fig jam on the shady veranda. *Children of all ages welcome.*

| Rooms | 2 doubles: €85-€155. |
| | Singles €85. |
| | Dinner, B&B €140 per person. |
| | Extra bed/sofabed available at no charge. |
| Meals | Dinner with wine, €55. |
| Closed | Rarely. |

Michael Frost
Mas de la Rabassière,
2137 chemin de la Rabassière,
13250 St Chamas, Bouches-du-Rhône

| Tel | +33 (0)4 90 50 70 40 |
| Email | michaelfrost@rabassiere.com |
| Web | www.rabassiere.com |

### Château de la Barben

The castle, all towers, turrets and terraces, is majestic; as is its position, high on impregnable rock, overlooking a lush valley. Join the museum visitors and enter to discover guardrooms, subterranean passages and watchtowers with pulleys, arrow slits, coats of arms and innumerable tapestried rooms. Madame is as elegant as you would hope her to be, Monsieur looks after the guests, with charm, and their daughter, a talented cook, delivers dinners to the big table in the 11th-century kitchen, shared with your hosts – or to the balustraded terrace for dinner à deux. Bedrooms range from 'Diane', a (relatively) modest symphony in celestial blue, to the 'Suite des Amours' in the tower, its four-poster dating from the Renaissance, its canopies of cream linen, its stone fireplace vast… take a bottle of bubbly to the private terrace and toast that exceptional view. Bathrooms are mostly huge, and scattered with L'Occitane potions. Heaps to do, from exploring the *orangeries*, topiaries and ornamental ponds in the gloriously historic grounds to discovering the sights, tastes and smells of delicious Provence.

| | |
|---|---|
| Rooms | 3 doubles: €150–€190. |
| | 2 suites for 2: €250–€270. |
| Meals | Dinner, 4 courses with wine, €50. |
| Closed | 17 November to 15 March. |

**Bertrand Pillivuyt**
Château de la Barben,
Route du Château, 13330 La Barben,
Bouches-du-Rhône

Tel       +33 (0)4 90 55 25 41
Email    info@chateau-de-la-barben.fr
Web      www.chateaudelabarben.fr

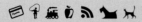

## Château d'Eoures

Just outside bustling Marseilles is a haven of civilisation and tranquillity. This 18th-century bastide, in Jean-Lou's family for generations, is surrounded by dappled grounds – enjoy peacocks, rabbits, hens and irresistible wicker-furnished terraces. Music room, library, salon – the house and garden are yours and your hosts love nothing better than to spoil you. Expect lavish breakfasts: cooked fruit, homemade jams, croissants, pastries and cakes. Madame is an excellent cook and gives dinner only to chambre d'hôtes guests – regional specialities such as terrines, tapenades and bouillabaisse, along with local wines. Find romance upstairs… a marble fireplace, a gilt mirror, a ciel-de-lit bed with beautiful linen in traditional rooms with antiques. Do discover the garden – a colourful vision, quite safe for children and with many secret places to hide yourself away. The swimming pool is lovely, among trees and shade, with wooden sunloungers and a summer kitchen which you may use to make pizzas or rustle up some lunch. Potted plants and flowers abound. Don't miss Aubagne, for fêtes, festivals and fountains.

| Rooms | 1 double: €150. |
| | 1 suite for 2-5 with separate bath: €100–€250. |
| Meals | Dinner with wine, €30. |
| | Summer kitchen. Restaurant 5km. |
| Closed | Rarely. |

M & Mme Chouvet
Château d'Eoures,
53 rue Arnould, 13011 Marseille,
Bouches-du-Rhône

| Tel | +33 (0)4 91 44 24 53 |
| Email | contact@chateau-eoures.com |
| Web | www.chateau-eoures.com |

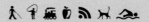

## Maison°9

A beautifully restored, impeccably decorated 19th-century winemaker's farmhouse on the side of a vineyard-braided hill, Maison°9 is elegantly ochre-pink with faded-green shutters under a flat curved-tile roof. The bedrooms, all different, all plush, are on the 'outskirts' of the main house, while the suite is at a discreet distance down a little path screened by bamboo. Expect big double beds, excellent linen, cool pink and weathered satin-finish terracotta floors, Italianate dipped-floor monsoon-head showers and small terrace gardens: simple, chic perfection. Paved paths lead through a delicious little garden bursting with pots of rosemary, thyme, lavender, sage, pebble beds of kentia palms and olive trees in wooden containers, to the centrepiece: a raised limestone pool lined with canvas loungers and surrounded by a sleek overflow wall with views across wooded hills to the grandiose 'Charlemagne's Crown' cliff face. A spectacular breakfast served in the main house sets you up for a ten-minute traipse to the beach, or you can just chill to the clonk of pétanque. Intimate, spoiling, special.

| | |
|---|---|
| Rooms | 3 doubles, 1 suite with sofabed: €215–€265. |
| Meals | Restaurant 2km. |
| Closed | November – March. |

**Cynthia Kayser-Maus**
Maison°9,
9 av du Docteur Yves Bourde,
13260 Cassis, Bouches-du-Rhône

| | |
|---|---|
| Tel | +33 (0)4 42 08 35 86 |
| Email | contact@maison9.net |
| Web | www.maison9.net |

## Bastide de Marie

A concert of colour sings from this handsome hotel: mellow old stone, pale blue shutters against creeper clad walls; a dash of turquoise in the two-tiered swimming pool, the pale green swathe of vines all around. In the lofty living room the high beams and neutral walls make the most of the light, while framed art and vast bookcases catch the eye. Bedrooms are all different, and wonderfully spoiling – one comes with a bright patterned canopy, another a four-poster and windows that point to the sunset. The deep elegance all around does not preclude a sense of warmth: guests to and fro with children and dogs in tow, all met as friends by the delightful Mireille. Many stay for the food, with a generous breakfast each morning and seasonal delights at night (a draw for the locals). You can dine outside, surrounded by the fragrant bouquet of wisteria, pink roses and oleander with a view across the lavender fields. There are bikes to hire, vineyards to visit, markets, galleries and a spa on site – in short, a Provençal paradise.

| | |
|---|---|
| Rooms | 4 doubles, 4 twin/doubles: €350-€650. 6 suites for 2-4: €500-€830. |
| Meals | Prices include breakfast & lunch or dinner with aperitif, wine & coffee. |
| Closed | 16 November to 19 December & 4 January to April. |

**Reservations & Enquiries**
Bastide de Marie,
64 chemin des Peirelles,
84560 Ménerbes, Vaucluse

| | |
|---|---|
| Tel | +33 (0)4 57 74 74 74 |
| Email | contact@labastidedemarie.com |
| Web | www.labastidedemarie.com |

## Le Clos du Buis

The gorgeous hilltop village of Bonnieux is renowned. Le Clos sits on one of its lower terraces, looking north to the surrounding hills and the legendary Mont Ventoux – a stunning view. Part of the building used to be the town bakery; the original front and the oven remain. Time and loving care have been distributed without restraint – Monsieur Maurin, a charming man, longed to return here – and everything appears to have been just so forever: Provençal country cupboards that rise to the ceiling, ancient patterned cement tiles, a stone staircase with an iron bannister leading to crisp, clean, uncluttered bedrooms, another bannister leading to the garden, a lovely surprise of a shady green oasis within the village. Provence is here on all sides, from the pretty quilts on the beds to the excellent breakfasts. The beautiful garden frames a large, delightful terrace, a pool and summer kitchen. If wine or weather keep you from the hills, days can be spent browsing the books by the old stone hearth – or playing the baby grand. Great staff, great value.

| | |
|---|---|
| Rooms | 2 doubles, 4 twin/doubles: €100–€165. 2 family rooms for 3: €130–€185. Extra bed €20. |
| Meals | Restaurants 2-minute walk. Occasional meals available upon request (larger groups only). |
| Closed | Mid-November to mid-March. |

**Monsieur & Madame Maurin**
Le Clos du Buis,
Rue Victor Hugo,
84480 Bonnieux, Vaucluse

| | |
|---|---|
| Tel | +33 (0)4 90 75 88 48 |
| Email | contact@leclosdubuis.com |
| Web | www.leclosdubuis.com |

Entry 309   Map 16

## La Bastide du Bois Bréant

You're in a peaceful hamlet – but near to bustling Lubéron markets, hilltop villages and great cycling routes. Find a handsome old farmhouse with pale blue shutters and clambering vines, a pretty pebbled courtyard with tables and chairs, ancient trees for shade and a pool area with plenty of loungers and views of the Lubéron hills. Most bedrooms are on the first floor of the main building: traditional but fresh, some heavily beamed, one 'romantically' themed (rose petals ahoy), all with good beds and modern bathrooms; a downstairs bedroom is perfect for the less than nimble and has its own entrance. You're free to loll about in the library with its pool table, grand fireplace, plenty of books and rather formal chairs, but there's plenty to do. After breakfast you could visit Avignon for a day out, or Mont Ventoux for serious cyclists (there's a good flat route round the villages for those who hate hills), clamber up rocks, have a round or two of golf or a guided walk. Cool off in the pool when you return: there are tree houses and a gypsy caravan in the grounds too, so plenty of opportunities to socialise.

| Rooms | 6 doubles, 5 twin/doubles: €155–€240. 1 suite for 2; 1 suite for 3 with separate shower: €155–€240. 1 gypsy caravan for 2: €170 per night. 1 treehouse for 4, 2 treehouses for 2 (1 with separate shower): €170–€320 per night. Extra bed €40–€45. Cot €20. Pets €10. |
|---|---|
| Meals | Restaurants 300m. |
| Closed | Never. |

**Sandrine Devis**
La Bastide du Bois Bréant,
501 chemin du Puits du Grandaou,
84660 Maubec en Lubéron, Vaucluse
Tel        +33 (0)4 90 05 86 78
Email    lemasdelalise@gmail.com
Web     www.hotel-bastide-bois-breant.com

## La Bastide de Voulonne

The utterly Provençal bastide sits in splendid isolation in lavender fields spread beneath the ancient hilltop villages of the Lubéron range. As you swing into the circular drive, there are ancient plane trees, wisps of tamarisk, tufts of lavender and blue shutters against golden ochre walls. Glorious – and a genuine family-friendly place, too: family suites, early children's suppers, DVDs galore, safe pool and lawn areas. The heart of this 18th-century farmhouse is a courtyard where you can breakfast to soft fountain music. Bedrooms (and beds) are huge, done in natural local colours, with tiled or parquet floors. The garden – it's more like a park – is vast, with a big pool not far from the house. The busy owners have refreshed the herb garden for the kitchen and menus focus on local food, while cherries, apricots, pears, figs and raspberries come from their orchards. After a convivial apéritif, with Julien if he's free, dinner is served at separate tables on the terrace or in a big dining hall whose centrepiece is the carefully restored bread oven.

| Rooms | 10 twin/doubles: €125–€155. 3 family suites for 3-5: €180–€275. |
|-------|------------------------------------------------------------------|
| Meals | Buffet breakfast €13. Dinner €36; children's menu €18. Wine €30. Early supper for children. |
| Closed | Mid-November to December (open January & February by arrangement). |

**Penny & Julien Hemery**
La Bastide de Voulonne,
Cabrières d'Avignon,
84220 Gordes, Vaucluse
Tel       +33 (0)4 90 76 77 55
Email    contact@bastide-voulonne.com
Web      www.bastide-voulonne.com

Entry 311   Map 16

## Château La Roque

Look an eagle in the eye, up here on the edge of the Lubéron, safe in the stony arms of the great fortress. Its history starts with the 8th-century Saracen invasion. Peace came at last in 1741 and, blissfully, still reigns, interrupted only by bees buzzing in the lime tree; the glorious views still stretch over the tranquil valley. Kind and interesting, Jean can tell you about the golden ratio used to build the castle; delightful Chantal speaks good English, too. The highly original rock-face pool will enchant you. Bedrooms, uncluttered but never cold, are huge, comfortable and furnished with carefully-chosen antiques, top-quality bedding and unostentatious designer fabrics. One has a deep-coral bed under vaulted ceilings and genuine 13th-century wardrobe doors. Each handsome, roomy bathroom, be it high-modern or new-old, is done with the best fittings. After visiting a pretty Provençal town or famous vineyard (Gigondas, Châteauneuf…), return to dinner of, for example, monkfish with a saffron sauce on a bed of green asparagus served on the vine-dappled terrace or in the garden. *Château can be rented as a whole.*

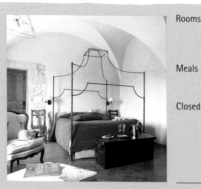

| Rooms | 2 doubles: €180–€220. |
|---|---|
| | 3 suites for 2: €320. |
| | Extra bed/sofabed available €35 per person per night. |
| Meals | Breakfast €20. Dinner, 4 courses, €46 (except Sunday); book ahead. Wine €22–€200. |
| Closed | Late November to mid-February. Open New Year. |

Chantal & Jean Tomasino
Château La Roque,
263 chemin du Château,
84210 La Roque sur Pernes, Vaucluse

Tel      +33 (0)4 90 61 68 77
Email    chateaularoque@wanadoo.fr
Web      www.chateaularoque.com

## La Prévôté

You're on an island, circled by a pretty river, and tucked down a network of wiggly streets. You can drive down to drop off your luggage, then head for a nearby car park. Walk through an ancient stone arch and straight into the sunny courtyard with its creeper-clad walls, convivial tables and canopy for shade. Inside, the bar has funky, colourful chairs and the talking point – a tributary of the Sorgue running right under the whole building; walk around an arch to the banks of the river. The hub of this bustling place though is its fabulous 'Maître Restaurateur' (always look for the symbol) restaurant and charming, friendly owners Severine and Jean-Marie: all is cooked completely from scratch and beautifully – no wonder locals flock here. Up stone stairs to bedrooms on the first and second floors: very understated and lovely, with good antique furniture rubbing shoulders with brocantes finds, a chaise longue here, an old trunk there. All feel roomy and airy, some have courtyard views; bathrooms are fresh with Italian marble. Wander around the antique shops in town, or head to Avignon or Orange in the car.

| | |
|---|---|
| Rooms | 2 doubles, 3 twin/doubles: €150–€230. Extra bed/sofabed available €40 per person per night. |
| Meals | Dinner, 3 courses, €41. |
| Closed | Rarely. |

Severine Alloin
La Prévôté,
4 rue Jean Jacques Rousseau,
84800 L'Isle sur la Sorgue, Vaucluse

| | |
|---|---|
| Tel | +33 (0)4 90 38 57 29 |
| Email | contact@la-prevote.fr |
| Web | www.la-prevote.fr |

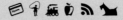

## Aux Augustins

German Sabine and French Patrick, both well travelled, spent two years renovating their 14th-century convent, creating a chic city retreat in the shadow of the neighbouring Augustin bell tower. Behind an unassuming shop front find peaceful rooms on three floors overlooking the tiled inner courtyard dotted with terracotta Anduze pots overflowing with flowering shrubs, the perfect spot for a breakfast of croissants, fruit and hot chocolate. German mattresses, Italian quilts and French linen come as standard, complementing wrought iron bedheads made by local artisans in rooms with exposed stone walls and original archways. Shower rooms are fresh and sparkling. Ground floor rooms have direct access to the courtyard, some first floor rooms have balconies, and the attic room comes with a landscaped roof terrace. Park nearby for a price or further out for less, or leave the car at home: it's just five minutes' walk to shops and restaurants. Soak up the historic city, take a summer lunch cruise on the Rhône to Arles, sample the wines at nearby Châteauneuf-du-Pape, or walk the hilltop villages of the Lubéron. *Min. stay: 2 nights, 7 during July festival.*

| Rooms | 2 doubles: €105–€130. |
| | 1 suite for 2: €135–€160. |
| | 2 studios for 2: €115–€145. |
| Meals | Restaurants 5-minute walk. |
| Closed | Rarely. |

Sabine & Patrick Eouagnignon
Aux Augustins,
16 rue Carreterie,
84000 Avignon, Vaucluse

Tel      +33 (0)4 90 81 00 42
Email    contact@autourdupetitparadis.com
Web      www.autourdupetitparadis.com

## Le Mas des Grès

A party atmosphere reigns at this spotless roadside hotel that the attentive owners – German-Swiss Nina and Franco-Italian Thierry – run with clockwork precision and sustainability in mind. Nina looks after you and Thierry conjures up superb food: inspiration from his Italian grandmother. Join in the preparations or sit and enjoy it all in the big beamed dining room or, in summer, under the soaring plane trees on a terrace lit by twinkling lights and candles. Children eat and then potter to their hearts' content. Plainish bedrooms vary in size, with neat quilts on firm beds and views over fields; bathrooms, some with superb Italian showers, are tiled top to toe. Nina knows everyone and can rustle up almost any local delight, from Châteauneuf-du-Pape wine tastings to Lubéron bike trips, trout fishing with the family or golf at one of 15 courses. A favourite is a guided nature hike to gather culinary plants and herbs; for collectors of brocante, popular L'Isle sur la Sorgue is up the road. Return to a kids' playground and a family-happy roadside pool.

| | |
|---|---|
| Rooms | 12 doubles (some rooms interconnect): €110–€270. 2 suites for 4: €200–€270. Price includes dinner, B&B. |
| Meals | Breakfast €12. Picnic €15. Buffet lunch €20, July /August only. Dinner €36. Wine €15–€100. |
| Closed | 11 November to 28 March. |

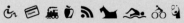

**Nina & Thierry Crovara**
Le Mas des Grès,
1651, RD 901, Four à Chaux Isle sur Sorgue, 84800 Lagnes, Vaucluse
Tel     +33 (0)4 90 20 32 85
Email    info@masdesgres.com
Web     www.masdesgres.com

## Le Château de Mazan

The Marquis de Sade's father and uncle were born here, an unexpected connection, given the luminosity inside. Though the infamous Marquis preferred Paris, he often stayed at Mazan, organising France's first theatre festival here in 1772. The château sits in an appealing little town at the foot of Mont Ventoux. Floors are tiled in white-and-terracotta squares that would drown a smaller space, ceilings are lofty, windows are huge with the lightest curtains. This is a family hotel and Frédéric, who speaks good English, runs a smooth team while Mother does the fabulous décor, each room an ethereal delight: pale pink walls, a velvet sofa, a touch of apricot taffeta, a flash of red. Ground-floor bedrooms have French windows to a private sitting area; a couple of the rooms in the annexe across the road have their own terraces. There are frondy palms and secluded spots in the garden – doze in the shade of the mulberry trees – and a beautiful terrace for dinner; the chef has worked in starred restaurants and is keen to win his own. Stay on a Friday and catch Carpentras market. Altogether wonderful. *Car park down hill.*

| | |
|---|---|
| Rooms | 12 doubles: €125–€310. |
| | 3 suites for 4: €335–€415. |
| | 14 family rooms for 3-4: €175–€345. |
| | Singles €125–€159. |
| | Dinner, B&B €164–€216 per person. |
| | Extra bed/sofabed available €35 per |
| | person per night. |
| Meals | Breakfast €18. Lunch from €16. |
| | Dinner from €39. Restaurant closed |
| | Tuesdays; Mondays out of season. |
| | Wine from €22. |
| Closed | January/February. |

**Danièle & Frédéric Lhermie**
Le Château de Mazan,
Place Napoléon,
84380 Mazan, Vaucluse
Tel      +33 (0)4 90 69 62 61
Email    reservation@chateaudemazan.com
Web     www.chateaudemazan.fr

## Château Juvenal

From the hall, peep through the double doorways at the sitting and dining rooms. Splendour! With two glorious chandeliers reflecting in the gilt-framed mirrors at each end of this long reception suite, you are transported back a couple of centuries. Surely the chamber orchestra will be tuning up soon, sending notes floating over the exquisite period furniture, high ceilings, tall windows? Yet this 19th-century gem is lived in and loved every day, thanks to delightful Anne-Marie and Bernard, who also produce an award-winning wine and delicious olive oil from their 600 trees. They nurture some superb specimen trees, too, out in the park. The traditional bedrooms are all on the first floor and range from cosy to spacious: 'Iris' the smallest in pure white and grey, 'Cerise', larger, with deep pink spread, 'Raisin' with Louis XIII chairs and marble-top dresser, 'Les Genêts', sunny yellow with a roll top bath. Grab your shopping basket and visit the local market, there is a summer kitchen next to the pool. There are wine visits, a pony for the kids, annual tango events, a spa and two lovely apartments for longer stays.

| Rooms | 1 double, 2 twin/doubles: €130–€150. 1 family suite for 2-3: €140–€170. 2 apartments for 6: €900–€1,700 per week. Singles €100–€150. Extra bed/sofabed available €40 per person per night. |
|---|---|
| Meals | Hosted dinner with wine, €45, once a week. Summer kitchen. |
| Closed | 1 November to 11 April. |

**Anne–Marie & Bernard Forestier**
120 chemin du Long Serre, 84330 St Hippolyte le Graveyron, Vaucluse

| Tel | +33 (0)4 90 62 31 76 |
| Mobile | +33 (0)6 07 13 11 47 |
| Email | chateau.juvenal@gmail.com |
| Web | www.chateaujuvenal.com |

## Les Florets

The setting is magical, the walks are outstanding, the greeting from the Bernard family, who bought Les Florets 60 years ago, is heartfelt. It sits at the foot of the majestic Dentelles de Montmirail, a small range crested with long, delicate stone fingers in the middle of Côtes du Rhône country. Over 40km of clearly marked paths call you, so appetites build for sublime food served beneath plane, chestnut and lime trees on the almost theatrical terrace; the low stone walls are bright with busy lizzies and the peonies were blooming in March. You'll also sample some of the wines that the family has been producing since the 1880s. Brightly-coloured corridors lead to simple but well-organised, well-renovated rooms, some with traditional florals, others in taupe and ivory, some housed in chalets above. Good bathrooms but no mozzie meshes or air con. We liked the quirky ceramic soup tureens in reception, the scintillating glass carafes in the warm red dining room and the beautiful new hillside pool. All this, and the wine list a work of art. Book well ahead, people return year after year.

| | |
|---|---|
| Rooms | 10 doubles, 4 twins: €105-€170. 1 suite for 2: €180. Dinner, B&B €130-€160 per person. |
| Meals | Breakfast €17. Lunch & dinner from €40. Restaurant closed Wednesdays all day & Thursday for lunch. |
| Closed | January to mid-March. |

**Thierry & Dominique Bernard**
Les Florets,
Route des Dentelles,
84190 Gigondas, Vaucluse
Tel      +33 (0)4 90 65 85 01
Email   accueil@hotel-lesflorets.com
Web     www.hotel-lesflorets.com

## Atelier du Renard Argenté

Come to be thoroughly pampered at this beautiful old farmhouse with a garden and pool in the enchanting Forêt d'Uchaux. Gail and Christian (a chef on the Orient Express) are brilliant hosts and food is taken seriously: breakfast on local yogurt and homemade cakes; lunch can be rustled up (or a picnic), dinner is sublime – maybe sea bass with truffle caviar, steak with mushrooms handpicked from the forest, homemade lavender and spelt bread, mango panna cotta; all with accompanying wines. You have your own, beautiful sitting room with a high ceiling and exposed stone walls: music will soothe you, candlelight will lull you. Sleep like a log in divine beds with clouds of goose down, slap on the 'Durance' goodies in spotless bathrooms, feel incredibly well looked after. There's an expansive garden to explore too, with fruit and olive trees, water features and private areas for couples – take your aperitif on a small island. Splash about in the outdoor pool in summer, or just lounge around here. If you can tear yourself away there's tons to do round and about from horse riding to truffle hunting, markets and cycling. Lovely.

| Rooms | 5 doubles: €130-€235. |
| Meals | Dinner €45-€150. |
| Closed | Rarely. |

**Gail Bodiguel**
Atelier du Renard Argenté, 90 chemin des Chevres, 84550 Mornas, Vaucluse

| Tel | +33 (0)9 67 25 71 99 |
| Mobile | +33 (0)6 09 39 33 14 |
| Email | contact@atelier-renard-argente.com |
| Web | www.renarda.com |

## Villa Noria

The garden sets the scene, a delightfully secluded enclave of mature cedars, palms, cherries, roses and manicured lawn. Within it is an elegant 18th-century house run by the thoroughly delightful Philippe and Sylvie who look after guests with immaculate professionalism. Sylvie ushers you up the stone farmhouse stair to beautiful bedrooms decorated in gloriously colourful Provençal style, the finest on the first floor. Cool tiles underfoot, beams overhead, walls colour-washed in cerise, blue and raspberry, beds opulently swathed in white linen and bathrooms boldly, diagonally tiled. You breakfast in an elegant, wraparound conservatory, there's a salon with fauteuils dressed in red and white checks, and the long oval dining table sits beneath a huge weeping fern. In summer you're under the trees. Philippe is an experienced chef: don't miss his hosted dinners. Noria is on the edge of the peaceful village of Modène, near several burgeoning villas, and the views sweep over vineyards to mountains beyond; recline by the saltwater pool on a handsome wooden lounger and drink them in. A stylish retreat.

| Rooms | 3 doubles, 1 twin: €75–€130. |
| | 1 suite for 4: €145–€170. |
| | Extra bed €30. |
| Meals | Hosted dinner with wine, €40. |
| | Restaurants 3km. |
| Closed | Rarely. |

**Philippe Monti**
Villa Noria,
4 route de Mazan,
84330 Modène, Vaucluse
Tel     +33 (0)4 90 62 50 66
Email   post@villa-noria.com
Web     www.villa-noria.com

## Le Domaine des Tilleuls

Bowl down the plane-tree lined road into the touristy, buzzing atmosphere of the town with its shops and good places to eat. Then step through an ancient gate to find peace and calm in this stone house (a silk farm in the late 1700s) with its huge garden, cooling pool and shading lime trees. You will be greeted by Louis and Florence Saint Joire who live on site and are always handy. There's plenty of space, so even if the place is full you can feel private: take breakfast in the large dining room with tiled floor, or the greenhouse-like annexe, or in the garden when the sun is out. Sleep peacefully in bedrooms split between the main house (bright and airy, some with beams, all relaxing and comfortable) and more compact rooms in the annexe (painted pastel colours with antique furniture). Cyclists are very happy (they return again and again) with the start of the Mont Ventoux ascent on the doorstep, good hiking around the Dentelles de Montmirail is a 10-minute drive, Roman excavations are nearby and lavender fields are abundant. But you can just don a straw hat (hanging by the garden door) and hang around here happily doing not very much. *Secure bike storage.*

| | |
|---|---|
| Rooms | 10 doubles: €76–€110. |
| | 7 family rooms for 2-3, |
| | 2 family rooms for 2-4: €86–€136. |
| | Extra bed €12–€15. |
| Meals | Breakfast €10–€13. |
| | Restaurants 1-minute walk. |
| Closed | 1 November to 25 March. |

**Louis & Florence Saint Joire**
Le Domaine des Tilleuls,
Route de Mont Ventoux,
84340 Malaucène, Vaucluse

| | |
|---|---|
| Tel | +33 (0)4 90 65 22 31 |
| Email | info@hotel-domainedestilleuls.com |
| Web | www.hotel-domainedestilleuls.com |

## Hostellerie du Val de Sault

This landscape has been called a 'sea of corn gold and lavender blue', and from your terrace you can contemplate Mont Ventoux – painters' mountain, cyclists' mecca. Lively, charming Yves knows everyone there is to know on the Provence scene and is full of good guidance. He also creates menus featuring truffles, lavender, spelt, game with mushrooms in the autumn... all beautifully served in the formal atmosphere of the light, airy restaurant. (Children can eat earlier if you wish.) This grouping of modern one-storey buildings is perched just above the woods in big gardens, with one structure dedicated to guest bedrooms. Wooden floors and pine-slatted walls bring warmth, soft colour schemes have oriental flashes, baths in the suites have jets, four-poster beds flaunt gauzy curtains reminiscent of mosquito nets. Each room feels like a very private space with its own terrace, and some of the suites have an exceptional view – worth splashing out on. Pool, bar and restaurant are there for conviviality; fitness room, tennis court and boules pitch are for exercise! Breakfasts are terrific.

| | |
|---|---|
| Rooms | 11 twin/doubles: €90–€180. |
| | 9 suites for 2: €230–€280. |
| Meals | Breakfast €21. |
| | Dinner, 4 courses, €47–€49. |
| | Dinner, B&B extra 60 p.p. Restaurant closed for lunch except Sundays. |
| Closed | 2 November to 30 April. |

Yves Gattechaut
Hostellerie du Val de Sault,
Route de St Trinit, Ancien chemin
d'Aurel, 84390 Sault, Vaucluse
Tel +33 (0)4 90 64 01 41
Email enter@valdesault.com
Web www.valdesault.com

## Auberge de Reillanne

The solid loveliness of this 18th-century house, so typical of the area, reassures you, invites you in. And you will not be disappointed: it feels good to be here, even if you can't quite define the source of the positive energy. Monique is clearly connected to the spirit of the place and has used all her flair and good taste to transform the old inn into a very special place to stay. Large, airy bedrooms are done in cool restful colours with big cupboards and rattan furniture. There are beams, properly whitewashed walls and books. Bathrooms are big and simple too. Downstairs, the sitting and dining areas are decorated in warm, embracing colours with terracotta tiles and flame-coloured curtains. On several levels of stream-fed rolling lawns and tree'd borders, the tranquil garden has hammocks and statues. This would be a place for a quiet holiday with long meditative walks in the hills, a place to come and write that novel under the shade of the ancient trees, or simply to get to know the gentle, delicate, smiling owner who loves nothing better than to receive people in her magical house. One of our favourites.

| | |
|---|---|
| Rooms | 4 doubles: €78–€82. 2 triples: €105. Singles €63. Dinner, B&B €74–€92 per person. Extra bed/sofabed available €10 per person per night. |
| Meals | Breakfast €9. Restaurants 5-minute drive. |
| Closed | Mid-October to early April. |

**Monique Balmand**
Auberge de Reillanne,
04110 Reillanne,
Alpes-de-Haute-Provence

| | |
|---|---|
| Tel | +33 (0)4 92 76 45 95 |
| Email | monique.balmand@wanadoo.fr |
| Web | www.auberge-de-reillanne.com |

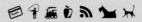

## La Bastide de Moustiers

The views of the lovely village of Moustiers-Sainte-Marie, the estate with its family of deer and the mountains all around give a magical feel. The hotel, however, has its feet firmly on the ground. This beautifully restored bastide rests at the foot of the cliffs of Moustiers: a 17th-century house, a cluster of stone cottages, and 13 bedrooms between them. For breakfast, lunch and divine dinner (the owner is Alain Ducasse) tables topped with white parasols sit on shaded terraces, and all is impeccable yet rustic. If you don't want to dine in, then the village, bustling with shops and restaurants, is a sprint up the hill or a three-minute drive. Staff are here to satisfy every whim and the attention to detail is striking, from your flip-flops and towels for the delicious pool to the helipad for the wealthy. Paragliders, riders, canoeists and climbers find heaven in the Parc Naturel du Verdon, and mountain bikes are available on request. Dreamy bedrooms to come home to (two with beds on mezzanines, most with private patios) complete the five-star picture. *Cot available.*

| | |
|---|---|
| Rooms | 7 doubles, 4 twin/doubles: €215–€415. 2 suites for 2: €365–€800. |
| Meals | Breakfast €24. Lunch €38. Dinner €79. Restaurants 5-minute drive. |
| Closed | 1 November to 4 March. |

Charlotte Loubier
La Bastide de Moustiers, Chemin de
Quinson, 04360 Moustiers Ste Marie,
Alpes-de-Haute-Provence
Tel    +33 (0)4 98 05 14 14
Email  cloubier@maisons-alainducasse.com
Web    www.bastide-moustiers.com

## Le Moulin du Château

A sleepy place – come to doze, your silence broken only by the call of the sparrowhawk or the distant rumble of a car. This 17th-century olive mill once belonged to the château and stands at the foot of a venerable grove; the vast press is now a reception area where modern art hangs on ancient walls. The Moulin, a long, low, stone building with lavender-blue shutters and the odd climbing vine, stands in its own gardens surrounded by lavender and fruit trees. In the bedrooms light filters though voile curtains, shadows dance upon the walls. The feel is uncluttered, cool, breezy, with vibrant colours: turquoise, lilac, lime – luminous yet restful. This is an easy-going 'green' hotel where the emphasis is on the simple things of life. Edith and Nicolas use regional and organic food, boules is played under the cherry tree, poppies grow on an old crumbling stone staircase and views stretch across fields to village and château. There are great walks, bikes for gentle country excursions, a swimming and boating lake nearby, and further afield are the Cistercian abbey of Le Thoronet, the Gorges du Verdon and Digne les Bains..

| | |
|---|---|
| Rooms | 6 doubles, 4 twin/doubles: €102–€130. Extra bed/sofabed available €16–€22 per person per night. |
| Meals | Breakfast €10. Picnic €10. Dinner, 3 courses, €28; 4 courses, €32 (except Mon & Thurs). Wine €6–€40. Restaurant 2-minute walk. |
| Closed | November – March. |

**Edith & Nicolas Stämpfli-Faoro**
Le Moulin du Château,
04500 St Laurent du Verdon,
Alpes-de-Haute-Provence

| | |
|---|---|
| Tel | +33 (0)4 92 74 02 47 |
| Email | info@moulin-du-chateau.com |
| Web | www.moulin-du-chateau.com |

Entry 325   Map 16

## Domaine de la Baume

This beautifully restored 18th-century classic bastide, tucked behind a discreet sign and gate, was the home of French painter Bernard Buffet. Exceptionally decorated by owner Jocelyne Sibuet, it is lavish, comfortable and tasteful with plenty of corners to cosy up in. Bedrooms are spacious and elegant in a colourful reinterpretation of 18th-century style with Indian prints and toile de Jouy. Cabriolet armchairs, delicately painted antique furniture, kilims, parquet flooring and pieces that nod to the splendour of the East India Company are tucked in every corner. Beds, mattresses and linens are top quality, while bathrooms have new loos, sinks and showers (two with bathtub only); the Annabel Suite has its original tiles and clubfoot tub. A buffet breakfast can be taken on the terrace when the weather is kind. Meals make splendid use of organic produce from the potager and herb garden and their own house wine from their sister hotel in the Lubéron. Visit beautiful Tourtour (4km) or wander the lovely gardens and seek out the caves and tumbling waterfalls. Who could fail to find delight here?

| | |
|---|---|
| Rooms | 11 doubles: €450–€730. 1 suite for 2-4, 3 suites for 2-4 with with sofabed: €690–€1,360. |
| Meals | Prices include breakfast & lunch or dinner with aperitif, wine & coffee. |
| Closed | 2 November to 1 April. |

**Reservations & Enquiries**
Domaine de la Baume,
2071 route d'Aups,
83690 Tourtour, Var

| | |
|---|---|
| Tel | +33 (0)4 57 74 74 74 |
| Email | contact@domaine-delabaume.com |
| Web | www.domaine-delabaume.com |

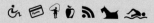

## La Bastide du Pin

It's a glamorous drive from Nice, through the Massif des Maures; bring the Raybans and the open-top car! This gorgeous hideaway, reached through a wide gate and a drive bordered by cypresses, sits in a garden of gravelled paths, sculptures, roses, lavender and a pool, and views as far as the eye can see. It is utterly, peacefully beautiful, and the shady patio – as much Tuscany as Provence – is a perfect place to laze away an afternoon with only the fountain to disturb you. Bedrooms, all upstairs, are spacious and elegant with an understated feel: dark wood and terracotta hues in one; lemon curtains, a dove-grey wardrobe, a sparkly chandelier in another. Cushions coordinate with bed linen and bathrooms are fresh with bathrobes and soaps. Best of all is Pierre, your friendly, interesting, attentive host, who offers you generous breakfasts in a lofty dining room. Stroll into Lorgues with its lovely abbey, buzzing summer market, shops and bars (it is equally alluring in spring). Quiet evenings in? There are books, billiards, WiFi, and a piano you may play.

| Rooms | 4 doubles, 1 twin/double: €100–€175. |
|---|---|
| | 1 family room for 2–3: €125–€170. |
| Meals | Restaurants 2km. |
| Closed | Rarely. |

**Pierre Gissinger**
La Bastide du Pin,
1017 route de Salernes,
83510 Lorgues, Var
Tel      +33 (0)4 94 73 90 38
Email    contact@bastidedupin.com
Web      www.bastidedupin.com

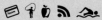

Entry 327   Map 16

## Château Nestuby

Bravo, Nathalie! – in calm, friendly control of this well-restored, soft-shuttered 19th-century bastide, in the family since 1949. Their rosé wines, smooth yet intense (one with touches of orange and sugared brioche, another with notes of vanilla and quince) are much admired; bliss to sit back with a glass under the stars, surrounded by a sea of vines. One whole wing has been set aside for guests, and the bedrooms are large, light and airy. Colours are cheerful, floors are pale and tiled, furniture is an uncluttered mix of old and new, tall windows overlook the vines. It's excellent value for what is included: a big bourgeois sitting room (little used: it's too lovely outside); a shop selling estate wines and 'produits du terroir'; a spa on the roof terrace; and a great spring-fed tank for summer swims. But best of all are the people who live here. Jean-François runs the vineyard, the tastings and the wine talk at dinner with sweet-natured ease; son Roman, equally passionate about the wines, gives unmissable tours; Nathalie, creator of superb jams for breakfast, is an adorable hostess. *Minimum stay: 3 nights July/August.*

| Rooms | 4 twin/doubles, 1 triple: €95. |
|---|---|
| | 1 family room for 4: €85. |
| | Extra bed/sofabed available €20 per person per night. Jacuzzi available in twin/double; extra charge €85. |
| Meals | Dinner with wine, €27. |
| Closed | Mid–December to February. |

Nathalie & Jean-François Roubaud
Château Nestuby, 4540 route de
Montfort, 83570 Cotignac, Var

| Tel | +33 (0)4 94 04 60 02 |
| Mobile | +33 (0)6 86 16 27 93 |
| Email | nestuby@wanadoo.fr |
| Web | www.nestuby-provence.com |

## Une Campagne en Provence

In spring, water gushes through the 400-acre estate: the 12th-century Knights Templar created myriad irrigation channels, the life-source of this stunning place. (Now it is proud possessor of the EU Ecolabel.) The bastide keeps it fortress-like proportions and bags of character and charm. Martina and Claude love it all, have planted 3,750 trees, and have a sense of fun that makes a stay a treat. The main house is arranged around a central patio, with stairs leading to the bedrooms above. Simple Provençal furnishings are lit by huge windows, floors are terracotta, there are cosy 'boutis' quilts and sumptuous towels and linen, and bathrooms cleverly worked around original features. Breakfasts are scrumptious; dinners put the accent on Provençal produce and their own wine. In the cellar: music and a mini cinema. Also table football and a pool with a view, a sauna, a Turkish bath and a well-stocked library. Beyond are the Gorges du Verdon, Cotignac, St-Maximin-la-Ste-Baume. An isolated paradise for all ages, overseen by a charming family, donkeys, Shetland ponies, swans, ducks, geese… and one dear old dog. *Min. stay: 2 nights in high season. Pets by arrangement.*

| Rooms | 3 doubles: €96-€128. |
|---|---|
| | 1 suite for 2: €123-€145. |
| | 1 studio for 2 with kitchenette: €135-€180. |
| Meals | Hosted dinner with wine, €38 (Thursday, Friday & Saturday). Restaurant 3km. |
| Closed | January to mid-March. |

Martina & Claude Fussler
Une Campagne en Provence,
Domaine le Peyrourier,
83149 Bras, Var

| Tel | +33 (0)4 98 05 10 20 |
| Email | info@provence4u.com |
| Web | www.provence4u.com |

## Bastide Avellanne

Deep comfort and incredible quiet await you in this beautifully renovated bastide with a 1616 build-date carved in stone; grounds, vineyards and glorious views over the Var surround you. Inside is a huge living and dining area with stone walls and fireplace, arched windows, red leather sofas and interesting paintings; eat here at large wooden tables or on the pretty front terrace. Dinner includes regional specialities mixed with Italian, French and Mediterranean dishes, with the emphasis on fresh and wholesome. Bedrooms (some upstairs, some down) are truly sumptuous, with ancient beams, local furniture and fabrics, tiled floors, fresh flowers, clouds of soft pillows and views over the gardens, front or back. Shower rooms are immaculate, luxurious, with mosaic floors, coordinated towels and sprigs of lavender; all is spacious and light. Friendly Steve and Valentina throw open their bougainvillea-bright grounds (also to gîte guests): find a lovely pool, blue sunbeds, boules, tennis courts and a giant chess set under the shade of a centuries-old oak tree. Deeply rural, heaps of charm. *Pets by arrangement.*

| | |
|---|---|
| Rooms | 3 twin/doubles: €140–€190. 2 suites for 4 (2 adults & 2 children): €200–€260. 2 apartments for 2, 2 apartments for 4 (2 adults & 2-3 children): €450–€1,590 per week. |
| Meals | Dinner, 3 courses, €32; children's menu €20. Wine from €20. Restaurant 3km. |
| Closed | Christmas. |

Steve & Valentina Dixon
Bastide Avellanne,
83890 Besse sur Issole, Var
Tel      +33 (0)4 94 69 89 91
Email    info@bastideavellanne.com
Web      www.bastideavellanne.com

### L'Hostellerie de l'Abbaye de la Celle

Rest your head (as did Brad and Angelina) in 'Perpétue de la Celle', one of five suites with its own pretty garden. Just what you'd expect of a Benedictine abbey (an abbey where the nuns once caused a scandal; the place has a fascinating history). The hotel is owned by Alain Ducasse so some serious cooking lies behind these abbey walls. Weekend lobsters are served, amongst other bounty, in a pale rustic-elegant restaurant (do book). Your alternatives are the village café and the town of Brignoles, six miles away. Breakfast is equally delicious, and authentic: homemade croissants, local cheeses and charcuterie, preserves from the orchard and potager. Chill out in the big contemporary conservatory on a shabby-chic leather sofa by a vintage wooden bar, where attentive staff dispatch whatever you fancy, and while there are wines in the cellar, let the wines rule. You'd never guess you were five minutes from the motorway: this is the perfect place to unwind. A pool in the garden, tennis nearby, golf, hiking and a couple of mountain bikes to borrow... Beyond? Aix, Nice, Cannes, St Rémy, St Tropez. Fabulous.

| Rooms | 3 doubles, 2 twin/doubles, extra bed available in 4 rooms: €250–€370. 3 suites for 2-3 with extra bed, 2 suites for 2-4 with 2 extra beds: €410–€550. Extra bed €50. |
|---|---|
| Meals | Breakfast €24. Dinner €38–€95. |
| Closed | January & Tuesday/Wednesday mid-October to mid-April. |

Charlotte Loubier
L'Hostellerie de l'Abbaye de la Celle,
10 place Général de Gaulle,
83170 La Celle, Var

| Tel | +33 (0)4 98 05 14 14 |
| Email | cloubier@maisons-alainducasse.com |
| Web | www.abbaye-celle.com |

Entry 331   Map 16

## Hostellerie Bérard & Spa

Bags of atmosphere, stunning gardens, exquisite gastronomy, a magical spa and possibly the best breakfasts in France. René's son Jean-François is now head chef of the Michelin-starred restaurant; Danièle is an expert in local wines. In both restaurant and bistro the emphasis is on Provençal gastronomy using organic seasonal produce from the kitchen garden; save up for a sumptuous treat. Madame and Monsieur are true belongers, who grew up in this hilltop village, opened in 1969 and have respectfully restored a complex of highly evocative buildings, an 11th-century monastery; a blue-shuttered bastide, a *maison bourgeoise*, an artist's pavilion. The views are framed visions of olive groves, of vines in their serried choreography and Templar strongholds on mountain tops in the distance. Each bedroom is a lovely French surprise – a delicate wrought-iron four-poster, a snowy counterpane, curtains in toile de Jouy – and the small spa is a delight; book in for a treatment. Daughter Sandra, full of friendly enthusiasm, handles the day-to-day running of this charming restaurant-hotel.

| Rooms | 36 doubles: €102–€210. |
| | 4 suites for 4: €267–€361. |
| Meals | Buffet breakfast €22. |
| | Lunch & dinner €36–€169. |
| | Wine from €27. |
| Closed | 10 January to 5 February. |

**Bérard Family**
Hostellerie Bérard & Spa,
Rue Gabriel Péri,
83740 La Cadière d'Azur, Var
Tel     +33 (0)4 94 90 11 43
Email   berard@hotel-berard.com
Web     www.hotel-berard.com

## Hôtel Notre Dame

On the edge of cobbled Collobrières, with wonderful views of the Massif des Maures, is an 18th-century staging post, a delicious modern hotel. Its inspired creators, Olivier and his wife (chef) Nili, speak several languages, embrace all nationalities and love what they do. Each elegant, simple room is named after a precious stone – sapphire, jade, coral; pick the colour of your choice on booking. Imagine cool floor tiles, glowing paintings, thick cream curtains, repro Louis XIV tables, bright mosaic'd showers and beautiful stone ceilings washed in white. The Pearl Suite has three windows and is full of light, and some rooms have divans that double up as child beds (families are welcomed with open arms). Outside: a secret garden with an eco-friendly pool, fenced and safe for children, and pretty tables at which guests linger over dinner under the trees and listen to the flowing river. As for the food, there are four different kinds of breakfast – from Scandinavian to continental – served until late. Dinner too is delicious; the wines are from the bio vineyards of Correns. Beyond: the palms and sands of Le Lavandou.

| Rooms | 5 doubles: €89–€135. |
| --- | --- |
| | 3 suites for 2: €119–€195. |
| | 1 family room for 4: €209–€245. |
| | 1 single: €89–€98. |
| Meals | Breakfast €12–€25. |
| | Dinner, 2-3 courses, €22–€28; book ahead. Restaurant closed Thursday. Wine €18.50–€109. Restaurant 1km. |
| Closed | 5 January to mid-March. |

Olivier Faivre
Hôtel Notre Dame,
15 av de la Libération,
83610 Collobrières, Var

Tel      +33 (0)4 94 48 07 13
Email    hotelnotredame@gmail.com
Web      www.hotel-collobrieres.com

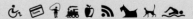

## La Villa d'Andrea

You travel through peaceful Var countryside to reach these oh-so-stylish studio apartments. Sandra's deft handiwork immediately catches the eye – driftwood furnished into her own designs, including a striking table and chairs in the most sought-after apartment: the studio with the beautiful stone interior. Provençal in style, with pale walls, blue shutters and terracotta roofs, the whole pretty place is divided into two sections: the more traditional Sud whose apartments are typified by wood, wicker and wrought-iron furniture, and softened by pastoral scenes from local artists; and the much more exotic Zen whose quirky touches – to bedheads, lamps, tiling and intricate pebble framed mirrors – run throughout. All but four come with tasteful kitchenettes and private terraces. Open windows wide to take in the gardens and two lovely pools, complete with stone bars, lush plants and pine trees, and roof supports made from tree bark. No communal indoors here, but outside is ideal for relaxation after a day spent on Pampelonne's legendary beach – or in St Tropez.

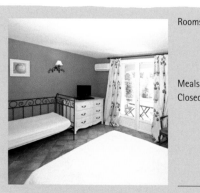

| Rooms | Sud building – 2 doubles; Zen building – 2 doubles: €100–€190. Sud building – 10 studios for 2; Zen building – 9 studios for 2: €150–€310. Extra beds available in some studios. |
|---|---|
| Meals | Breakfast €15. |
| Closed | 7 October to 18 April. |

**The Owner**
La Villa d'Andrea,
321 chemin de la Pinède,
83350 Ramatuelle, Var

| Tel | +33 (0)4 94 79 22 84 |
| Email | contact@lavilladandrea.com |
| Web | www.lavilladandrea.com |

## La Ferme d'Augustin

A 13th-century gateway heralds your arrival to the olive farm that opened to guests (just a few wanderers and celebrities) in the early days of Brigitte Bardot… she still lives nearby. Fifty years on: fabrics from Provence, tiles from Salernes and *objets* stylishly scattered by owner Ninette. The décor is wonderfully relaxed, the pool is discreet and the place is filled with garden roses. The farm rests in a relatively untouched spot of this legendary peninsula, a minute from Tahiti Beach and two miles from St Tropez, reached by a road known only to the locals, or a 15-mile coastal path: the position is among the best on the Riviera. Couples, families, foodies flock. Organic veg from the potager, wines from the vines, fruits from the orchard and their own olive oil structure a cuisine that is as authentic as it is simple; savour the flavours of Provence from the terrace or the pergola. Their very own bath soaps and gels express the same Provençal spirit; bedrooms in apartments are cosy and characterful, some with whirlpool baths and sea views. A rich, relaxed Riviera retreat.

| | |
|---|---|
| Rooms | 22 doubles: €205–€460.<br>24 suites for 2: €400–€985.<br>Extra bed/sofabed available €50 per person per night. |
| Meals | Breakfast €20.<br>Lunch à la carte €15–€50.<br>Dinner à la carte €30–€60. |
| Closed | 19 October to 20 March. |

|  | |
|---|---|
| | Vallet Family<br>La Ferme d'Augustin,<br>Route de Tahiti, St Tropez,<br>83350 Ramatuelle, Var |
| Tel | +33 (0)4 94 55 97 00 |
| Email | info@fermeaugustin.com |
| Web | www.fermeaugustin.com |

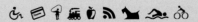

Entry 335   Map 16

## Hôtel Le Cavendish

Civilised and convivial, the Cavendish is a joy, offering a drink on arrival and a complimentary bar in the evening. Set back from the bustle of Cannes, this splendid rebirth of a Napoleon III mansion displays Madame Welter's talents. Subtle modern comforts and splendid rooms, some with balcony or terrace, are the frame. Sensuous, exuberant, almost edible choices of fabric and colour that are never overdone – crunchy raspberry taffeta, tasselled pistachio green, twilight mauve – clothe the frame. Quirky old-fashioned charm enfolds it all. It's like being a guest in the grand house of a *grand homme*, such as its namesake, Lord Cavendish. How attentive to offer leaf teas for breakfast, how attractive to dress the curvy Carrara marble staircase with candles at dusk, how delightful to slip between lavender-scented sheets at night. Freshly baked croissants, cakes and crumbles, homemade jams and cheerful staff make mornings easy, especially if you are attending one of the events at the Festival Hall, ten minutes away. Superb.

| | |
|---|---|
| Rooms | 23 doubles, 12 twins: €125-€330. Private beach nearby €20 p.p. Valet parking €25. |
| Meals | Breakfast €20 (included for Sawday's guests). Complimentary bar 6-9pm. |
| Closed | 1 to 26 December & 6 January to 15 March. |

**Christine & Guy Welter**
Hôtel Le Cavendish,
11 bd Carnot, 06400 Cannes,
Alpes-Maritimes

| | |
|---|---|
| Tel | +33 (0)4 97 06 26 00 |
| Email | reservation@cavendish-cannes.com |
| Web | www.cavendish-cannes.com |

## Villa Garbo

A sparrow's spit from the heart of Cannes, its railway station and myriad fleshpots, the elegant and evocatively re-named Villa Garbo brings you the luxury of a smart hotel and the practicality of a serviced apartment. Choose your breakfast from the buffet and have it on the terrace or in your room. Your suite or apartment, done in taupe and pink, has an immaculate stylish kitchen, good lighting, comfy beds and a contemporary marble bathroom with a striking black mirror. The whole place is carefully furnished and colour-coordinated in period and modern style – antique chandeliers and tonic lime green chairs, marble fireplaces and ethnic touches, 1890s candlesticks and leather sofas. The owners and staff are genuinely friendly, always ready to answer your questions round a (free) aperitif and expertly creating a convivial house-party atmosphere. The private beach is the height of indulgence in bustling, celeb-ridden Cannes. You will feel like a guest in a high-class mansion with impeccable servants at your beck and call. The Penthouse is a wow with its own roof terrace. *Minimum stay: 2 nights.*

| Rooms | 2 suites for 4, each with separate bathroom: €220-€450. 8 apartments for 2 (extra bed available for 2 children/1 adult): €180-€330 per night. |
|---|---|
| Meals | Restaurants 2-minute walk. |
| Closed | November – March. |

Christine & Guy Welter
Villa Garbo,
62 bd d'Alsace, 06400 Cannes,
Alpes-Maritimes

| Tel | +33 (0)4 93 46 66 00 |
| Email | direction@cavendish-cannes.com |
| Web | www.villagarbo-cannes.com |

## Hôtel La Jabotte

What makes La Jabotte special? Is it the courtyard scented with oranges or the bedrooms the colours of jewels? Or is it Pierre and Nathalie, new owners of this delightful little hotel, an explosion of colour, beautifully clean and inviting? Enthusiastic and inspired, they are hard at work updating things (new bedding all round, air-conditioning too) while their three cool cats breathe that inimitable feline calm. Down a small side street, 60 metres from the beach, you will find polished stone floors, cherry-red walls and pots of roses. Pass the deep aubergine sofa, go through the gliding wall of glass and into the enchanting pebbled courtyard off which lie the bedrooms. Each has table and chairs outside the door and lovingly labelled plants; it feels more home than hotel and you get to know your neighbours (the family suites are sensibly separate in the villa). Bedrooms are small but charming, shower rooms have delicious lotions and fulsome towels. After fresh fruit and croissants, saunter into Old Antibes – or drift down to the free sandy beach and your own parasol. *Extra beds available in suites.*

| | |
|---|---|
| Rooms | 5 doubles, 3 twin/doubles: €80–€159. 2 suites for 2-4: €169–€209. |
| Meals | Breakfast €12. Restaurants 2-minute walk. |
| Closed | Never. |

**Nathalie & Pierre Lesjean**
Hôtel La Jabotte,
13 av Max Maurey,
06160 Cap d'Antibes, Alpes-Maritimes
Tel      +33 (0)4 93 61 45 89
Email   info@jabotte.com
Web     www.jabotte.com

## Hôtel Windsor

A 1930s Riviera hotel with a pool in a palm grove and exotic birds in cages – a lush escape in the heart of Nice. Indoors, Hôtel Windsor has introduced the Thirties to the 21st century by asking contemporary artists to decorate some of the rooms. The result is gifts of wit, provocation, flights of fancy and minimalist sobriety: Joan Mas's *Cage à Mouches*, cosmopolitan Ben's writing on the walls, Antoine Beaudoin's frescoes of Venice, Egypt, India – and Tintin, all-time favourite. Plain white beds have contrasting cushions or quilts, furniture is minimal but interesting, little bathrooms are delightful and one room is painted in glimmering gold. Clear bright colours everywhere, including the richly exotic public areas; the charming Odile is passionate about contemporary art and chooses a different artist every year to reinvent the lobby. Outside, a tropical garden gives space for reflection among bamboo, fruiting trees and bougainvillea. Light filters through onto warmly smiling staff who prepare sumptuous buffet breakfasts under the palms in summer and run a superb spa, with gym, on the fifth floor.

| | |
|---|---|
| Rooms | 57 twin/doubles: €89-€205. Breakfast & dinner €36 extra per person. Extra bed/sofabed €20-€30 per person per night. |
| Meals | Breakfast €6-€13. Dinner à la carte €29-€40. Wine from €21. Restaurant closed Sunday. |
| Closed | Never. |

**Odile Redolfi-Payen**
Hôtel Windsor,
11 rue Dalpozzo, 06000 Nice,
Alpes-Maritimes

| | |
|---|---|
| Tel | +33 (0)4 93 88 59 35 |
| Email | contact@hotelwindsornice.com |
| Web | www.hotelwindsornice.com |

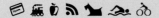

Entry 339  Map 16

Quick reference indices

**Wheelchair-accessible**
At least one bedroom and bathroom accessible for wheelchair users. Phone for details.

**Pets welcome**
Please let the owner know if you want to bring pets.

## Bikes
Bikes on the premises to hire
or borrow.

## Public transport
Places within 10 miles of a
bus/coach/train station and
the owner can arrange
collection.

Quick reference indices

Quick reference indices

Swimming pool
Pool on the premises; use
may be by arrangement.

Photo: Hôtel Arraya, entry 235

# Sawday's

# GO SNOW

## COLLECTION

It's time to hit the slopes! From the
cosy to the grand, find a chalet with
a heated pool, an underground spa
or a Michelin- starred restaurant.
With handy tips about distances to lifts,
the best places to hire equipment,
and some great après-ski pampering,
this is a superb place to start planning
your close encounter of the snowy kind.

www.sawdays.co.uk/gosnow

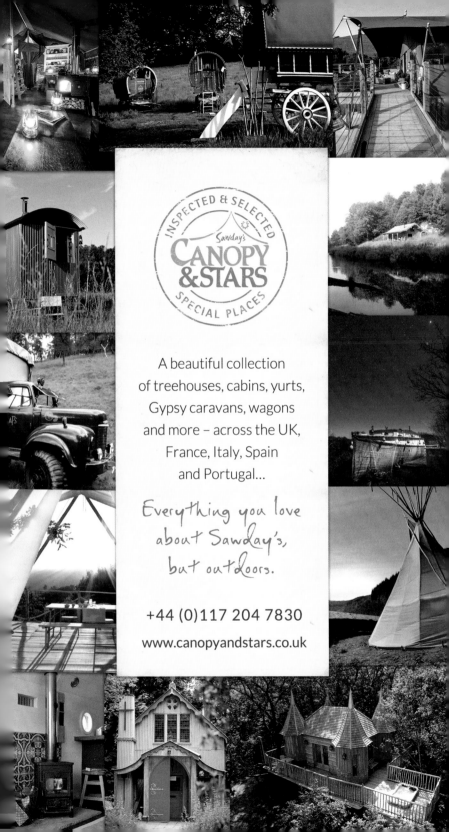

Photo: Hostellerie Bérard
Et Spa, entry 332

Alastair Sawday has been publishing books for over 20 years, finding Special Places to Stay in Britain and abroad. All our properties are inspected by us and are chosen for their charm and individuality. And there are many more to explore on our perennially popular website: www.sawdays.co.uk. You can buy any of our books at a reader discount of 25%* on the RRP.

| List of titles: | RRP | Discount price |
|---|---|---|
| British Bed & Breakfast | £15.99 | £11.99 |
| British Hotels and Inns | £15.99 | £11.99 |
| Pubs & Inns of England & Wales | £15.99 | £11.99 |
| Dog-friendly Breaks in Britain | £14.99 | £11.24 |
| French Bed & Breakfast | £15.99 | £11.99 |
| French Châteaux & Hotels | £15.99 | £11.99 |
| Italy | £15.99 | £11.99 |

*postage and packaging is added to each order

How to order:
You can order online at: www.sawdays.co.uk/bookshop/
or call: **+44 (0)**117 204 7810

Photo: Mas de l'Oulivié, entry 299

# Sawday's

'More than a bed
for the night…'

Britain
France
Ireland
Italy
Portugal
Spain

www.sawdays.co.uk

Self-Catering | B&B | Hotel | Pub | Treehouses, Cabins, Yurts & More

Photo: La Cour de Rémi, entry 7

# Join us

## TIME AWAY IS FAR TOO PRECIOUS TO SPEND IN THE WRONG PLACE. THAT'S WHY, BACK IN 1994, WE STARTED SAWDAY'S.

Twenty years on, we're still a family concern – and still on a crusade to stamp out the bland and predictable, and help our guests find truly special places to stay.

If you have one, we do hope you'll decide to take the plunge and join us.

———

ALASTAIR & TOBY SAWDAY

"Trustworthy, friendly and helpful – with a reputation for offering wonderful places and discerning visitors."

JULIA NAISMITH, HOLLYTREE COTTAGE

"Sawday's. Is there any other?"

SONIA HODGSON, HORRY MILL